World University Library

The World University Library is an international series
of books, each of which has been specially commissioned.
The authors are leading scientists and scholars from all over
the world who, in an age of increasing specialization, see the
need for a broad, up-to-date presentation of their subject.
The aim is to provide authoritative introductory books for
university students which will be of interest also to the general
reader. Publication of the series takes place in Britain,
France, Germany, Holland, Italy, Spain, Sweden and
the United States.

Bryan Wilson

Religious Sects

a sociological study

World University Library

McGraw-Hill Book Company
New York Toronto

For Terry

© Bryan Wilson, 1970
Library of Congress Catalog Card Number: 68-13141
All rights reserved. No part of this publication may be reproduced,
stored in a retrieval system, or transmitted, in any form or by any
means, electronic, mechanical, photocopying, recording or otherwise,
without the prior permission of the copyright owner.

Photoset by BAS Printers Limited, Wallop, Hampshire, England.
Manufactured by LIBREX, Italy.

Contents

1 Introduction: sects in sociological perspective

Sects are movements of religious protest. Their members separate themselves from other men in respect of their religious beliefs, practices and institutions, and often in many other departments of their lives. They reject the authority of orthodox religious leaders, and often, also, of the secular government. Allegiance to a sect is voluntary, but individuals are admitted only on proof of conviction, or by some other test of merit: continuing affiliation rests on sustained evidence of commitment to sect beliefs and practices. Sectarians put their faith first: they order their lives in accordance with it. The orthodox, in contrast, compromise faith with other interests, and their religion accommodates the demands of the secular culture.

At first glance, sects may appear to be marginal and incidental phenomena in history – odd groups of alienated men with outlandish ideas. Yet, at times, sects have had an immense significance for the course of history. After all, Christianity itself was only a Jewish sect at the beginning. The Mahdi movement in the Sudan in the 1880s, or the Tai-ping movement in China a couple of decades earlier, each significantly affected the history of their own peoples and that of people far from the places where these sects arose. Sects sometimes act as catalysts in history, crystallising in acute form social discontents and aspirations, and marking the moments of social structural collapse, and sometimes heralding, or even promoting, social reintegration. Three examples, drawn from very different societies and historical periods, will illustrate these points.

Social collapse and millennial hopes

In Münster, Westphalia, at a time of acute social, religious and political dissension, in the 1530s, just over a decade after Luther had taken the first steps leading to the Reformation, there occurred one of the most extraordinary sectarian outbursts in European history.[1] All over northern and central Europe men were challenging the church, and the most radical of these dissenters were the Anabaptists (so-called from their insistence on adult baptism of believers). They looked forward to the establishment of the kingdom of

God, and whilst many of them – particularly those in Switzerland, south Germany and Austria – were pacifists, excitement about the imminence of Christ's second coming induced some, in Holland and north Germany, to advocate practical steps towards the establishment of new forms of government, suitable to the interim until God's wrath should be felt in the world.

Under the influence of the preaching of Bernt Rothmann and of the millennial prophet Melchior Hoffmann, a large part of the population of Münster espoused the idea of the imminent second advent, with the millennium to follow. Jan Matthys of Haarlem initially associated these millennial ideas with pacifism, but gradually as excitement increased a more militant note emerged, particularly once it had been prophesied that Münster was the New Jerusalem which alone should stand when the earth perished in a few months' time. Matthys and his associate, Jan Bockelson (or Beukels) known as John of Leiden, established themselves in Münster, and their prophecies induced nuns to abandon their orders, drew in hordes of vagabonds and visionaries from Holland, as well as affecting the local citizens. The Anabaptists gained control of the town, expelled the Catholics and Protestants, and by a reign of terror established communism of property and polygyny. John of Leiden proclaimed himself king, the messiah of the last days. The siege of Münster and the eventual triumph of the besieging forces after about eighteen months of Anabaptist rule are events fully chronicled. A combination of general causes and particular local events and personalities brought sectarian fury to Münster. It was a city divided between Catholics and Protestants; its people had been heavily taxed for the maintenance of its many religious houses; it had been afflicted by repeated depressions and famines in the years preceding the Anabaptist reign of terror. The prophecy of its destiny was enough to make it the cockpit of dissension and unrest, the microcosm of confusion that threatened the social order of all Europe.

Missionaries and misconceptions

Missionaries have often bewildered aboriginals whom they have sought to convert, but sometimes the misconceptions of natives about their purposes have had strange, unintended consequences, particularly so in the case of sectarian missionaries, who appear as a direct challenge to the orthodox missions that natives had hitherto regarded as the 'white man's medicine'. A particular case was the impact of the Salvation Army on the (then Belgian) Congo in the 1930s (though it is an episode with many parallels – conspicuously in the history of Seventh Day Adventist missioning in the South Seas, Jehovah's Witness activity in Zambia, and Pentecostal incursions into Nigeria). The apparent success of the Salvationists in the Congo was phenomenal. Their uniforms, hand-shaking, flags, and their emphasis on joy, made an immense impact on the natives. Only belatedly did the Army discover that their symbols were regarded as agencies effective in witch-cleansing in territory over which various witch-finding cults had recently spread (and where the tribal witch-finding methods by poison ordeals had been prohibited). Worse than this, the letter 'S' on the lapels of the Salvationists' uniforms was regarded by many Congolese as connoting devotion to Simon Kimbangu, the Baptist catechist who had gained a rapid reputation as a healer in 1921, and who, after his arrest and trial, had been imprisoned by the Belgian authorities. Kimbangu had become a martyr for the natives, whom they identified with Christ: his early second advent was eagerly awaited. Disarray and fragmentation occurred once misunderstandings were made apparent: some converts, such as Simon Mpadi, led Kimbanguist schisms whilst retaining the ideas and paraphernalia of the Salvationists who had simply not appreciated the factors that were at work in their early success in the Congo.

Cultural confusion and sectarian reintegration

Perhaps no country has experienced the rapidity of change in such measure as Japan, which has passed from feudalism to modernity, from traditionalism to the age of mass-media in less than a century, and from military ascendancy to devastating defeat within a few years. The process of adjustment cannot have been easy for the Japanese, and it is not surprising, in these circumstances, that there should be a proliferation of sects, all peculiar to Japan. Weaving new patterns from received ideas of Buddhism, Shinto, Christianity and modern secularism, these sects appear as almost conscious attempts to restructure personal and social relations as well as the nation's social order. None is more remarkable than *Sōka Gakkai.*

Like many other movements, Sōka Gakkai ('Value-Creation Society') claims to be neither a sect nor a religion, but simply a lay association to promote the teachings of Nichiren, a thirteenth-century Buddhist monk. (In adopting this dual structure, Sōka Gakkai is somewhat reminiscent of Jehovah's Witnesses, who have also denied being a religious movement.) Nichiren propounded a nationalistic and intolerant version of Buddhism, emphasising the Lotus Sutra, the recitation of the *Daimoku* (an adoration of this Sutra) and devotion to the *Mandala,* the scroll on which this invocation was inscribed. Sōka Gakkai today regards Nichiren as the true Buddha.

The movement was organised in 1937 with about sixty members, but its leaders were imprisoned in the 1942-5 war for refusing to participate in the rites of the Shinto faith. In 1946, Toda Josei, a former teacher, first disciple of Tsunesaburō Makiguchi, founder of the sect and author of its basic philosophical work, re-formed the movement. Its aim was to bring peace and happiness to all mankind. It adopted fanatical techniques of evangelisation, *shakubuku* ('browbeat into submission') appropriate to its intolerance, and spread rapidly in the 1950s, claiming hundreds of thousands of families as adherents. It promoted regular discussion groups, lectures, a wide range of literature, and conducted examinations in its teachings, awarding academic titles to the successful. It organised candidates for the Upper House of the Japanese Parliament, and in 1965 with twenty members was the third largest party in the house. In 1964, it formed a party for Clean Government to fight elections for the Lower House: in 1969 forty-seven of its candidates were elected. The sect has its own university, and has created organisations for the mass diffusion of 'wholesome' culture.

The spectacular appeal of Sōka Gakkai, which now claims over a million and a half families, can be explained only by its relevance to Japan's recent fortunes. Culturally rootless people, lost between the authoritarian world of the past and the exercises in freedom and democracy imposed upon Japan by the Americans, find security in the martial quality of the mass movement, and new goals and new hope in its promise of happiness for everyone. Sōka Gakkai combines elements of traditional folk religion with the rational bureaucratic efficiency of a well-organised mass movement in its devotion to the Mandala, in carefully organised pilgrimages to view the relics of Nichiren, and in the magical benefit to be had from reciting the Daimoku. Like Jehovah's Witnesses, members of Sōka Gakkai are kept busy disseminating propaganda – the main activity of adherents: the textbook on shakubuku is the guide to their daily lives.

Data, problems and approach

These are dramatic examples of the socially-transformative role that sects have sometimes played. Sects have also influenced society in much less conspicuous, but perhaps not less significant ways. The re-socialisation of whole generations and the transmission of new moral perspectives to the uprooted lower classes by the Methodists in late eighteenth- and nineteenth-century Britain and America, or among Pentecostalists in many parts of the world today, are largely consequences of sectarian impulse.

Even apart from their influence on the development of society, however, sects are an important social phenomenon in their own

Table 1 Jehovah's Witnesses and Seventh Day Adventists in advanced countries in 1966

	Population (in millions)	Seventh Day Adventists		Jehovah's Witnesses	
		Churches	Members	Congrs.	Publrs.
United States	196·7	3,164	378,737	5,242	302,450
Canada	19·6	176	16,830	897	39,554
Australia	11·5	316	30,144	400	16,588
Austria	7·2	44	2,622	176	7,762
Belgium	9·4	19	1,164	157	8,370
Denmark (including Faroes)	4·7	65	4,035	220	10,250
Finland	4·7	63	5,647	324	9,005
France (and Luxembourg)	49·3	83	4,742	453	22,656
Germany (West)	59·2	464	26,576	1,032	76,693
Gt Britain *	50·2	126	10,740	896	49,073
Greece	10·3	10	251	376	10,849
Italy	51·8	59	3,230	275	9,798
Netherlands	12·0	45	3,228	223	13,758
New Zealand	2·7	60	6,711	116	4,391
Norway	3·6	68	5,349	129	3,984
Portugal	10·3	36	3,257	61	3,105
Spain	31·7	20	2,280	80	4,302
Sweden	7·6	48	3,323	228	9,886
Switzerland	5·8	61	3,842	129	6,138

* Referred to as 'British Isles' in Jehovah's Witness literature, but since Eire is entered separately this presumably means Great Britain.
Congrs. = Congregations, Publrs. = Publishers

right. No one knows how many sects there are in the world, nor even in Christendom, much less how many sectarians. Jehovah's Witnesses alone number perhaps two millions, and Seventh Day Adventists well over a million. Pentecostalists of one sort or another are perhaps twice as numerous as both these together. The new sects of Japan have millions of adherents; there are hundreds of sects in South Africa and new dynamic movements in west and central Africa.

There is a rich descriptive literature that grows steadily about Christian sectarianism, and the sects themselves produce a voluminous quantity of tracts, books and periodicals every year. But sects are extremely diverse, and the cultural conditions in which they have arisen are various: no one volume could present them in anything approaching descriptive completeness. But what we know of sects, extensive as it is, is merely a fragment of what might be known, had all the first-hand research been done. The research will of course never be undertaken. Sects are very closed communities, sometimes unwelcoming even to those outsiders who might want to join, and hostile to those who wish to enquire, record and analyse. Merely by pursuing his investigation, the researcher appears to sectarians to be commenting unfavourably on their priorities and values.

This book is not a catalogue of sects. The particular character of individual sects is presented both for its own importance, and to bring out the similarities in sectarianism as well as the diversity and differences among sects. The circumstances in which sects emerge; the influence that they exert; the functions that they perform for their votaries; and the changes that they undergo over time – are all issues worth examining and explaining. From such an investigation we may hope to learn something about fundamental social processes.

Although the sects about which we know most, and with which this book is almost exclusively concerned, are sects within or at the fringe of the Christian tradition, useful comparison may be made with sects that have developed in countries with traditions received from more than one of the great religions. Japan particularly will be shown to provide material for such comparison. Our use of Christian cases should not, however, mislead. Sectarianism is being viewed sociologically and not theologically. The term *sect* is not used pejoratively, as it has been in Christian history. Normative assumptions about what men should believe and practise as their religion are eschewed. Sects are taken simply as self-evident and significant social facts. The truth of beliefs, and warranty of practice are not here at issue. The writer is manifestly not a sectarian, and he does not seek to commend, condone or condemn, but only to present a detached discussion of origins, persistence and significance of sects.

The sect as a social phenomenon and as a sociological concept

In a loose sense of the word, sects, as separated groups, exist within or at the fringe of all the major religions: but the concept of the sect differs according to the organisational structure of different parent religions. In Hinduism, which is diffuse, uncentralised and pluralist, sectarianism exists only in a much more limited sense than in Christendom. Diverse traditions of worship and divergent philosophical schools have existed side by side in Hinduism over centuries, and devotees of particular cults have not felt the need for separation from other people in order to practise the rituals that they have regarded as especially beneficial. Yet the term *sect* is widely if loosely used for such groups as the Lingayat movements among the Brahmins, even though these were merely movements cultivating particular styles of devotion. It is clear then that the specific connotations of the word, when used of Christian movements, are not all relevant for those outside the Christian tradition.

The early association of church and empire, and the early development of agencies of political control in the Christian church, enhanced when the church inherited the Roman Empire's administrative structure and something of its civilising mission, all conferred on Christianity a degree of centralisation and coherence lacking in Hinduism and Buddhism. The church authorities were enabled more effectively both to impose Christianity on pagan populations, and to systematise and bring into general conformity the beliefs and practices of Christians. Clearly, neither the elimination of pagan magic nor the establishment of uniformity in Christian usage was ever completely achieved. Before ancient magic had been rooted out in the rural areas of Europe, the church itself had been broken asunder at the Reformation. True as this is, the co-ordinated hierarchy and effectiveness of control of the Roman church was quite unequalled in the older world religions.

Because of this degree of religious cohesion, dissenters who deliberately departed from the accepted beliefs and practices of the faith were more emphatically distinguishable in Christianity. Sects were regarded as opposed to the church, even though sectarians saw themselves as reformers or restorers of the faith itself. Their real sin was to reject sacerdotalism, church organisation and to believe that they alone possessed the truth about God. With such ideas went distinctive conceptions of social relationships and ethics.

Sects had, of course, arisen before the establishment of Christianity in Rome, but since we are, in this book, concerned with modern sects, and primarily with those arising in Christianity, it is important to recognise the specific colouring that the concept has acquired in Christian history.

The Christian concept of the sect

To Christian theologians a sect was expected to manifest distinctiveness both in doctrine and in its conception of authority. The Christian church, whilst concerned with uniformity in religious practice, always made doctrine the central criterion of orthodoxy. The power struggles of the early church were fought, if not always about belief, at least always in terms of it. There emerged in Christendom, often in finely-stated formulae, a distinct idea that only those who held the same beliefs belonged to the true faith and the true church. Whilst variations in liturgy, social practice, local tradition (especially in the celebration of local saints) might be tolerated, all

The Amish Mennonites of Pennsylvania
have retained the dress, customs
and life-style which they brought
to America from Switzerland.

must proceed under the rubric of the same doctrines. This intellectual orientation came in consequence to colour the character of
sectarianism in Christendom. Sectaries were those who voluntarily
professed beliefs different from those of the church, and associated
together in common faith outside the church's control. New sects
thus took the same criterion for the identification of the in-group as
the early church had taken when it spread to include Greek and
Jew, bond and free – shared common belief. Nominally, this idea of
voluntary subscription was still claimed by the church, but in
practice subscription to its tenets and obedience to its clergy were
enforced wherever its political writ, or that of faithful princes, ran.
This principle contrasts sharply with the criteria of ethnicity and the
fulfilment of ritual demands associated with ethnicity which were
typical of Judaism (once it ceased to proselytise) and of Hinduism.

Thus divergent belief, separation and rejection of church authority
were the defining characteristics of Christian sects. Heresy and
schism, together with denial of sacerdotal claims, were the essence
of sectarianism as the Christian church saw it. Sects challenged the
monopoly of churchly access to the supernatural and to salvation
which the church had claimed for itself in suppressing earlier pagan-
ism. Since sects were enemies of the clergy, the clergy defined them
as enemies of God, of his church, and of all legitimate princes.

Christian theologians and Christian-influenced sociologists have
tended to ascribe to sects either conscious and articulated organisation, or charismatic leadership. So strongly have these elements
been associated with sectarianism that some scholars have denied
the designation of *sect* to movements that conspicuously lacked
conscious organisation, and have applied the term *cult* to movements
that lacked either a central hierarchy or that failed to convene their
members as congregations. In this book, the term *sect* is applied
broadly to all religious movements that emphasise their separateness and distinctiveness of mission, regardless of their organisational character. Indeed, even among groups to which none would
deny the name *sect*, there are very considerable differences. Thus, on
the one hand, Jehovah's Witnesses, although nominally merely the

company of faithful Bible students, have in the Watchtower Society an elaborate and highly routinised publishing organisation; on the other hand, the Amish Mennonites use their religious ideas to sanctify and justify their distinctive, segregated communal way of life, in which religious practice is scarcely distinguishable from the folk-culture that they have perpetuated. Both are sects. Were the sects of Islam and Buddhism to pass under review, wider divergences might be found in organisation. Yet all could be described as sects – as separated and voluntary minority religious movements.

Some common misconceptions

Religions may begin as sects, and in the Christian case the sect preceded the church. But once established, the church anathematised all new sects. Precisely because of its tighter organisational structure and its claim to monopoly of religious concerns, official Christianity has been more conscious and more intolerant of sects than have other world religions. Sectarians have been regarded not only as heretics but as revolutionaries, and church anathema has been used to justify political oppression. These charges have not always been warranted. Although sects do envisage some transformation of man's condition and do represent a breach of the institutional social order, they do not always consciously intend to disrupt society much less to mobilise men for its overthrow. That some sect believe that God intends to overturn the world must not obscur the fact that other sects expect salvation in quite different ways Church pronouncements about sects have often been misleading, and have little relevance to dispassionate sociological study.

The other common error that persists about sects, even among Christian theologians, is an inherited idea that had rather more validity in the past than it does today. This is to suppose that al sects arise around a charismatic leader, a man who claims divinity or at least strong divine inspiration. Prophets have always been the enemies of priests. Institutionalised religion is challenged by those who claim new inspiration which threatens the monopoly o access to divine knowledge that priests claim for themselves. It ha often been easier to blame a leader as a false prophet for misleading men, than to accept the idea that some men conscientiously and sincerely disagreed with orthodoxy. The church had ready-made enemies in the figures of devils and Anti-Christ, who could clearly be made to symbolise sectaries. Again, when little was known about the social structural causes of tensions in society, or about the divergence of social perspective among different social groups, it was easier to blame a particular man for disturbances from the norm than to look for social causes. But the central fact in explaining this misconception is that pre-industrial societies relied considerably on at least a diluted form of charisma, on exceptional men (found in such concepts as men of high birth, nobility, genius, saintliness). And since all these mystical qualities appeared to have their distorted forms, there were prophets and there were scapegoats.

Before the nineteenth century many sects did arise around a charismatic leader. Men more readily believed in inspired or messianic personages, around whom movements sometimes came into being. The movements were often ephemeral, the leaders deluded, and sometimes demented. But they drew on a persisting element in the Christian tradition, without which Christianity itself might not have captured so readily the imaginations of its early followers – the belief in the second coming and the inauguration of a new social dispensation in the millennium. Such messianic hopes recrudesced frequently, and churchmen became used to the misguided ideas of charismatic figures, and tended to attribute all sectarianism to them. Sects in industrial societies, however, are less frequently attributable to charismatic leaders, and it is perhaps important to understand why this should be so.

Sects and charismatic leadership

To its members the traditional society appears to be a sacred order: customs, *mores*, relationships and authority are seen as a continuation of the divine order that embraces both nature and society. (Even the sophisticated classical societies of antiquity, where the man-made quality of the state was apparent, believed social *mores* and values to be divinely natural.) Where challenge to the existing order occurs in such societies – and in the most primitive it follows only from disturbances arising from external sources – it is necessarily a religious challenge based on a new apprehension of the divine: hence the importance of the charismatic leader. In primitive societies such a figure is almost always the source of new religious movements, and is often so in feudal societies. Occasionally such charisma has become the basis for the re-structuring of the social order; more usually it has led to the emergence of a sect. Sects facilitate the crystallisation of new social groupings, and provide social cohesion within a self-selected community, but it is not always the case that sects are charismatically inspired, particularly in industrial societies.

Advanced societies are marked by increasing division of labour, in which men are increasingly related according to their roles. In most social relationships the total personalities of individuals are not engaged; they are involved only in role obligations and role expectations. Consequently, *personal* trust is not invoked in the way in which it is essential to primary relationships. 'Put not your trust in persons' might be the motto of advanced societies – but only in specialists performing their roles, in routine procedures an technical facilities. It follows that in these societies there tends to b disbelief of the special powers of any individual. But personal trus of course is crucial to the concept of the charismatic.

Advanced societies leave little room for the manifestation c charisma, except perhaps in extreme conditions of social strai when whole societies feel their way of life threatened. When charismatic figure does arise, it becomes evident to all that the trus he wins itself depends on the manipulation of highly technica facilities, particularly in the mass-media, and these things are ir themselves profoundly anti-charismatic. Charismatic claims ar found only at the fringe of the social system, in the least routinise activities of society – at the very top level in politics (and ther decreasingly), in entertainment and in marginal religious groups.

Religion is that social institution in which non-rational disposi tions and super-rational claims are stock-in-trade. Supernatura power is expected to operate in religious gatherings, even if, a among Quakers and Pentecostalists, the expectation is for a highl diffused charismatic experience. There are modern sects that aris in response to charismatic claims of a more traditional type, such a the followers of the Dutch fisherman, Lou, and the group tha accepts the messianic claims of George Roux in France. But these sects become more marginal and less typical of sects in general. The extent to which charismatic claims have become tempered by rational considerations is also evident. Thus Mrs Eddy, founder o Christian Science, who was regarded by many of her followers as 'the woman clothed with the sun' and who did not discourage these ideas, evolved a religion that claimed to be a science and, as well as churches, instituted teachers and courses of instruction in imitation of the rational, educational every-day world. The religious prophet now acquired new appeal by adopting the model of the scientist and educationalist. These are indications of the waning of the credi- bility of charismatic claims in the modern world. Modern sects cannot be regarded as simply new examples of the type of sectari- anism that was common in the medieval world.

The religious quest in sectarian guise

Theologians often overlook the basic similarities of concern of orthodox churches and aberrant sects. Religion is always concerned with salvation – sects no less than orthodoxy. The central religious question is, 'What shall we do to be saved?' The answers to it justify religious practice. Just what salvation means varies from one culture to another, and so do the ways of attaining it. Men may seek salvation from immediate and pressing ills that afflict them; or salvation may be seen as the liberation of a people and the establishment of a new political dispensation; or it may be a preoccupation with benefit after death. Salvation extends from therapeutic relief to transcendental reassurance or social transformation. Sects reject the conception of salvation and/or the means of attaining it advanced by orthodox religion. In particular they react against the institutional character of the means, and usually, as lay movements, against sacerdotalism and sacramentalism, since these are the bases of monopolistic control exercised by the orthodox religious authorities. It is frequently the case that sectarians believe that salvation is scarce and that few will attain it, but they often also believe that the means are essentially simple and direct.

2 The problem of definition

The importance of sects to sociologists is that they provide by far the most numerous examples of self-conscious attempts by men to construct their own societies, not merely as political entities with constitutions, but as groups with a firm set of values and *mores*, of which they are conscious. Such groups have a carefully ordered structure of social relationships and clearly established patterns of social behaviour and control. As persisting social entities, they exhibit mechanisms of socialisation of the young and identifiable processes of social change. A sociology of sects, however, requires more than a collection of historical and contemporary data about the numerous individual movements. It requires a conceptual apparatus by which we recognise the central features of sects and significant differences among them. The pioneer of the study of sects was Ernst Troeltsch,[2] who took as his basic data information about sects that had arisen in medieval and modern Christendom.

He contrasted the sect with the church. He saw in Christianity a dialectic principle at work, with sectarian and churchly strains as alternating forces that had been there since the beginning. This scheme has been criticised, both for its limited conception of sects and its restricted view of the church and also for the implication that sects as such depend on the church towards which they are antithetical. These are serious shortcomings, but it is still useful to recall how Troeltsch envisaged the sect.

Whereas the church was hierarchic and conservative, appealing to ruling classes for whom it operated as an agency of social control, the sect was egalitarian, radical and an expression of the depressed condition of underprivileged groups. The church, both socially and ecclesiologically, saw itself as an order established from above, whereas the sect saw itself as working up from below. The church had a certain objective quality. It was an external institution administering grace; it stood over against individuals as an entity similar to the state, emphasising its permanence and its transcendence over human and social conditions. The sect, on the other hand, was a subjective fellowship, a community in which personal holiness was emphasised. Its members were aware of each other and aware that they constituted the brotherhood. They did not so much administer the means of grace as share the fellowship of love. The sect then was depicted as an inner community lacking external qualities; unlike the church it was not itself an object of reverence. Yet, almost paradoxically, the sect saw itself in some ways as a lay élite, whereas the élite of the church, the clergy, served the masses. The status of the sectarian was *achieved,* requiring voluntary submission and subscription; the status of the church member was *ascribed,* a consequence of birth into society, solemnised by rites of baptism. The church was integrated with the world, but the sect was in tension with it, rejecting many of its associations and much of its culture. The church had a division of labour which also indicated differing degrees of commitment: thus there were priests, monks, lay orders and lay members, and for the most dedicated of these there was a distinctive – heroic – ascetic ethic. But the sect was totalitarian. Being egalitarian, it recognised no differences in commitment; all subscribed to an ethic of the same degree of rigour and asceticism. Over time, however, and because of their subjectivity, sects tended to lose spontaneity; lacking spiritual breadth they had little capacity for adaptation in changing circumstances; being egalitarian they had difficulties in finding direction, once initial enthusiasm had become attenuated.

Troeltsch produced an 'ideal type' for the sect – a construct in which particular elements found in sects are systematically presented in an arbitrary statement of what is typical. The 'ideal type' is a shorthand statement which attempts to clarify common usage and which permits us to examine and compare particular cases and processes of change by the use of a standard measuring rod. But all 'ideal type' constructs rely ultimately on a range of empirical material, and if this is not in itself sufficiently broad, particular elements in the construct may be stated in too concrete a manner. Clearly, the wider the range of cases and the greater their diversity, the more likely it is that summary statements purporting to draw together the essential elements in all cases must be at a high level of abstraction. But beyond a certain point, abstractness of formulation may itself limit the usefulness of the construct – practical utility and value in research may then be surrendered in the desire for formulations with a high degree of comprehensiveness. This of course is a central problem of sociological theory. The builder of constructs must in consequence compromise with historical specificity. How far might one talk about the *sect* without specifying particular historical periods, particular cultural contexts, and particular religious traditions? The historian and the theologian may be impatient with any such discussion: the sociologist, committed to comparative method, as far as it can usefully help in the explanation of social processes and social organisation, cannot avoid the problem.

The sects that provided Troeltsch with his data were principally those that attached great importance to the second advent of Christ and the subsequent millennium, and his concept of the sect was unduly coloured by this. Again, although the idea that sects are fellowships of love does tell us something about the sectarian spirit as it is contrasted with the church, we know that many sects today are very large organisations. Although the sense of fellowship is undoubtedly fostered in the local congregation, sectarians in such movements have, nonetheless, a conception of 'headquarters' and sometimes of decisions taken at levels quite remote from that of their own local fraternal group.

Troeltsch's contrast of sect and church was no doubt an appropriate dichotomy in most European countries until relatively recent times. But in Britain, and more emphatically in America, the growth of tolerance permitted the development of religious pluralism. Many organisations grew up, and thus sects came to have some relationship to each other, a relationship of an ordered, systematic and recognised kind. The very concept of sect was less appropriate for the American case, where, in the absence of any federal established church, the dichotomy of church and sect broke down. The culturally accommodative, religious movements have long been recognised as denominations – the distinctive organisational form of American religion. In a society without a church, but with several important denominations, sectarianism necessarily takes on rather a different character.

For Troeltsch, sects recruited from the lower class, and in feudal societies this was perhaps often the case. But as class structure has been diversified, and as industrial societies have grown complex, other forms of social differentation have become evident. There have been unaccommodated ethnic groups, immigrants, frontiers populations cut off from the culture of cities and the assumptions of orthodoxy, people moving rapidly up the social scale seeking agencies of adjustment to new social status; there has been a diversification of class positions with fine (but to those in the situation, real) differences of status, assumptions and *Weltanschauungen*. Add to these structural changes, the rapid, and now perhaps overwhelming diffusion of information, the challenge to traditional religion from humanist and secularist sources and from the purveyors of religious ideas from other cultures, and one sees that men are very variously exposed to diverse philosophies, ideologies, gobbets of knowledge and propaganda that are now available. Thus structurally and intellectually there are many possible new situations in which sects might spring up.

Even a cursory survey of the sects now active in Christendom must at once indicate the inadequacy of the Troeltschean analysis – and this without regard for the many sectarian movements outside Christendom (to which, in all fairness, the 'ideal type' constructed by Troeltsch was not intended to have specific application). Although some of the old styles of sect characterised by Troeltsch still function, there are many new styles of movements, many different foci of concern that have arisen at many points of tension, which did not exist in the pre-industrial past or in the early stages of industrialisation. Equally, although Troeltsch saw that sects might, over time, lose spontaneity, it is now evident that this may occur in a variety of ways, or may be resisted consciously by sectarians; we know much more about the process of sect development.

The sect defined

The task of formulating general characterisations of sects has become more, rather than less, difficult since Troeltsch wrote, because of the many new combinations of elements that sects might now embrace in a world where men have far more diversified social experience. Particular styles of organisation, doctrine and ethical practice cannot now be said to be necessarily associated with each other, or with recruitment of a sect's personnel from particular strata. We are obliged to recognise the diversity among sects, as well as their similarity, if our characterisations are to be useful.

Before we turn to the variety of postures that sects adopt in registering their protest against society, what may be said that is generally true of sects in different cultural contexts and epochs? Any such statement must avoid the contrast of church and sect, since the church is no longer the central entity claiming monopoly of access to the supernatural. Necessarily, it must not allow specific cultural and historical factors to obscure social uniformities of structure and development.

Sects are voluntary bodies. Individuals have some choice, theoretically complete choice, in subscribing to sect tenets. The very concept of *sect* implies at least division, and usually diversity, of religious belief within a given society. The votary must choose the sect, but choice is mutual – the sect receives or rejects the man. Membership is by some test of merit: the individual must be worthy of membership. The sect then has a strong sense of self-identity: who is admitted becomes 'one of us'. And this 'us' is set over against all others, the more compellingly so because sects lay claim to special and usually exclusive access to supernatural truths. The sect is a body which claims complete and conscious allegiance of its members, that should transcend where it does not eclipse all other allegiances, whether to state, tribe, class or kin-group.

Associated with these characteristics is the self-conception of the sect as an élite. The sect, as the sole possessor of true doctrine, of appropriate ritual and of warranted standards of rectitude in social behaviour, regards itself as a people set apart, making claim, if not always to absolutely exclusive salvation, at least to the fullest blessings. Sects are also disposed to exclusivity. Membership takes precedence over all other secular allegiances and normally precludes other religious allegiance. In separating from other groups, sects impugn their sanctity and their warranty: belonging to a particular sect implies distance from, and perhaps hostility to, other sects and religious bodies.

It follows from the rigour of these attributes that most sects, being voluntary, intense and in insisting on merit in their members, also have procedures for expulsion of the wayward. The sect is not – as a caste or a clan might be in some social circumstances – an unconscious entity. It is not in other words a social body which sees itself as a 'natural' unit. In contrast to the way in which Jews traditionally regarded their faith, or in which Latin peoples regard Catholicism, the sect is self-conscious, and its formation and recruitment are deliberate and conscious processes. Thus it is also a body with a sense of its own integrity, and a recognition that that integrity might be impugned by the careless or insufficiently committed member. Hence the sect expels the unworthy.

This in turn imposes standards on the individual sect member. He is expected to live the life of a good sectarian, and in consequence the voluntariness of his allegiance and the test of merit to which it is exposed are possible only if he has a personal sense of commitment. Because sects reject differential commitments, the integrity of the sect is simply the integrity diffused among the members. Self-control, conscience and conscientiousness are significant characteristics of sectarianism.

Although sects assert an alternative set of teachings, commandments and practices from the orthodox, this alternative is never a complete and total rejection of all elements in orthodox tradition – otherwise we should not recognise the sect as being such. It is essentially a set of different emphases, with some elements added and some omitted. To propound this alternative the sect must espouse some other principle of authority than that which inheres in the orthodox tradition, and claim superiority for it. The authority that a sect invokes may be the superior revelation of a charismatic leader, it may be a re-interpretation of sacred writings, or it may be an idea that revelation will be given to the truly faithful. Whatever it is, the sect rejects the authorities of the orthodox faith.

General formulations and actual cases

The foregoing formulation is both general and 'ideal typical'. In consequence, it is a rather abstract, somewhat reified depiction of a sect. In actual sects we must expect that each of these general attributes will show some variation from the formulation. Sects undergo change, both in response to changes in the external environment, and by a process of what might be called mutation. Consequently, some attributes may be receding in importance, and others growing, at particular times in a sect's life history.

Voluntariness Although sects are voluntary bodies, there is a tendency for the children of sectarians to join the same faith as their parents. In western Christendom, a sect may continue to exact from young recruits explicit subscription to its tenets much as it did from their parents, because in these societies – and this is particularly true of the United States, Britain, Germany, Switzerland, Scandinavia and Holland, and increasingly true even in Catholic countries – choice of religion is abundant. Highly segregated sects that have established very effective means of insulating themselves (often in part by vicinal segregation – by removal into relatively-closed locations) narrow the prospect of choice for their young people. The adolescent Amish Mennonite in Pennsylvania, or the young Hutterian in Alberta is, by the age of fifteen or sixteen so thoroughly socialised to the way of life of the sect and to the community that is coterminous with it, that choice is very much less evident than for a contemporary Quaker, Pentecostalist or Christian Scientist. Some Amish do leave their sect, but to do so they must also leave their kinsfolk, and then they usually affiliate to other, less rigorous Mennonite groups. Some Hutterians leave their colonies, but very few abandon their beliefs: most young men who leave return to their colony after a few years in the wider world.

Exclusivity It is one of the essential characteristics of a sect to demand over-riding allegiance of its votaries. The principle of exclusive affiliation in Christianity that stems from the jealous God of the Hebrews, is a basis for this attitude among Christian sects. Typically, the sectarian is identified by his sect allegiance in a way which is not true for other men: it becomes the most important thing about him. When he is being mentioned, it is more important to know that he is a Plymouth Brother, a Christian Scientist or a Seventh Day Adventist than any other piece of information. This is not true for an Anglican or a Presbyterian or even for a Baptist if he belongs to one of the major Baptist denominations. The commitment is thus primary, and it must be unequivocal. Yet even on this issue it is possible to recognise that, at least at certain stages of sect development, this last point might have to be qualified. It is common for sects to begin with a strong affirmation of their hostility to sectarianism. They frequently arise to unite all Christians, and there is strong expression of indifference to denominational boundaries. Thus Alexander Campbell, leader of the American movement which eventually split into the Disciples and the Churches of Christ, rejected all the divisions of Christendom. So too did the early Plymouth Brethren, who were intent on providing a simple form of worship for all who lived the Christian life. At this stage, a movement is being called out, and its leaders have not yet worked out the implications of their activity. Strictly, we may be justified in calling this stage 'pre-sectarian', a period of incipient crystallisation, when commitment is still somewhat equivocal. As hostility is met and as followers need to know who are reliable associates, who are Christians to be accepted at worship or for social intercourse – so boundaries come to be drawn and the sect acquires real shape.

Merit Sects require an act of subscription. But when sects persist for a very long time, such tests of merit may become nominal. The history of the Quakers affords an extreme example of diminished rigour in this regard. The Quakers undoubtedly began with a strong sense of separateness and of the need for real worthiness in recruits. Separateness persisted, but eighteenth- and early nineteenth-century English Quakers were often admitted virtually on the strength of birth-right. The sect came near to being a set-apart, self-recruiting people, a type of descent group. Although this tendency changed under the strong evangelical influences that affected Quakerism in the mid-nineteenth century, the tests of merit now imposed upon would-be recruits vary considerably in rigour according to the traditions of particular meetings, and perhaps according to the dispositions of the two Friends who interview the candidate. More generally, as a sect becomes more accepted in the world and takes its place among the denominations, so it places less and less emphasis on tests of merit for admission.

Self-identification In our desire to establish conceptual order in the world, we are all disposed to seek firm boundaries and unambiguous categories. Sects appear as an almost natural affirmation of the same principle. Why should they not, since sects are indeed man-made, self-conscious social entities? Our general formulation suggests that sects have a strong sense of self-identification, and hence enjoy clear boundaries. Without abandoning that generalisation, we must also recognise that in the real world a sect may sometimes be almost as hard to identify with certainty as are those frequently vague entities *tribes* in anthropological reports. Sects, like tribes, do entertain a strong conception of 'us' in contradistinction to all others. But this 'us' may, as with tribes, be variable in its application, and unclear at the boundaries. For the thoroughly committed there is usually no problem, but sects also have attached to them those called 'adherents' who have never sought, or have never attained, admission. They have young people who are believers, but who may not be admissible until a certain age. Most conspicuously of all, sects may recognise certain other movements as being, in some ways, nearer to the truth than others. This may occur when there has been schism within a sect. At first the mutually schismatic groups may anathe-matise each other, and gain considerably in their sense of self-identification from having a recognisable enemy. But once the initial breach has been forgotten, the two groups may come to recognise each other as having more in common than either have with the world outside. Such was the case with the two schismatic branches of Christadelphians in Britain, in the 1930s and 40s, when two periods of common wartime experience had come to define the essential similarity of their differences from the world outside. Old mutual antagonisms subsided. A similar case arises where two movements crystallise at similar times to support generally similar positions, but independently of each other, and often with marginal doctrinal differences. In this instance, separate organisations are in being and some differences of practice and belief may prevail, but each movement may at times regard the other as 'our people'. This has been conspicuously the case of Pentecostal sects – groups emphasising speaking in unknown tongues – many of which have arisen independently of each other. Although some amalgamations have taken place, most European countries have their own Pente-costal movement and some have several. Pentecostalists may see themselves at times as simply members of their own particular group: at others they may use 'us' in reference to all Pentecostalists.

Elite status The exact extent to which a sect sees itself as a social élite varies with a number of specific factors, most important of which are the received tradition of eschatology, and the character of the relationships that sect members conduct with outsiders. In Christianity, the concept of an elect is fundamental: the old ethnic idea of a chosen people was inherited from Judaism and conferred upon the voluntary subscribers to the Christian faith. But even in the Christian tradition, those sects that have sought their legitim-ation in the scriptures have not always found it easy to assert that they and they alone were the elect of God. Thus Salvationists and Pentecostalists, whilst clear that they enjoyed a fuller blessing (and

Hutterian women farming. After centuries of intermittent persecution the Hutterians – originally of German and Tyrolean stock – now prosper on the Canadian prairies where their numbers have increased from a few hundreds to over 17,000 in less than a century. They still speak dialect German.

perhaps a more God-inspired organisation) than other Christians, were generally prepared to concede, even in the early days of their pristine rigour, that other fundamentalists might be included among the saved.

Expulsion Tests of merit for admission to a sect might generally be held to imply criteria for continued membership. But in practice we find that although most sects maintain rigorous standards some become lax about the standards of those already in fellowship. This occurs when a sect has taken extreme steps to insulate itself from the wider society, and has come to recruit its following largely among those in-born. English Quakers in the early nineteenth century were one example; another, more extreme, is the case of the Amish Mennonites, who are not interested in recruiting from people outside and whose way of life is dictated more by the seventeenth-century standards of a peasantry than by severe religious scruples. The Old Order Amish, indeed, sometimes express concern for those of their young people who show squeamishness about bawdy jokes, or who begin to show doubts about drinking alcohol, since such youngsters must have picked up such ideas of being 'good' from outsiders.

Conscience The extent to which the sect relies on high degrees of self-consciousness and conscientious commitment may vary. This is particularly so where the inborn principle has developed, although sectarians such as the Hutterians, Doukhobors and Amish all become intensely conscious of their differences once they have passed early childhood. This sense of apartness may, however, be more like that of an ethnic group than of a voluntary religious group. Indeed, in all these cases ethnic difference is also an important fact in the environments in which they have settled: the Canadian prairies and the Dakotas, the prairies and British Columbia, and Pennsylvania and Ohio, respectively. What must also be recognised is that conscience and conscious commitment do not spring up immediately when a sect first emerges. These qualities are found

most fully in established sects in which the voluntary principle is strong. They are not evident in new movements, when the clientele has not yet been socialised and when the stable demands of allegiance have not yet been formulated. The sect may have arisen in anticipation of the second advent or of some cataclysmic event, in the face of which saving measures are deemed necessary. Such movements are at given points in time only incipiently self-conscious, and conscience and integrity of commitment are undeveloped.

There is one other circumstance in which conscience, if not self-consciousness, appears to undergo an unusual transformation in some sectarian movements. These are cases where the concept of élite status is so strongly accepted that the faithful believe that they are a chosen people regardless of their moral behaviour. Being chosen, they might come to see themselves as perfect: thus behaviour that would be sinful in others cannot by definition be sinful for them. This tendency – antinomianism – has occurred in a number of

Christian sects, particularly in the sixteenth and seventeenth centuries. It has always met fierce disapproval, since it is a teaching that licenses sectarians to behave entirely as they like. It contrasts sharply with the normal disposition of sects to impose standards of decorum and behaviour on their members more rigorous than those of other men in order to manifest their adherence to a higher truth.

Legitimation No sect arises without ideological justification. Sects claim sacred authority to persuade men to abandon the orthodox system of religion. There must be a man – or men – under authority to make this legitimation known. Where a sect arises around a charismatic leader (who may be both the sacred source and its interpreter) charisma is legitimation. In other cases there is a recognised leadership, and methods for appointing or electing leaders. But there are sects which trenchantly deny that they have any intermediaries between God or the divine word and themselves. They reject all forms of human organisation: they believe themselves called out to do what God enjoins. Thus Jehovah's Witnesses assert that they have no organisation (although they acknowledge that they have set up a publishing house, which has an elaborate organisation). The Quakers proceed with a minimum of formal leadership, and so do the Christadelphians. These sects oppose authority and become intensely anti-clerical; their opposition is as much to the organisation of the church as to its teachings. Christian sects often see the two as equally pernicious. In other traditions, however, the focus of dissent has not been to clerical caste, and of course the concept of a priesthood is not appropriate to Islam or contemporary Judaism. But all religious systems have their authorities, and all sects are opposed to them, whether, as in many Christian cases, they emphasise lay involvement and the adequacy of laymen to perform all functions (the doctrine of the priesthood of all believers) or whether, as in many of the cases of syncretistic sects of Africa, they establish their own elaborate hierarchies of authority.

All these exceptions to the general characterisation of sects that I have offered are intended, not to dispute the value of clear categories in sociological analysis, but only to remind us that our categories are often clearer than the actual cases. The danger of sociology is that its constructs may easily be mistaken for summary statements of reality, for formulae in terms of which the world is to be grasped. By emphasising that the empirical data is richer than the categories, we remind ourselves that the categories are merely convenient ways of handling large bodies of data that approximately fit. The specific cultural and historical circumstances will always render our typifications false in detail: this is the price that we consciously pay in order to have some comparative over-view of a range of social phenomena – sects – which, despite their diversity, may be examined in terms of their salient similarities.

3 Sectarian responses to the world

The general characterisation of sects presented in chapter 2 has concentrated on their distinguishing features as social groups or movements. Two elements that were deliberately left aside were the specific pattern of organisation and the specific status of adherents. One advantage of the more general, if therefore somewhat more abstract, formulation provided above is that it is a depiction of the sect without the suggestion that sects are necessarily set over against a church. Sects do exist in a religiously plural environment of many denominations. They arise within a distinctly secular society, against which – rather than against a church – their protest may be directed.

The general formulation provides a framework. But sects are not all of a piece. *Within* the general frame of reference, we must now provide some categories that allow for their differences. Of the utmost importance is the choice of criteria by which we shall establish the different types of sect. Ideally, this should be consistent with, but should also refine, the central features of sectarianism that are emphasised in the general framework. Consequently, styles of organisation – charismatic, democratic, communitarian and other organisational patterns – are not adequate. Nor is categorisation in terms of the social class of votaries, as can be seen from the very different types of sect recruited largely from the poor in, say, the eighteenth and nineteenth centuries in western Europe. Both organisation and class show marked variations, apparently dependent on specific circumstances. Our best guide would seem to be to take up the basic and universal issue with which sects, and all religions, are concerned – namely, what should be done to attain salvation.

The answer to the question, 'What shall we do to be saved?' determines the entire quality of the sect. In settling this question, sectarians necessarily establish their conception of the world and of the supernatural, and how to behave towards them. Their response to conditions reflects their response to this ultimate religious concern. Their doctrine, social ethic, relationships within the group, posture to the outside world, and their conception of what it is expedient to do in their meeting together reveal what sectarians think is the way to be saved. Their conception of the supernatural and of appropriate action towards it lies in the field of descriptive study known as comparative symbolics: the social relations of the group and its response to the world is in the field of the sociology of religion.

The orthodox respond to the world by accepting it. They accept the prevailing culture and the means of salvation provided in the established religious system. Thus, in traditional Christendom men accept the church as the institution distributing the means of salvation and assisting them to attain a state of grace. They accept its authority, its pronouncements on ethical questions, and revere its leaders as agencies through whom the divine will might be more accurately known, at times to a point of belief in the infallibility of their pronouncements.

Sects reject the orthodox way to salvation, but the terms of rejection differ. The sectarian defines his need for salvation, as salvation from the evil apparent in the world. How that salvation will be vouchsafed, and how and when it operates, are significant differences in belief among sects. There are a limited number of ways of assessing the world from which one seeks salvation and of responding to it.

Deviant responses to the world

First we must recognise the range of deviant religious response, then we must examine the general sectarian organisation of each of these responses as it occurs in Christendom. The different responses may be simply stated.

Men may say that the world and its institutions (usually including orthodox religion) are evil, and that salvation is to be had only by a profound change of oneself. Only by acquiring a new conception of himself, by being born again, will a man be saved. In some measure this idea is embraced in orthodox Christianity, particularly in evangelical Protestantism, of course, but it is an idea that has been considerably diluted in practice. As the rituals of the church were established, so they were felt to be adequate for man to gain some assurance – on certain conditions – of a prospect of salvation. The change of the self ceased to be so explicitly demanded in daily life.

As a deviant response, however, the process of conversion is radically set over against institutionalised procedures and rituals. It must occur at a given time, as a known experience. Thereafter the individual may believe himself touched of God, inspired by the Spirit, redeemed by the Saviour. The experience may need frequent recollection, and the emotions attendant upon it might be rekindled in circumstances in which the converted meet to offer praise and thanksgiving. It is believed that this experience, and acknowledgment of it are essential to salvation; that men will be saved by no other agency, whether it be priests saying prayers, performing ritual, or social reformers or revolutionaries seeking to improve social conditions. All of these activities are irrelevant. What men need is a 'heart experience', and only when men have had such an experience of salvation, can society hope for betterment. This response, with its emphasis on conversion of men, we shall call *conversionist*.

A second answer to the problem of salvation is to declare that the world is evil, and that the only prospect of salvation is the overturning of the world by supernatural action. Nothing can be done to improve or redeem the present order, but men – some men, true believers – might be saved when the divinely-ordained overturning of this dispensation occurs. This response to the world then is to demand, not that men change, but that the world be changed, and to anticipate this event. It must be noted that the sectarians do not necessarily, or usually, expect to initiate this transformation of the world themselves, although they might be called to act on the side of divine forces at some signal from on high. Thus, instead of demanding that men experience inner change, their response is to demand that the world change. This response we shall designate *revolutionist* (or *transformative*)[3] implying, not that sectarians are actively preparing revolution, but that they think that God intends to.

A third response to the human situation is to recognise the evil of man's circumstance, and to seek salvation by withdrawing from it.

and by attempting to cut oneself off from the taint of the world. Instead then of saying man must be changed, or the world must be changed, this response demands that the world be abandoned. Those who retreat hope to preserve and cultivate their own holiness. Salvation is to be found in the community of those who withdraw from involvement in the affairs of mankind. This response may be designated *introversionist*.

The fourth response is to seek salvation in the world, but essentially by the employment of means not generally known in the world. The character of salvation is in this case seen as much more proximate, the attainment of those goals that are generally well-regarded in the world, but which, in the nature of human life, are elusive and ephemeral. Bodily vigour and mental ability are perhaps the most universal of these ideals, but in some cultures, status, power or control of economic resources may be associated with them. These are much more worldly aims than are embraced by some sectarians, but salvation is not always seen as other-worldly or transcendental. The religious character of this response comes in the belief that by religious knowledge, or through supernatural agencies, better means than are otherwise available will be found to attain these desired ends. By the use of these supernatural and often esoteric or occult means, the world is to be manipulated for benefit. This is how men will be saved. This response we shall call *manipulationist*.

The fifth response involves a narrow particularistic conception of salvation. The individual's concern is to be relieved from present ills, whether physical or mental, and salvation is gained by special, almost magical dispensation by supernatural agencies from the normal laws of causality. There is here no conception of the world being saved, but only of immediate release from tensions and difficulties, and vague ideas of transformation into conditions of bliss. This response differs from the fourth in the highly particular nature of salvation, and by the absence of any clear idea of benefits likely to accrue. The operation of salvation is personal and local, and the means of its attainment are neither available universally, nor capable of being stated in universal terms. This response is in fact a demand for miracles, not the expectation that principles are to be discovered for the salvation of the initiated. We shall refer to this response as *thaumaturgical*.

Two other responses remain, although neither need be specifically religious (that is to say, invoking supernatural agencies and explanations). The first of these responses is one which sees the world as a place in which there is evil, but evil which might in some of its manifestations be overcome by reform in accordance with the dictates of conscience. Conscience is here made the insight that derives from apprehension of the divine. This is, as will be seen, a rather special type of response, in which rational procedures are justified by religious (extra-rational) inspiration. This response we designate *reformist*.

Finally, there is the search for salvation by an attitude which wishes neither to abandon nor overturn the world, but is an attempt to find a basis for a radical reconstruction, based on religious principles. The world is evil because men have created an evil system. Salvation is to be attained by returning to the basic principles by which the creator intended men to live. These principles may be had from revelation or from received sacred scriptures, and on this basis the world might be rebuilt as a place in which men should experience no tension. The means to this reconstructed society may, in themselves, be rational, but the choice of ends (and perhaps even the choice of means, in some respects) is defined by acquaintance with the supernatural. This response we shall designate *utopian*.

Excluding only the conformist response – the acceptance of existing agencies of salvation – these appear to be the seven possible types of solution to the central religious quest. All of them assert that salvation is to be attained, and that supernatural agencies intend that at least some men should attain it. The supernatural agencies are said to have acted, to be acting, or to be intending to act to this end. Men must acknowledge this, and do as they are enjoined in order to be saved.

The sectarian expressions of response

Each of these responses is to be found institutionalised in different movements, and if the scheme exhausts the different ways in which men may reject conformity to social and religious norms, it should provide a useful provisional basis for the classification of sects. Clearly, sects sometimes may embrace more than one response, either because they believe that there are more ways than one to attain salvation or because the possible contradictions in doing so are not apprehended. Again, sects may change response with time, moving from one expectation about the supernatural to another, and from one set of practices to another. We shall see that there are some regularities to be observed in the way in which responses change, and these probably hold for sects outside as well as within Christendom. My concern is primarily with Christian sects, however, and the particular received traditions of that religion are, it appears, sufficiently diverse for every sectarian group, organised to express one or other of these orientations, to claim for itself Christian precedents. Now that the range of deviant religious responses to the world has been explored, I shall examine the way in which they are represented through the specific cultural material of Christian teaching, myth and ritual.

Sects which I label conversionist, because they seek to change men's hearts, find justification for devoting their resources to proselytising, for which they favour revivalist techniques. Proselytising is a way of keeping members busy, providing them with positive goals of action, maintaining emotional involvement, and providing concrete results as 'proofs of faith'. These sects are highly emotional in character. They emphasise feeling, particularly in their conception of the relation of the sinner to his Saviour, Jesus, and they express intense emotion in their meetings. Revivalism reinforces this disposition. There is acute emphasis on man's guilt, but this is less for sins actually committed, than for man's inherited condition of sinfulness. As fundamentalists they concentrate on simple Bible truths and 'felt faith' which they oppose to the dead ritualism of the hierarchic churches, particularly the Roman church, to which strong antipathy is felt.

Conversionist tendencies were evident in evangelical Protestantism in the eighteenth and nineteenth centuries, but from the beginning this response found sectarian expression initially perhaps in the teachings of grace of the Herrnhuter community which had so much influence on Wesley and the Methodist movement that he brought into being. This orientation in religion reflected the strong individualism of the period, which these sects communicated to the working classes from which they recruited most of their following.

Although conversionist sects are very strongly concerned with the recruitment of new members, recruiting is not to be identified with conversion as such. Conversion is a 'heart experience' in which the individual accepts Christ as Saviour. That does not in itself draw him into the ranks of any particular sect. Such is Christian teaching that it is not possible for any sect of this sort to claim that its ministrations *alone* effect true conversion of the heart. None claims to be the exact replica on earth of that spiritual church which is the body of Christ. They usually admit that there are saved people in other movements, particularly in movements similar to their own. Thus, fundamentalist Baptists acknowledge that Pentecostalists, Salvationists, and even evangelical members of the Church of England, may very possibly be saved. Sects of this kind do attempt to convert people on a large scale, but converting them is bringing them to Christ, not necessarily causing them to join a particular movement – although the two processes are often simultaneous. In loose usage, we may refer to men being converted to the Pentecostalists, but it is as well to recognise a distinction which the sects themselves make.

Revolutionist sects in Christianity make biblical prophecy their guide to salvation. The tribulations of the world are seen as foreordained of God. History moves on a relentless course, and men, drawn together into evil combinations as nations and empires, leagues and organisations, unknowingly act out God's grand design that leads to the battle of Armageddon and the end of this world. The sign of their impending end is already to be read in the scriptures. Orthodox churches, too, as agencies of the Anti-Christ, and all in them, are equally doomed.

Neither faith nor works ensure salvation, but only knowledge of God's word and obedience to his commands. Most men will not find salvation, but since God directed that all men should hear the truth, these sects feel obliged to preach God's word whilst there is still time. Understandably they reject the conventional eschatology of Christendom, fixing on the resurrection of the body rather than the migration of the soul (a concept denied by many of these sects). Their approach is more materialist and matter-of-fact than that of orthodox Christianity. They eschew emotionalism: for them converting men is persuading them intellectually of the truth of prophecy, not inducing an emotionally defined 'heart experience'. They sustain an aggressive orientation to the world, and draw in those profoundly disillusioned with society – or communicate such disillusionment to those whom they draw in. They lay no emphasis on joy and a loving God. Religion is serious, and God is a judge and governor who has already determined the fate of men.

Christian introversionist sects seek to withdraw into a life of inner holiness, which is both a quality of an individual and of the sect's community life. The community is the only place of salvation, initially as a place of preservation (until death or the second advent) but in practice as salvation in this life, too. The community is itself 'the gathered remnant'. There is little interest in evangelising others, since inner illumination or inspiration is not readily communicated to outsiders who may, indeed, be regarded as contaminating the faithful. Inspiration may be diffused among participants, or it may come through chosen vessels. It is regarded as the manifestation of the deity, who is seen not as a suffering Saviour but as the Holy Spirit, deepening the spiritual piety and perfection of the fellowship. Doctrine has less relevance for salvation than inspired utterance, and sustained moral rectitude, even when the scriptures are retained for general spiritual guidance. As the sect cultivates its intense community experience, eschatological ideas may recede in significance.

Introversionist sects emerge only in certain sorts of social conditions, and since they do not arise quickly, their development depends on sustained conditions of religious toleration. Some come into being in the expectation of attaining salvation in other ways – typically by the second advent – and become introversionist after disappointment. Others, particularly in Germany, evolved within the eighteenth-century Pietiest tradition. Sects of this type insulate themselves, avoiding other men in all but the most essential concerns of daily life. At times they have established themselves as isolated communities, which was possible for them in eighteenth- and nineteenth-century North America and Russia, and in twentieth-century Central and South America, when frontiers were expanding, when land was available and diligent settlers were needed. (Not all sects that adopted communitarian arrangements have been introversionist, of course, and not all communitarian introversionist sects have established communism, although some have done so.)

Manipulationist sects have flourished at different periods in Christian history emphasising their monopoly of special, and sometimes secret knowledge as the way of salvation. The teaching itself is held to be new, recovered or secret, but its principles are held to be universal, and might be taught to anyone. Their deity is not a redeemer, but an abstract idea of great power, which men can be taught to apply for their own benefit in this world. These sectarians do not avoid the world, but remain in it, enjoying it, and gaining all they can from it by the manipulation of their special knowledge. They re-learn the truths of scripture, and may increasingly abandon its literal meaning for emphasis on healing and the transcendence of evil experience by divine intelligence.

The appeal of sects such as the Christian Scientists and Scientologists is largely to the somewhat more sophisticated sections of the public. They flourish in urban contexts, among people who are usually middle-class, who are used to at least the style of abstract thinking, and who are impressed by education and progress, even though – in their manipulationist practice – they are seeking a short-cut to knowledge of greater power than is available in secular systems. The religious gatherings of these sects are unemotional, and indeed, there is sometimes little occasion for members to come to-gether, except to rehearse their blessings, undergo instruction or examination, and to claim prestige for their success in and with 'the truth'. Worship is marginal; ritual and the Bible are viewed symboli-cally, although they provide an important line of continuity with traditional Christianity, which is regarded not as being evil so much as blind, inadequate and backward.

Thaumaturgical sects cultivate that belief in oracles and miracles that has atrophied in Christianity. The search for salvation from immediate evils by involving spirits is common in all other cultures, although the higher religions in their pure form have rejected it. Jesus was a thaumaturge, and Christian myth attributes miracles to apostles and saints, although the Roman church has subsequently sought to institutionalise the thaumaturgical. Although Protestan-tism rejected magical practice, demand for it persisted in faith-healing movements before new impetus was given to this orientation to the world in modern spiritualism. Spiritualistic sects generally lack any coherent eschatology, but emphasise life after death and communication with the dead. More sophisticated spiritualist sects as they develop sometimes pick up metaphysical ideas similar to some of those found among manipulationist sects, but spiritu-alists seek a much more personal salvation by reliance on particular mediums and spirits, and these particularist concerns contrast sharply with the universal general principles espoused by manipul-ationists. Ethical practice is less important than spirit guidance. As extreme Protestant sects abandon rites in favour of words (the Bible, sermons, hymns, 'tongues' and tracts), so spiritualists abandon words in favour of 'communications', knockings, promptings, transfigurations and manifestations. What is communicated is not

narrative or homily but personal reassurance from a supernatural
source. The central relationship is not saviour and sinner, mediated
by preachers, as among conversionists, but spirit and client, represented to each other through a medium.

Reformist sects are rare, and perhaps the only thoroughly
developed example is modern Quakerism: it is a secondary or
tertiary response rather than the initial orientation of a sect. Such a
sect is aware of social organisation, and concerned to improve it by
use of that religious insight that they regard as uniquely their own.
Salvation is gained by communicating an ethic by which men may
live. The sects remain separate and apart, the better to provide a
commentary and critique for the society towards which it is no
longer either hostile or indifferent. Its own separateness is largely a
matter of tradition, transmuted into a profound sense of ethical
obligation and intensity of conscience. It is scarcely a recruiting
organisation. It hopes to influence the world more by leavening the
lump than by winning members for itself. Their salvation is
identified with the salvation of all men and with the salvation of
society. Whilst the sectarians themselves are often disposed to be
individualists, they see salvation as very largely a matter of transforming social organisation.

A meeting of Friends (Quakers) in the
eighteenth century: men and women
are separated. Except for announcements
and inspirational utterances, more
traditional groups of Quakers still
worship in silence.

Utopian sects are impressed by the possibility of salvation in
society, but for this society must be re-made entirely, not by an act
of God, but by men working on God-given principles. These sects
withdraw from society not to cultivate holiness, but to provide the
social organisation for salvation. Their conception of morality is
strongly conditioned by the requirements of men in the social
relations of the new society that they seek to form frequently by
founding colonies in the wilderness. They differ from secular
Utopians in their demand for common religious belief, usually
based on the Bible, and sometimes explicitly on the church at
Jerusalem as described in the book of Acts. They may propagate
their ideas, but they do not readily accept would-be entrants to the
societies without careful scrutiny, and in practice they often become
more closed than their original conception warrants. Such was the
case with the *Bruderhof* community founded by Eberhardt Arnold.
Their communities differ from those that introversionists sometimes set up, because they are committed, as a matter of principle, to
rediscovering the model for the way of life for all men, which has
been corrupted by existing social organisation. Introversionist communities, on the other hand, are often only a defence mechanism to
preserve their own distinctive piety.

The general framework that we have now developed in application to Christianity will permit us in the following chapters to
look at actual sects in some detail, and in particular at the origin and
development of particular movements, their organisation, the
classes from which they have recruited, the means by which they
have grown, or the causes of their decay, their social practices, and
the way in which their patterns of response have shifted in the
process of social change. A discussion of sects without an apparatus
for analysis and comparison, such as that of our first three chapters,
would not be sociology: but the theoretical framework must now
prove its value in the examination of the sects of contemporary
society.

4 The early Fundamentalists

Salvation by faith and the acquisition of grace and personal holiness is an important element in the Protestant tradition. Even in England there had been numerous lay religious societies in the late seventeenth century, in which the search for a holy way of life was very much the central concern. Although these groups were sometimes led by laymen, they were in no sense sects. They sought intensification of religious experience in devotional meetings, but did not separate themselves from the Church of England. Preachers from Count Zinzendorf's Herrnhut community, who visited England in the 1730s, preached the doctrine of grace in some of these societies and at their hands John Wesley was converted in 1738. Subsequently he undertook his lifelong itinerant evangelism throughout England, and shares with George Whitefield and Howell Harris responsibility for the dissemination of this new orientation throughout England and Wales. From their activities arose the Methodist movement in its various branches, and also the Whitefield-inspired and more Calvinistic denomination known as the Countess of Huntingdon's Connexion.

Revivalism and individualism

Methodism itself went through a distinctly sectarian phase,[4] but, more important, by disseminating teachings of free will and grace, it stimulated revivalism and produced a climate conducive to individualistic religion that dispensed with the forms and procedures of the churches. If salvation might be attained by a 'heart experience', what need could there be for bishops, priests, sacraments and ceremonial? Rejecting the need for the mediation of society or its agents, Methodism unwittingly diffused the theory of individualism to the masses – obscured as this was by the cohesive, but separated, chapel communities that arose in its name.

In the United States, and particularly among frontiersmen, this religious individualism was quick to flourish. The social system was without the traditional legitimation of social organisation that prevailed in Europe and was therefore less firmly grounded. In any case, at the frontier, men found themselves more isolated and necessarily more self-reliant. Salvation by individual decision to accept Christ fitted circumstances in which men had to decide things for themselves, without the strong social pressures of a settled social order. Established and sacerdotal churches were not available, and the social role of the priest was unaccommodated to frontier conditions. Priests fit into a society as fully institutionalised as their own role: cultural frontiers are places for prophets, or at least, for revivalists.

Revival had occurred in America before Methodism came – in New Jersey in 1720, and in the Great Awakening led by Jonathan Edwards in Northampton, Massachusetts, between 1735-40. Methodism provided a better doctrinal justification for this religious style, however, with its assertion of free will, than did even much-modified Calvinism. With few indigenous institutions to check emotionalism, revivalism became a powerful social force in frontier religion. With limited cultural, educational and recreative opportunities, and no other very effective religious institutions, revivalism was suited to the atomised character of frontier society, and was one of the few agencies that could bring man together momentarily and often ecstatically en masse. The intoxication of the revival was itself a caricature of the ordered meetings of the religious assembly for high ceremonial, by which more settled societies reinforced their sense of unity and cohesion.

The Methodist circuit riders were the principal early agents of religion and revival in America, and next to them the Baptists. Some Presbyterians also participated, but their inheritance of Calvinism and the echoes of the doctrine of predestination (contrary to the Methodists' emphasis on free will) inhibited their participation and caused divisions in their ranks. But some Presbyterians espoused revivalism: one of the two McGee brothers prominent in the great Kentucky Revival in 1799-1801 was a Presbyterian. On that occasion, as on others, the converted frontiersmen were powerfully affected: some lay prostrate for hours under the impact of the message of conversion; others jerked obsessively, barked like dogs

Methodist circuit rider,
Bishop McKendrie, riding through
southern Illinois and Missouri.

51

or danced and shrieked in joy or anguish. Although the preachers on these occasions belonged to the powerful denominations, the sober assemblies of ministers and respectable laymen in the cities on the East Coast looked askance at revivalistic fervour that led to such excesses. Their disapproval of extreme manifestations of the conversionist faith which, in more tempered form, they subscribed to themselves, was the occasion for the emergence of new movements that were less inhibited in their enthusiasm. Just as the Primitive Methodists and Bible Christians arose in England in the early years of the nineteenth century to accuse the settled leadership of the parent Wesleyan Methodists with the abandonment of true Methodist spirit and fervour, so in the United States, in even more extreme form, new movements – in particular the Cumberland Presbyterians and the forerunners of the Disciples – were coming into being with the same justification. As religious movements continue, their procedures become routinised, and their initial ardour settles into comfortable security and respectability. Schism may then occur as a radical, energetic and enthusiastic protest against this. This process has been particularly marked among the denominations espousing an evangelical conversionist approach to salvation and in conversionist sects themselves.

Sects that arise in distinct schism from a parent body of which their own members have been an integral part begin with a definite self-conception, and often inherit a pattern of organisation. But sects that arise from revival, that may have had nominal association with larger denominations (the members of which may have not always wanted to receive less sophisticated revival-recruited people), more typically begin as inchoate and ill-defined collectivities depending often on the one revivalist whose activity has led to their conversion. Rapidly recruited converts, whose knowledge of Christ and Christianity is largely what they have experienced in a few intense hours of conversion, are not readily drawn into and accommodated to the established congregations of existing denominations.

A frontier sect

In the conversionist tradition an early sect that arose from mixed motives of revivalistic freedom and naive ecumenicalism was the group that came to be known as Disciples of Christ (sometimes known simply as Christians). The Kentucky Revival of 1800 had very much impressed one evangelical preacher, Barton W. Stone who thereafter steadily acquired a following that sought to be free from the hindrances of all denominations. Not long afterwards a Northern Irish Presbyterian minister, Thomas Campbell, became convinced that isolated frontiersmen ought to have the opportunity of hearing the message of salvation and participating in Christian worship, even though they were not Presbyterians. His 'Christian Association' was expelled by the Presbyterians, and Campbell, becoming convinced of the unscriptural character of infant baptism, joined a Baptist association. The group retained something of its separate identity, and under Campbell's son, Alexander, became a well marked radical group among the Baptists. Campbell's strong anti-clerical opinions, voiced in a magazine he edited, together with his vigorous demand for purely scriptural authority in Christianity eventually led to his following leaving the Baptists and uniting with the larger part of the group led by Barton Stone.

The Campbellites (and the followers of Stone) had always insisted that they were strongly opposed to sectarianism. Their aim – a common one among sects, particularly conversionist sects – was to unite Christians around simple scriptural truths. If men would see that all that they needed was to accept Jesus and to obey the scriptures, then ecclesiastical institutions would be clearly redundant. But this very assertion created resentment in other movements, not least because the clergy were a principal target of Alexander Campbell's vigorous polemic. To them the Campbellites were merely a sect. Such indeed they became. In the 1830s, a period of diverse religious excitement in the United States, when the Millerite enthusiasms (see chapter 6) and the Mormons both grew vigorously, the Campbellites or Disciples were one of the most prominent and vigorous new movements in the frontier territories.

The Disciples were almost a prototype of the essentially biblical sect, dedicated to converting men as the only way to salvation. But as others increasingly recognised them as an independent group, so they themselves had to become concerned about their self-definition and their organisation. A central problem for conversionist sects that begin with a broad definition of themselves as simply 'Christians' is to know just by what criteria a Christian is defined. The Plymouth Brethren (known as Darbisten in Switzerland and Germany) encountered the same problem. Since the Campbellites were prepared to join in fellowship with all Christians, but *only* with Christians, and in communion with them, the problem was more than academic. In the 1830s, when the Campbellites were crystallising into a sect, these issues were keenly discussed.

They already had from Campbell's strong leadership a well-defined social ethic, although this did not differ radically from that of other fundamentalist groups. Dancing, drinking, even keeping a shop where alcohol was sold, were all prohibited. These things were part of the worldliness which, as converted men, they had abandoned. The range of expected asceticism among them is apparent from these lines from an early edition of their periodical:

> Renounce the world, the preacher cries;
> We do, the multitude replies.
> While one as innocent regards
> A snug and friendly game of cards;
> And one, whatever you may say,
> Can see no evil in a play;
> Some love a concert, or a race;
> And others shooting, and the chase;
> E'en dames, their fortune to enhance,
> Will have their children learn to dance,
> And ape the fashions late from France.[5]

Like other fundamentalist sects, the Disciples, in this period, condemned the professional ministry of the churches and denominations, although they had their own itinerant preachers. They urged

54

mutual ministry one unto another by the lay members. They disapproved strongly of worldly styles in religion, not only in Catholicism, which was the principal enemy of American evangelical Protestantism, but also in the evangelical denominations, particularly of their use of musical instruments to accompany church singing, and their imitation of formal church architecture. Most of all, simple frontiers-people that they were, they distrusted intellectualism in religion and the theological institutions which debated scholarly matters far removed from what to them was the one overriding issue – the conversion of sinners.

The impact of the Holiness Movement

The Disciples steadily lost their rigour and became a denomination, as did other sects that emerged in the conversionist tradition. Here it is their sectarian phase that concerns us. In the United States, and to a lesser degree in Britain, a group of movements sprang up to revitalise Methodism and subsequently to form new sects outside Methodism. The leaders of these movements were not all Methodists, but it was from the Methodist inheritance that the new movements acquired their doctrinal legitimation, particularly in the doctrines of assurance of salvation and of personal holiness.

John Wesley had paid special attention to the concept of holiness of heart, at times suggesting that this was the central truth for Methodism to promulgate. Men could be entirely sanctified by the experience of salvation, and their lives should show forth their saved condition. The idea of entire sanctification had not been embraced by other Christian denominations, and as for the teaching of assurance, the more Calvinistic among the Baptists used to refer to it as 'the doctrine of cock-sureness'. In the United States, however, revival traditions and the ideal of individual self-help combined with the strong lay emphasis in American Protestantism to make the doctrine of entire sanctification specially attractive to some fundamentalists outside the confines of Methodism. The doctrine had the appeal of asserting spiritual equality of opportunity, and demanded by implication the capacity to achieve holiness in daily life in manifestation of the grace that God had granted. Equality and achievement were primary American virtues, and the doctrine was well matched with the values of the wider society, where the traditions of equality and self-help of the frontier were still strong, and where the ideas of improvement and progress were complemented by the ideas of holiness and behaviour free from sin. In the 1830s, holiness teachings received explicit endorsement even from some prominent Congregationalists – men brought up in a Calvinist tradition. Charles G. Finney and Asa Mahan, professors at the Congregationalist Oberlin College, Ohio, canvassed holiness ideas in their vigorous revival campaigns throughout America and Britain also. Finney's acceptance of the doctrine of disinterested goodwill as the model for Christian behaviour led him to accept the teachings of entire consecration, or entire sanctification as it was known in the Methodist tradition from which it sprang. Other Congregationalists and the more established Methodists disapproved of revivalism, and the holiness ideas – 'Oberlin Perfectionism' as they called it – which Finney and others adopted in the hope of making revivals more effective and results more lasting.

Methodism was the more natural soil for the growth of holiness, and even one or two American Methodist bishops endorsed the private meetings at which many experienced instantaneous sanctification in 'the second blessing', that is, an experience of God's blessing different from, additional to and following conversion itself. From the 1830s, these private devotional meetings grew in number, but increasingly the claim of holiness people to immediate cleansing from sin was regarded by others as potentially dangerous to orderly Christian life, as presumptuous in relation to themselves, and perhaps also to God. Others disliked the threat which the interdenominational character of holiness teachings posed to the distinctive teachings and organisation of Methodism. Holiness ideas spread, however, particularly after the revivalist, Dwight L. Moody, who had already experienced the 'second blessing' himself, learned from a Plymouth Brother that the most effective

revival message was not the threat of divine sanctions but the omni-presence of divine love. His revival campaigns in Britain in the 1870s, and those of Pearsall Smith (who had also preached with great success among the Lutherans in Germany), communicated a more positive and joyous form of evangelical Christianity and led to the establishment of the Keswick Conference, once Moody's ideas had found support among Anglican and Free Church evangelicals. A modified form of holiness teaching was accepted: instead of claiming that a man's 'sinful nature' was instantaneously rooted out at the second blessing, the emphasis was rather that a 'cleansing process' was begun.

Holiness as a basis for sectarianism

Growing differences among holiness preachers themselves and official attempts to curb the various associations that had sprung up among Methodists in America led some holiness people into separation. Frequently this step, undertaken in the name of all united true Christians, led nonetheless to the appearance, in only a short time, of distinctly sectarian characteristics. One early separ-

D. L. Moody, here seen preaching in the Islington
Agricultural Hall, London, was the most successful
American revivalist of the 1860s and 1870s.
Although Moody's revivals were interdenominational,
many of those whom he inspired came to
favour the emerging Holiness movements.

ated group was the movement that began in 1880 under the leadership of Daniel Warner and that came to be known as the Church of
God (Anderson, Indiana). Organisation was rejected, and congregations did not maintain membership lists: the fraternity was bound
together by shared fellowship of the Spirit. This radical rejection of
ecclesiastical machinery drew a considerable following, and
although still emphasising its ecumenical spirit, this movement has
in effect become a sect.

To many orthodox Methodists, the enthusiasts for holiness
appeared fanatical, intensely emotional and given to anarchy.
These characteristics, together with their severe taboos against
jewellery, tobacco, musical instruments and adornments of dress,
made it difficult for them to continue their association with the
Methodists, who had come to accept the general values of the
prevailing secular culture. But even for the more restrained members
of the National Holiness Movement, which was sponsoring separate
meetings and publishing its own literature, a parting from Methodism was becoming inevitable. Little by little, different independent
missions and assemblies sprang up, many of which proclaimed
themselves to be non-denominational.

Several of these bodies were steadily brought into association,
and for practical ends such as organising missionary work, distributing literature and establishing theological institutions, the economies of scale worked to bring about the familiar process of routinisation of procedures and the development of a bureaucratic structure.
Minimal creeds were sometimes adopted, the holiness leaders being
careful to dissociate their following from faith-healing movements
and from the enthusiastic watchers for the second advent. They
sought to maintain spontaneity and freedom of worship by watching
for the Spirit and the gift of sanctification. Discipline was left to the
Spirit. The vital emphasis, for example in the Church of Nazarene,
Los Angeles, was 'getting the glory down' (from heaven to the
congregation). People would shout, cry out in ecstasy, and the
unsanctified would sometimes go down under the power of the
Spirit to experience the 'second blessing'.

The Los Angeles congregations of a former Methodist minister, Phineas F. Bresee, known as the 'Church of the Nazarene', united in 1907 with the Association of American Pentecostal Churches, calling themselves *The Pentecostal Church of the Nazarene* and emphasising the evangelical, evangelistic and emotional inclinations of the movement: each side being anxious to show that 'the Pentecostalers and the Nazarenes could shout as loud as the holiness folks in Texas', who were to join the union within a few months. The enthusiastic character of the movement was revealed in the first assembly held in Chicago, when again and again the president 'had to call the people back to business which had been interrupted by testimonies, singing, praise and shouts of joy'. The eventual basis of union was holiness of heart and life, with liberty on non-essential doctrines. This permitted those so inclined to preach the second coming and faith healing, and to condemn tobacco. (Alcohol was, in any case, prohibited.)

The new movement was by no means the union of the most extreme and emotional advocates of holiness, however, and in its organisation it resembled Methodism, adopting, despite the experience of independence of many of its congregations, a mixed constitution between superintendency and congregationalism. A number of more radical holiness groups, in particular the Metropolitan Church Association with its headquarters in Chicago, and the Pillar of Fire Church, organised by Mrs Alma Kent White at Denver, Colorado, adopted more rigorous conventions about dress and adornment, and even freer forms of uninhibited worship; the former also prohibited private property beyond immediate need.

The Pentecostal Church of the Nazarene spread rapidly, both by drawing in independent holiness missions and associations and by its own evangelism in the United States and in various mission territories. In Europe its principal strength is in Britain, arising mainly from its drawing in the dozen or so congregations of the Pentecostal Church of Scotland in 1915. All holiness bodies have by no means sought such union. Many other holiness sects have persisted in the United States and Great Britain, some of miniscule proportions. The strong non-denominational character of the movement has persisted in the isolation of small independent missions and churches, and the pre-sectarian stage of the development is evident in those movements that maintain a purely auxiliary function. Thus the Faith Mission operates widely in rural areas in Scotland, Ireland and parts of England. It continues the activities of typical holiness associations, bringing people together for prayer, for conversion and the second blessing, but does not seek to create separate new church fellowships.

The Pentecostal Church of the Nazarene strongly emphasised 'spirit-leading', experiences of glory and freedom of worship, with vigorous assertions that worship should include expression of joy. The Holiness Movement in general, however, dissociated itself from the more ecstatic developments that began to occur in the conversionist tradition at the beginning of the twentieth century when the Pentecostal movement began. Much as holiness people taught the second blessing, they had not taught that the blessing was marked by signs of the Spirit's action, except in the utterance of the believer himself. The distinction is important, even though both Holiness and Pentecostal movements belong to the same sub-species of sect. It was sufficiently keenly felt to cause the Pentecostal Church of the Nazarene, which was becoming somewhat more respectable, to drop the word Pentecostal from its title, just as some of the loosely-knit holiness associations in Britain, for example, the Pentecostal League, changed their names.

The Holiness Movement in its varied forms brought women to the fore, perhaps more than any previous development in Christianity. This was not through the leadership of any one woman, but was a widely diffused tendency. From the early days of Mrs Palmer's weekly holiness meetings, women appeared as conspicuous figures in holiness associations. As a movement with strong lay traditions, arising at a time of women's increasing emancipation in western countries, this is perhaps not surprising. It was the first development in Christianity which admitted them to positions of influence on any wide scale, both because external influences sanctioned it, and

because the freedom emphasised in the new movement ignored traditional Christian precepts on the subject.

The Salvation Army

One extremely significant sect, the influence of which has been felt throughout the world, emerged in England at least partly as a result of the influence of holiness ideas. This was the Salvation Army – the creation of William Booth, a former minister of the schismatic Methodist group known as the New Connexion. Striking out on his own, Booth settled in the East End of London in the mid-1860s, seeking by revival methods to persuade the slum-dwellers to go to church. Booth was a dramatic preacher, who used styles of oratory that were new in religion. His vivid metaphors and trick effects met with thorough disapproval from most ministers, but he had rapid success with the poorest classes. The very name, Salvation Army, which he adopted in 1878, and the military styles: officers and other ranks, barracks, bullets, knee-drill, enemy, and many other terms,

William Booth, who founded the
Salvation Army in the 1870s,
preaching from a lorry.

61

were an extended and colourful metaphor, which captured the
imagination of the working classes. By 1881 the movement had
grown from little more than 4,000 in 1877 to over 72,000. The
General had set his face against forming a sect, but in the event, the
Salvation Army became as distinctive and separate an organisation
as the Plymouth Brethren had been at an earlier date, and more so
than the looser-knit holiness groups then flourishing in Britain.

The Salvation Army did not arise directly from the inspiration of
holiness preachers and teachings, but it shared the extreme evange-
licalism of the period. Revivalism and open-air evangelism were its
chosen methods of recruitment, and the pouring out of the Holy
Spirit, the search for a new Pentecost, and the expectation of a full
and complete conversion with sanctification, were among its
essentials. In rejecting the sacraments of communion and baptism,
the movement came even closer to the sectarian ideal, and went
further than some holiness meetings. Nominally, and despite its
hierarchic structure, it was committed to the priesthood of all
believers, and it remained a firmly lay organisation.

There was a strong touch of the charismatic about 'General'
William Booth himself, of course, and an indication of hereditary
charisma in the transmission of leadership to his son and subsequently to others in his family. The General vested the movement's
property initially in himself and swept away the committee that had
kept his earlier Christian Mission in order. He had something of the
autocrat about him, much as had Wesley, and many were drawn to
the movement to follow him. Working-class movements – particularly those with a rather strong emotional orientation, such as
characterises conversionist sects – have not infrequently demanded
a strong autocratic leader.

Salvation and social welfare
The Salvationists had a rather stronger social commitment than
usually marked holiness sects. From early days Booth recognised
that saving souls was not easy when men had empty stomachs and

cold feet: he wanted to redeem the slums in more than a strictly spiritual way. Perhaps he understood that religion, whilst ostensibly directed solely to heavenly salvation, also gave men respectability and earthly prospects. Whereas Wesley had seen the tendency of the pious to become prosperous as a danger to their spiritual condition, Booth, perhaps because so many of his early converts lived in the degrading conditions of the large cities, endorsed social welfare as an aid to spiritual regeneration. His campaigns for hostels for the down-and-out, and the enthusiasm with which his followers demanded social legislation for a variety of social ills, led to the publication of his dramatic plan for material salvation, published in 1890 as *In Darkest England and the Way Out*. Booth's vision was of a utopia of colonies to be set up by some measure of totalitarian government. A strict almost puritanical discipline and a strong work-ethic would enable all but the most feckless to improve their social condition, and vigorous evangelism would help them to accept salvation.

Booth's scheme was over-ambitious but he was far from being a revolutionary. His plan was not in the usual sense a millennial dream: he did not advocate overturning the social system, nor did he expect the advent of Christ to signal the time when his plan might be implemented. It was rather a reformatory scheme to be run in harness with revivalist and evangelistic effort. He rejected as a central tenet of religion the pre-millennialist adventism of some Christian sects just as much as he rejected socialism. Indeed the Army was closer to espousing post-millennialism (the teaching that Christ would return to earth *after* the thousand years of peace and harmony, rather than returning before to usher in such a period). This is somewhat unusual for conversionist sects, but none of them make the advent the central issue of their concern, although, as literal biblicists, all have some way of interpreting those scriptural texts that promise the return of Christ, and most conversionist sects are pre-millennialist.

The Salvation Army has always been conspicuous for its sustained efforts to redeem men socially as well as spiritually. Salvationist women sell the Salvationist newspaper, *The War Cry*, in pubs and clubs and wherever alcohol is sold. The movement has never relaxed the vigour of its temperance work. More dramatic, and perhaps without parallel among Christian sects, was the work that the Salvation Army undertook, especially in the early days, to save girls from the extensive white-slave traffic that flourished in the great cities of the western world. Although the work had already begun, it came into prominence when Bramwell Booth, the General's son and 'Chief of Staff', and subsequently his father's successor, persuaded William T. Stead, the editor of a vigorous London paper, the *Pall Mall Gazette,* and a supporter of the Salvation Army, to bring to the notice of the public details of the way in which girls were abducted and forced into prostitution. Stead contrived to have a young girl procured and transported to France in order to expose the ease with which such traffic was conducted, and behind him in his enterprise stood the Salvation Army, whose officers presented a petition with hundreds of thousands of signatures to Parliament seeking changes in the law. (Incidentally, the law reacted by convicting and imprisoning Stead for his part in the affair.)

Such efforts have been unusual among sects, although some have occasionally tried to mount public protest about legislation that they have considered to be vicious. Conversionist sects, frequently employing revival techniques for recruitment, are of course much more disposed to attempt to influence the public than are other types of sect. The demonstration, the rally and the techniques of persuasion are part of their stock-in-trade; even so, it is not very often that they are used for purposes other than strictly religious ones. The Salvation Army has been alone among sects of this type in its sustained commitment to social work and social welfare.

The Salvation Army very quickly spread to other countries of the English-speaking world, and beyond. It met severe police regulation in Prussia and even in Württemberg, which had a reputation for greater toleration towards sectarians. In France, Booth's daughter Catherine led the movement. In Switzerland, hostile crowds attacked the first meetings held by Catherine Booth, and in 1883 in the

Cantons of Geneva and Neuchâtel the movement was proscribed: to wear its uniform became an offence. Part of the hostility was occasioned by the prominence of women among the Salvationist leaders. In America, too, the Army met with hostility, despite the diversity of sects there and the long acquaintance of Americans with revivalists.

The social impact of the early conversionist sects

Despite their diversity, what the conversionist sects such as the Disciples, the various holiness groups of which the Church of the Nazarene is the largest, and the Salvationists, have in common is their reliance on swift conversion as the basis of Christian commitment. Doctrines are not elaborate; rituals are minimal, and where they are performed no sacramental import is attached to them. Salvation is easily obtained, and it can be obtained by anyone, anywhere. Of special importance is the way in which these sects accepted, and perhaps stimulated, the emanicipation of women, especially in the lower classes. This was not merely a matter of the occasional emergence of a semi-charismatic woman leader. Women became full participants with more equal opportunity than in other types of religion available to the same social classes. The intense emotionalism, subjectivism and the rejection of formal education in these sects facilitated the greater involvement of women. These sects, especially in their early days, adopted revivalism as the means of bringing people to salvation. Mass gatherings in which men were shorn of their social status (usually it was negative status) and in which they were levelled to a commonality of condition, were the usual places where converts took the radical decision to be 'washed in the blood', to be 'born again'. The emotionalism of such occasions, as well as their colourfulness and vigour, were most attractive to the least educated and poorest members of western society, and from them these sects drew their recruits. The development of mass communications and the diffusion of elaborate and tempting recreational facilities has undermined the appeal of their methods, but some more modern conversionist sects have other characteristics that are attractive to many among the least privileged sections of the population.

5 The Pentecostal movements

Conversionist sects and emotional expression

Conversionist movements have a direct continuity with the evangelical branch of Protestantism in their return to the scriptures for the fundamentals of Christianity. Because their mission was to restore what they considered to be lost elements in Christianity, their ardour and their insistence on a 'heart experience' as the real criterion of true faith were embarrassing to settled, conventional and respectable Christians, and appeared to the clergy as a challenge to their role and function. The gulf was widened when, in addition to this, special claims of instant sanctification and of Spirit baptism were made. The division grew more profound even between new sects and old churches in the same tradition as the churches adjusted to the secular styles of modern society. The increased demand for decorum in social life and the growing inhibitions against easy emotional expression, even among the lower classes, that has marked advancing civilisation, would make a Wesley or the McGee brothers far less acceptable in today's Anglican or Presbyterian churches than they were in their own times. As religious exercises have become more decorous and as less room has been left for lay spontaneity, so the newly emerging conversionist sects (and these are the emotional sects) have seemed increasingly outlandish. The sects, for their part, have interpreted their mission all the more intensely, since there was now so much more of the Christian message of a 'heart religion' to restore.

The emotionality of early Methodist meetings was a normal expression of the uninhibited moods of the workers of the eighteenth century, and the exhibitionism of the early Salvationists was part of the response of conversionists to the new, showy and increasingly organised and well-equipped styles of public entertainment. As General Booth said, defending the adaptation of music-hall ditties as hymns, 'Why should the Devil have all the best tunes?' But, by the end of the nineteenth-century, emotional religion probably needed some legitimation that was more impressive than the excuse that men were overjoyed at getting the truth. This justification came in the form of crediting intense religious expression of the emotions to God himself. The Christian God, diversified in three persons, has always had the advantage of being able to sustain, as a dialogue or as a threefold operation in the world, a drama of which all the parts were played by him. The Holy Spirit in particular as the form of Deity capable of being diffused as an influence among men, and as the form in which modern men almost exclusively claimed to encounter God, has always been available to legitimate particular ideas or inspirations in religious life.

Emotionalism and doctrinal justification

Conversionist sectarians gained a sudden new impetus in the early years of the twentieth-century, and this development may be at least in part attributable to new styles of emotion in religious life and to the scriptural way in which they could be justified. As there had never been any lack since Wesley's day of new conversionist groups in the holiness tradition, particularly in the United States, the rapid and dramatic success of the new wave of these sects appears to be associated with the form of expression that it re-discovered and the scriptural sanctions that could be invoked to explain it, defend it and sanctify it. The new wave of conversionist sects were the Pentecostalists.

The particular teachings of the various Pentecostal sects did not spring up fully formed when the movement first began. What happened rather was that at various holiness meetings, at which the significance of the sanctifying experience of the inspiration of the Holy Ghost was emphasised, particular converts began to break out into 'unknown tongues' in the intensity of the highly charged situation in which the second blessing was awaited. Some of the outbreaks may have been little more than a few rhythmic utterances, but they were sufficient to touch off a new expectation that the Holy Ghost would again descend and baptize men in the Spirit.

Pentecostalists are all fundamentalists, accepting the literal inerrancy of the scriptures. They are generally orthodox about the

Trinity (as indeed to justify the Pentecostal phenomena, they virtually must be), accepting the conventional eschatology of evangelical Protestants (although they often also accept premillennial adventist ideas that in the nineteenth century were also part of orthodox evangelical Protestantism). Many Pentecostalists came from holiness meetings and were already committed to the conversionist position with regard to the attainment of salvation and the prospect of sanctification. What came to be added to these beliefs was the strong conviction that the gifts of the Spirit, as described by St Paul in I Corinthians, were still in operation in the modern age, and that their conferment on a converted believer would be signalled by a baptism of the Holy Spirit with charismatic manifestations. Emphasis on the gifts and on the signs occurring at Spirit baptism distinguish Pentecostal sects from holiness movements. The holiness movements expected no evident charisma, and although there might be shouts, cries of 'Hallelujah', and groaning and weeping at many holiness meetings (particularly those in backwoods areas where participants were often known as 'Holy Rollers' from their tendency to roll about in anguish or joy), these occurrences were attributed not to the Holy Ghost, but were regarded simply as appropriate expressions of emotion by men being saved and sanctified.

Speaking in tongues *(glossalalia)* is the most frequent of the gifts of the Spirit. Such phenomena had occurred in revivals throughout history, but it was only with modern Pentecostalism that they were fitted into the regular pattern of church life as a permanent feature of worship. Thus inward experience is confirmed by outward manifestations, and it is largely for these signs of Spirit blessing that Pentecostalists pray, seeking them first in the Spirit Baptism, and then in the gifts conferred by the Spirit. Gradually the regulations for exercise of the gifts became institutionalised in the more settled Pentecostal sects, and the regulations of St Paul concerning the frequency of such utterance in a church service were accepted as the appropriate pattern of order. Pentecostalists believe that the gifts, whilst given to individuals, are intended for the benefit of congregations, and although individuals may privately sing 'in the Spirit', tongues and the gift of interpretation are for the church. It became established too that messages in tongues, being at the Spirit's bidding, could not conflict with the Bible. They are a sign of the 'latter rain' mentioned in the Books of Joel and James, and portend the second advent of Christ. The idea of the advent is often used in Pentecostal meetings to impress the urgency of salvation and the need to experience the fuller blessings of the Spirit before the end of this dispensation. Apart from this, however, Pentecostalists generally behave as if salvation occurred with the soul's ascent to heaven, as conventionally understood by fundamentalist Christians.

Pentecostalists accept the theory of sanctification as promulgated by the holiness movement, i.e., that sanctification does not mean an immediately sinless life. Whilst sin is a central concern of these sects, especially in the activities leading to conversion, it is sin in the abstract as a theological category and sinfulness as a quality of man, rather than sinful behaviour, that is emphasised.

Pentecostalists are not primarily interested in doctrine. Theirs is rather a religion of congregational devotional exercises in which the intense excitement generated is attributed to the action of the Holy Ghost. In general only the ministers of the Pentecostal movements know much about doctrine. But although the laity are doctrinally uninformed, doctrine is important for Pentecostalism, since it justifies Pentecostal phenomena through the scriptures, and these phenomena justify separation from other churches.

The emergence of Pentecostalism

In the development of the Pentecostal sects, the new interpretation of Pentecostal phenomena was more important than the phenomena *per se*. The holiness movement had excited some preachers to examine scriptural discussion of Spirit Baptism, and evangelists, perhaps led by Charles F. Parham, at Bethel College, a newly founded Bible school at Topeka, Kansas, concluded in 1900 that speaking in tongues was proof of Spirit experience attested by the Bible.

Tongues were spoken by some of these students, and the claims grew that by the power of the Spirit they spoke in languages that they had never learned, but that others recognised as real languages. From this beginning developed a movement that quickly spread.

At first the charismata were not ordered into any pattern of stable religious life, but were demonstrated at revival gatherings; healings and many conversions were claimed. Visions, messages of guidance, and dubious interpretations of scripture came through these manifestations. The revival spread to Houston, Texas, and to Los Angeles, where W. J. Seymour, a holiness preacher, taught that the Spirit Baptism should be confirmed by speaking in tongues. For many people Pentecostalism seemed a logical development of holiness ideas, transforming belief into real action, excitement and supernatural power, and providing an easier and more immediate demonstration of Holy Ghost power than could be made by leading a sanctified life. The charismata made religion appear efficacious again. The new teachings also provided justification for the continuance of revival excitement as a daily and thoroughly respectable experience. Conversion was a once-and-forever event; the 'second blessing' was another; so even was the Spirit Baptism. But beyond these successive horizons of spiritual growth now opened the limitless prospect of the continued power of using the Spirit gifts. So Pentecostal groups could justify their sustained emotional pitch. Many (but not all) holiness people were convinced, and Pentecostalism proved far more effective in winning converts from those outside the Christian churches than holiness teachings had ever been.

The effects of Pentecostalism were sometimes to produce more emotional heat than spiritual light, for excesses and deviations certainly occurred among the early devotees. The sense of power in the meetings was exactly the experience that provided compensation for those otherwise poor, neglected, uneducated and powerless. It was called the real 'power', and because of its supernatural source it was greater than the power of the rich and worldly. The meetings appeared to be manifestations of divine force, and individuals could feel the communication of power as they prayed and succumbed to inner compulsions to express and assert themselves.

American cities in this period were at a stage of extremely rapid growth. They were full of immigrants, both from rural areas and from Europe, many of whom expected opportunities to make money and increase their social status. The psychology of the immigrant has, of course, left a deep impression on the American character and way of life. America was presented as a land of opportunity, and the ideal of social mobility became an irradicable element in the American social ethos. The myth of improving social status was, however, always greater than the reality, even though the reality did exist. But many people were disappointed and their worldly hopes repeatedly frustrated. The cities were places of wrecked aspirations, as well as places where fortunes might be made and the comfortable conditions of secure livelihood might be enjoyed.

Worse perhaps than the failure to achieve the expected wealth and security, was the loss of the warm associations of rural communities from which many of the new townspeople had come. Cities were impersonal in character; men were on the move; relationships were shallow, and dominated by role performances rather than by total personality dispositions. The normative structure of life was confused. People from widely different cultural backgrounds tried to work out their lives in a complex new situation and the normal expectations about behaviour broke down. There was no received tradition of custom and convention; no aristocratic class with a chivalrous code that might be admired and imitated; no settled middle class with firm conventions bent – as had been the English gentry and city merchants – on communicating their values in order to gentle the people. Crime in many forms flourished, and constantly took new forms as opportunities for exploitation, parasitism and political corruption grew. These characteristics of American cities amounted to a condition of *anomie* (confusion of social norms). In this context Pentecostalism burgeoned.

Immigrants presented one rather important characteristic that may have been of significance in the rapid spread of the new movement. Many were not long settled in America, and English was for most a new language. Speaking in another tongue can be a traumatic experience, and many first generation Americans knew that a major hindrance in making their way in American society was their deficiency of language. In the cities of the east coast, where particular ethnic colonies settled, the immigrant had at least one reference group in which he might speak easily. In the cities of the west this was less commonly the case. Even the migrants from the rural areas, who were not usually first generation Americans, might find the speed and the slickness of the urban context disconcerting. They, too, were hindered by poor verbal skills in a society that coined neologisms, and conducted its affairs in constantly changing jargon. Thus a movement promising power, and, in particular, power by the supernatural acquisition of verbal facility, was well fitted to make a dramatic appeal to the first generation of urban dwellers, even if it only symbolised their difficulties and the solution for them. Both in the specific point of emphasis – and the gift of tongues has always received so much more attention than the other spirit gifts that the movement has been known as 'the tongues movement' – and in its encouragement of free and uninhibited expression of the emotions, Pentecostalism was appropriate to the needs of many Americans.

Pentecostal teaching legitimised the expression of intense feelings for which there was so little opportunity otherwise. The meetings provided a real sense of relief from oppressive, frustrating and even bewildering social circumstances. Their social experience made men want to run away to God, and to run away sobbing and screaming. Religions often function to legitimate necessities, and to solace men for feeling as they do. From the solace there may emerge a new adjustment to situations and a new capacity for dealing with the world. Religions also solemnise in ritual activities the every-day experience of men. Primitive religions often re-enact the day-to-day concerns of a tribe, particularly in fertility rituals: so Pentecostalism re-enacted the traumas of daily life for many of their adherents. It did so with the additional invocation of the divine to give meaning to their expressions of dismay. It provided a rationale for attributing blame and praise and conferring reward, and it channelled pent-up and inhibited feelings into harmless and gratifying activities. Most important of all – and here Pentecostalism fulfilled functions common to other sects – it brought the distressed together into a warm social context, where they could confirm the appropriateness and acceptability of evangelical interpretations of their condition, and reassure each other by their shared beliefs and, more especially, by their shared activities. The sect became the surrogate community, resting on voluntary adherence, but drawing together those who chose salvation into a community of love.

Other sects would also have provided community life, but for many only the expressiveness and intensity of Pentecostalism was really adequate to their conditions. Its demands were light and its gratifications immediate. These were not people who were to be drawn into introversionist groups emphasising quiet searching of the scriptures, nor were they sufficiently educated to accept the elaborate ideological explanations and metaphysical arguments of mani-pulationist sects. The religion they needed had to be group-centred. They needed social support, and they needed a permissive context for the expression of their emotional troubles. Pentecostalism was the fullest manifestation of a faith sanctioning, indeed sanctifying, expressive emotionalism. It provided instantaneous relief.

It would be unfair to Pentecostalism, however, if it were taken to be group therapy. Pentecostalism was part of the evangelical tradition: it saw man as a sinner who needed redemption through Christ, and subsequently needed the extra blessings of the Holy Spirit. Although at the beginning of the movement the operation of the Holy Ghost was emphasised, Pentecostalists never abandoned their insistence on conversion as a first, and, indeed only, essential for salvation. Although in the days of its first enthusiasm little attention was paid to the 'fruit of the Spirit', and the insistence on good behaviour was secondary, nonetheless Pentecostalism has communicated standards to its adherents. In this it has tended to socialise its followers in a particular way. Its emphasis was less direct than that of some of the holiness movements, which, especially in their modified expression, came to exercise a powerful influence in presenting their followers with a strong set of values and norms, but its influence has been in the same direction. Pentecostalists were introduced to the dominant, if somewhat idealised, values of evangelical Protestantism, and these have been values important in the development of industrial society.

Converts drawn in for emotional gratification, and little acquainted with formal moral injunctions, steadily learned – often by rather rigorous injunctions and taboos – the styles appropriate for the ideal moral man in the modern west. Such a process of adjustment could begin only by accommodating the emotional needs of adherents in the first place, and by subsequently introducing them to a more orderly and disciplined pattern of life. This, without conscious intention, is exactly what happened in Pentecostal sects. They have steadily regulated the operation of the Spirit in their assemblies: disorder has been reduced and increased decorousness imposed. Rules have emerged about how the gifts should be manifested, and when. And this process of institutionalising the charismata has gone on alongside the establishment of more settled systems of government, and more sedate forms of group activity.

The spread of Pentecostalism

Most commentators have noticed that considerable numbers of immigrants joined Pentecostal groups, and might have noticed more had the rural migrants to the city been added to foreigners. Pentecostalism also quickly took root among Negroes in the United States and in the West Indies, and the West Indian sects in Britain, after the large-scale migration to Britain in the 1950s, are principally Pentecostalist. The vast expansion of Pentecostalism in many parts of the world, particularly in Latin America, is easily correlated with the processes of urbanisation.

In the early days the dramatic spread of Pentecostalism often brought exaggerated expectations of the power which the Spirit gifts conferred. Enthusiasm had its dangers. Some expected the messages in tongues to give direct and personal guidance for daily concerns. Others believed that the gift of tongues was given so that they might go to the mission field and preach. Elements of spiritual élitism were not absent, as some who had received the Spirit Baptism sought to establish positions of greater status for themselves. The gift of interpretation and the gift of discernment of spirits were sometimes used as supernatural justification in quarrels between members. The theory of Spirit inspiration was used to justify all sorts of behaviour in the meeting, and to resist any imposition of order. The leaders of Pentecostal assemblies (some of whom were ordained holiness ministers, others of whom were lay leaders) had difficulty in asserting any sort of authority, or in legitimating their own roles. Since the charismata were diffused, leaders could claim no more authority than others who enjoyed Spirit blessing.

These difficulties were only slowly resolved. The establishment of authorised leadership and regulation of the operation of the Spirit (without quenching the Spirit, Pentecostalists are always eager to add) was brought about only as the early interdenominationalism gave place to separate Pentecostal sects. Before this occurred, however, Pentecostal meetings sprang up throughout the United States and Canada. No one leader emerged to foster this spread and this is perhaps accounted for by the central theory of diffused Spirit power throughout a congregation. Once Pentecostal phenomena became known, the congruity of the new teaching to holiness ideas of sanctification led to rapid spread. It is precisely this facility of communication that has made difficult the assessment of the number of Pentecostal groups and of their membership, for Pentecostal practices might simply begin in a meeting hitherto of a more conventional type. Even relatively unemotional sect meetings have, even in recent years, been suddenly affected by Pentecostal practice, and some sects of quite different character, some orthodox evangelicals, for instance, have suddenly become convinced of the reality of Spirit Baptism. The Renewal Movement has led to Pentecostal ideas being accepted by some Anglican clergymen and even some Roman Catholics in Britain and the United States.

The statistics for the United States showed that there were about a thousand people in recognisably Pentecostal sects in 1906; some 22,000 in 1916; 126,000 in 1926; and over 350,000 in 1936, the last year in which the official American census of religious bodies was taken. The Pentecostalists themselves counted over a million American adherents in 1950, and by the mid-1950s, about a million and a half people belonged to thirty-six Pentecostal denominations which together had nearly 19,000 churches. Pentecostalism is particularly strong in the Southern States, with many Negro congregations, as well as congregations of poor whites, and in the states of the West Coast: it has made much less impact in the states of New England and in the Mormon stronghold, Utah.

The divisions of American Pentecostalism

Early Pentecostalism at Los Angeles did not lead to the emergence of a denomination, perhaps because Parham was a man of unstable and dubious moral character, or because his Negro associate, Seymour, lacked organising ability. One of the first effective Pentecostal sects was a small holiness movement on the borders of Tennessee and North Carolina, which accepted Pentecostal teachings in about 1906. The movement gave itself the name of the Church of God, and A.J. Tomlinson, who became its leader, drew other groups into fellowship with his organisation. The movement grew, but, as in other Pentecostal groups, divisions occurred, Tomlinson's leadership was disputed, and the church fragmented. The branch remaining under Tomlinson's direction divided after his death when his two sons disputed the right to leadership. This particular movement gained many adherents in the West Indies, and most of the Pentecostal sects founded by Jamaican immigrants to Britain of which details are known are associated with one or other of the movements which have developed from Tomlinson's movement, in particular the Church of God of Prophecy, and the New Testament Church of God. The actual distinctions between these churches are, however, of very little consequence to the adherents, who move fairly readily from one to another. This appears to be a common characteristic of Pentecostalism wherever it is found.

An early Negro movement which is now the largest Negro Pentecostal sect is the Church of God in Christ, which was founded as a holiness body in Mississippi in 1897, and adopted Pentecostal teachings in 1906. Like the various other bodies known as the Church of God, this sect regards foot-washing as a biblical injunction. This movement had over 328,000 members in the mid-1950s, compared with the 75,000 of the next largest Negro group, the Apostolic Overcoming Holy Church of God which was founded in Alabama in 1916.

By far the largest Pentecostal body in America is the movement which takes the name Assemblies of God (not necessarily identified with movements of that name elsewhere). The Assemblies of God bears less trace of the distinctive pre-Pentecostal holiness ideas than do groups like the Church of God (in its various branches) which were holiness movements before the days of the Pentecostal revival. Those sects emphasise conversion, sanctification and Spirit Baptism as separate experiences: for the Assemblies of God, Spirit Baptism replaces a sanctification experience with gradual rather than instantaneous sanctification following. This gives this branch of Pentecostalism closer association with the more moderate wing of the holiness movement, and particularly with those who espoused holiness ideas whilst remaining in other churches and denominations.

The Assemblies of God was formed from a conference of the pastors of independent churches, and it has in consequence always emphasised the congregational autonomy of individual chapels whilst uniting for general denominational purposes, particularly for missionary activity and publishing. A mixed form of congregational and Presbyterian government has evolved. The steady development of theological institutions for the training of missionaries and of ministers has drawn this movement somewhat closer to the general denominational pattern, although it remains fundamentalist and relatively puritanical in its moral injunctions. Meetings no longer

A preacher at a Berlin Pentecostal
meeting prays with a woman member
seeking the Baptism of the Holy Ghos

have the fervour of the early Pentecostal assemblies, and regulation inducing decorum and order have steadily been evolved and imple mented. With over 400,000 followers in the United States in mor than 7,000 churches, the movement has also sent out many hundred of missionaries. It has also established branches in Europe, and i the late 1950s claimed 1,700 members and 30,000 adherents i Germany, and 700 members in Austria, as well as churches i Switzerland. The *Assemblées de Dieu de France* claimed to have on hundred churches in France, although some of these may well b quite small.

Perhaps more than most emerging movements, Pentecostalism has shown an extraordinary capacity for schism, independen developments, reunions, and repeated division. This follows fron the diffused charismatic authority to which it appeals, and perhap also reflects the relatively limited capacity for organisation and th emotional disposition of many of its votaries. Only rarely ar doctrinal issues involved in such divisions, which appear often t arise from disputes about power. There are, however, divergence about the extent to which the Spirit should be free in the meetings The extraordinary freedom of the Pentecostalist meeting, and th ease with which a following has been recruited has given laymer and, quite often, laywomen opportunity to bring into being a nev sect. This has been especially true in the United States, where th authority of a regular and established ministry has been lacking and where religious pluralism has prevailed: it has been particularly sc among the Negro population.

Of the numerous Pentecostal sects, the *International Church of th Foursquare Gospel* is one of the few that owed its inspiration and continuance very much to the charisma of a leader – Aimée Sempl McPherson. After a period as a successful revivalist (like many others she required only the divine commission to qualify her as a preacher) Mrs McPherson settled in Los Angeles in 1918 and decided to build a temple there. By the use of dramatic methods – she once drove a motorcycle onto the stage of her church, pulled up sharply and shouted 'STOP – You're driving straight to Hell' – she found a

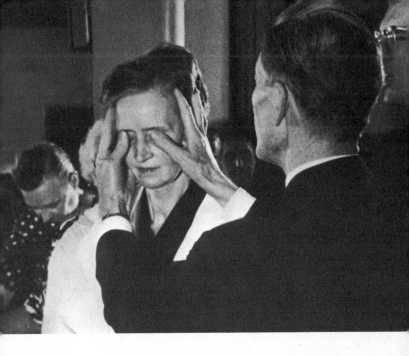

eady and enthusiastic following. Her style of preaching was as innovatory in Los Angeles in the 1920s as that of Booth in Britain fifty years earlier. She brought elements of sex appeal to the pulpit, and made her services into a great show. She was, despite her vulgarity, a vigorous campaigner against vice in Los Angeles, and undertook a variety of good works. Many of these were characterised as much by showmanship as by systematic commitment, and no activity which could yield publicity went unexploited. A series of scandals (including an occasion when Mrs McPherson was 'kidnapped' and held to ransom but which the press largely thought was merely a holiday of a rather amorous kind), marked her career, but appeared to do nothing to diminish her appeal to her followers, who were exhorted to maintain strict and exacting standards of personal behaviour. In the mid-1950s, the movement claimed some 60,000 adherents and some 600 churches in the United States, and ten churches in Switzerland.

Just as the early converts to Pentecostalism were often immigrants, either from the country or from Europe, so many more recent immigrants to the United States have adopted Pentecostalism as their faith. The store-front church is a common feature of districts in which immigrants settle, and in recent years East Harlem, the part of New York in which Puerto Ricans have very largely settled, has become heavily populated with such sectarian meetings, most of which are Pentecostal. It has been estimated by two Roman Catholic commentators that perhaps seventy per cent of the Spanish-speaking population of New York may be called Pentecostalists, and most of these were at least nominal Roman Catholics before immigration.

Pentecostalism in Europe

Among those who were quite early affected by Pentecostalism in the United States were a number of foreigners, in particular several Scandinavians, and it was T. B. Barratt, an Englishman, founder of the Oslo Methodist City Mission, who first brought back the news of Pentecost to Europe, initially to Norway. Barratt learned of the Pentecostal outbreaks whilst in America at a time when, because he was low in funds, he was almost certainly going without meals. In such a physical condition, hallucinations, visions and inspiration come easily. Barratt was, in any case, more than willing to be convinced, and after receiving Spirit Baptism and speaking in tongues, he returned to Norway as a Pentecostal evangelist. In many ways Norway, and Scandinavia generally, was well-prepared ground. Various waves of revivalism had occurred in the nineteenth-century, including the preaching sickness in the mid-century, when even children had broken out into eloquent expression, in prayer and praise, sometimes in unknown tongues. Adventist ideas had also been a subject of enthusiastic demonstrations, and holiness teachings had also spread widely, not being regarded as particularly heretical by many Lutherans, in whose traditions (particularly in Spener, Zinzendorf and Schleiermacher) strong subjectivist, pietistical strains had existed. Pentecostalism quickly became successful in Norway, and when the Methodist church opposed it, Barratt resigned to devote himself to the new movement.

Almost at the same time, the Reverend Alexander A. Boddy, Anglican vicar of All Saints, Monkwearmouth, Sunderland, told his church of the healings, conversions and attendant phenomena he had witnessed in the Welsh Revival in 1904-5, and led his congregation to pray for Holy Ghost visitation. Boddy invited Barratt to the Keswick Conference of 1907, and under Barratt's preaching at Sunderland several people received the Spirit Baptism. Annual conferences were now held at Sunderland, and the new teaching found temporary lodgment there in the ever-tolerant Church of England. A Pentecostal Missionary Union was founded in 1909, giving expression to the evangelistic character of the movement.

Barratt spread Pentecostalism to continental Europe, first to Sweden where some Methodist and Baptist ministers accepted it; most prominent among them being a young Baptist minister, Lewi Pethrus, who became the leader of the thriving Pentecostal movement in Sweden. Barratt visited sympathisers in Germany and Denmark, and other Norwegians visted Hamburg, Kassel and Zürich. In Finland the ground had been prepared by Adventist and holiness movements, and by the curious Finnish phenomenon of the 'sleeping preachers' – usually women who preached in a somatic or semi-somatic state, and who were widely famed in the country. Finnish Pentecostalism, led by the Norwegian Baptist, Gerhard Olsen Smidt, adopted the practice of adult Baptism, which has been usual in America and Britain and which gradually became general except among some movements arising among former Methodist and Reformed Church members.

Pentecostalism received its first welcome in Europe from among the faithful in existing churches, and originally presented itself as a restoration of apostolic experience, and as an intensifying and enriching of evangelical faith. To many it was presented as the outpouring of the 'latter rain', and was taken as a prophetic sign of the imminent return of Christ.

It was slower to take root among the Reformed Calvinistic Churches than in Lutheranism and Methodism, which shared the inheritance of holiness ideas. In Switzerland, it was among followers

The impact of American sects on Europe

The new American sects of the nineteenth century inherited the American tradition of proselytising religion. Within a few years of their foundation, the Mormons, and later the Witnesses and Pentecostalists, were sending their missionaries to Europe.

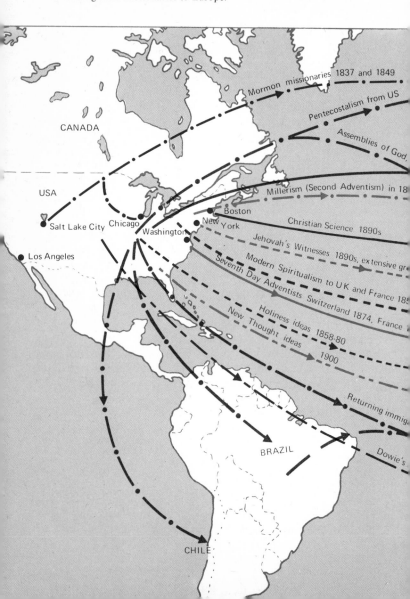

CANADA

USA

Salt Lake City

Los Angeles

Chicago

Washington

Boston

New York

Mormon missionaries 1837 and 1849

Pentecostalism from US

Assemblies of God,

Millerism (Second Adventism) in 18

Christian Science 1890s

Jehovah's Witnesses 1890s, extensive gr

Modern Spiritualism to UK and France 185

Seventh Day Adventists Switzerland 1874, France

Holiness ideas 1858-80

New Thought ideas 1900

Returning immig

BRAZIL

Dowie's

CHILE

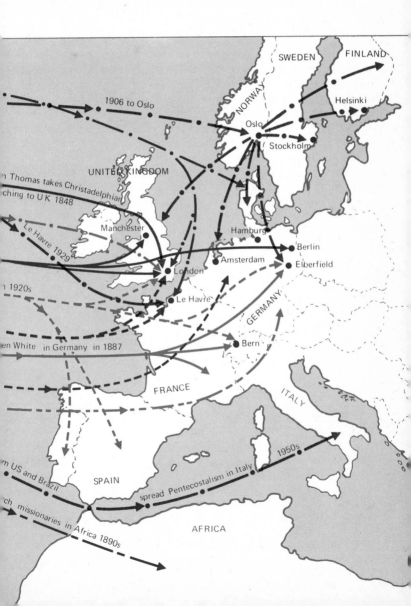

83

SWEDEN   FINLAND

NORWAY

Helsinki

1906 to Oslo

Oslo

Stockholm

UNITED KINGDOM

n Thomas takes Christadelphian
ching to UK 1848

Le Havre 1929

Manchester

Hamburg

Berlin

Amsterdam

Elberfield

n 1920s

London

GERMANY

Le Havre

en White in Germany in 1887

Bern

FRANCE

ITALY

1950s

m US and Brazil

SPAIN

spread Pentecostalism in Italy

ch missionaries in Africa 1890s

AFRICA

of Alexander Dowie's Zion Church in Illinois – itself a conversionist sect with adventist, faith healing and communitarian elements – that the new movement took root. In Holland, another country dominated by Catholic and Reformed churches, although early beginnings were made, Pentecostalism has never assumed the proportions it had quickly attained in Scandinavia, especially in Sweden.

By the 1960s there were over three hundred congregations in Norway, with perhaps 35,000 members, the largest being that at Filsdelfiamenigheten, Oslo, with 2,600 worshippers. There, and in other Scandinavian countries, the movement remained congregationalist in polity, and this makes difficult an exact assessment of its strength. In Sweden, the movement had some 90,000 members by 1960, with particularly large followings in Stockholm under Lewi Petrus, and in Öbebro; in Denmark, there were at that time only 4,000 Pentecostalists. In Switzerland about thirty different Pentecostal sects operate, although none of them is large, and some are single congregation sects. The largest movement is the *Schweitzerische Pfingstmission*, with some hundred communities and 3,000 members in 1960. The number of Pentecostalists in France is disputed, and recent estimates have varied between 8,000 and 25,000.

In European Catholic countries Pentecostalism had less success except in Italy. From the 1920s, Italian Pentecostal churches sprang up among immigrants in the United States, who found the institutionalised Catholic churches unwelcoming. The Catholic church saw little need for special missionary work among these Catholic immigrants, but Protestants did: in 1911 there were over 250 Protestant churches and missions for Italians in the United States, and only 150 Catholic ones. Although many Italian immigrants relatively quickly became unchurched, Presbyterians, Methodists and Pentecostalists made considerable numbers of conversions. In Brazil and Argentina, as well as in the United States, many Italians became Pentecostalists, and the migrants to South America were often well-educated, skilled workers.

Many Italian immigrants returned to Europe, and this was the basis for the establishment of Pentecostal churches in Italy itself.

Evangelising began in the 1930s, and the *Assemblies di Dio in Italia* has become the largest Protestant church in the country, with about 400 assemblies and perhaps 100,000 adherents, of whom nearly a half are members (thus far surpassing the pre-Reformation Waldensians in Savoy and Piedmont, who today number about 27,000, with a further few thousand 'sympathisers'). Of these groups belonging to the *Assemblies di Dio,* over 360 are in Mezzogiorno, and fewer than 40 in central and north Italy.

In Britain Pentecostalists eventually separated from other churches from which they were sometimes expelled. Of the many independent assemblies a large proportion joined, in 1925, to form the Assemblies of God in Great Britain – a body with some considerable similarities to the movement of the same name in America, and with some connections with it. There are about 450 churches, with over 18,000 members and some 60,000 adherents in Great Britain.

The Assemblies of God is a rather less enthusiastic form of Pentecostalism than the other two principal sects of the movement in Britain, the Elim Foursquare Gospel Church, and the Apostolic Church, each of which was more completely brought into being by revival campaigns. The Apostolic Church traces its history to the Welsh Revival of 1904-5, and its headquarters are in Wales. It has about 230 communities and 10,000 votaries in all, a considerable proportion of whom are in Wales and Scotland. This movement regards Pentecostalism as not simply an endowment of Spirit gifts for the congregation, but also as a pattern of church life. Thus the prophetic gift becomes the basis for church leadership in this sect, and its elaborate hierarchy of offices – Apostles, Prophets, Pastors, Teachers, Evangelists, Elders, Deacons and Deaconesses – are all appointed according to spirit guidance. This sect also permits spirit guidance on ethical, personal and ecclesiastical subjects, and it may be this facility, together with its elaborate structure of offices, which for a time gave the Apostolic Church such dramatic success in the revivals in Nigeria, where it helped to bring into being several movements which later asserted their independence and which have grown rapidly throughout west Africa.

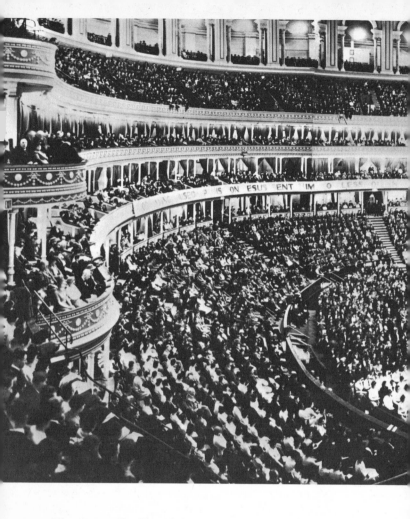

The Apostolic Church is governed by those who are appointed Apostoles: it is they who 'recognise' Prophets. The sect is thus much more authoritarian in government than are the Assemblies of God, with much less congregational autonomy. In doctrine, too, the Apostolic Church differs in espousing the principle of instantaneous sanctification, although allowing also that some will attain entire sanctification more gradually. The Apostolic Church has fifteen

churches in Germany, and fifty in Switzerland, and one or two in
Italy and France.

The Elim Church was the creation of an exceptional revivalist,
George Jeffreys, who, though a Pentecostalist himself, was a free-
lance revivalist in Britain, and especially in Northern Ireland, in the
second decade of this century. From his campaigns there developed
a clear need for the after-care of the converted. By an inevitable

process of routinisation, his revival campaigns eventually came to be *designed* to establish churches, and his associates became increasingly preoccupied with building up Elim, although Jeffreys himself clung for a long time to a vision of interdenominational revivalism. Differences over government of the movement, and a subsidiary issue about the prophetic exegesis that the movement should accept, caused a schism in 1939, and Jeffreys left to found the Bible Pattern Fellowship, a small Pentecostal movement most of whose leaders were, like Jeffreys, British-Israelites who believed that the British were the descendants of the last ten tribes of Israel, to whom all biblical prophecies related. The Elim Church has remained centrally organised, on a denominational pattern somewhat similar to that of Methodism, with a rather powerful central executive controlling its 25,000 members.

Pentecostalism elsewhere in the world

No account of Pentecostalism would be complete without reference to the movement's dramatic growth in other parts of the world. In Canada, the Pentecostal Assemblies claim over 100,000 members and the movement has grown vigorously in Australia, New Zealand and South Africa. It has also, particularly since the end of the Second World War, become the most flourishing Protestant movement in many parts of Latin America, Indonesia and perhaps also in Russia. In Chile, where Pentecostalism began in 1909, some fourteen per cent of the population are now claimed as Pentecostalists, and one commentator has even suggested that on a typical Sunday morning in Chile there are more worshippers in Pentecostal churches than are attending mass in Catholic churches. Undoubtedly this degree of success relates to the closeness of the Pentecostal movement to the mood and circumstances of the people. The informality, directness and enthusiasm of Pentecostalism gives it a powerful missionary appeal, especially among less educated and less sophisticated populations. Many of the Chilean assemblies are more ecstatic than their European counterparts; many are without regular control; some permit dancing and emphasise both prayer and the receipt of answers to prayer.

In Brazil, although there has been a steady increase in diocesan Roman Catholic priests since 1912, the population per diocesan priest in 1960 was 15,800 (per priest of all kinds, including those in religious orders, 6,400 people). Such a situation of spiritual neglect has facilitated the growth of local, intense, fraternal Pentecostalist sects. There are some fifty denominations of Pentecostalists, including the *Congregação Cristã do Brasil*, the *Assembléias de Deus*, and the *Igreja Evangélica Pentecostal*, which altogether are estimated to have a following of perhaps four millions. Faith-healing occurs significantly in a country with too few hospitals. Like other Latin American countries, Brazil is undergoing rapid transition, and Pentecostalism thrives especially among dislocated populations experiencing disruptive cultural contact and social change.

Instances of the ease with which Pentecostalism can be accepted by indigenous populations are abundant in Latin America and in Africa. The Toba Indians, who occupy the Chaco region of northern Argentina, had become a completely demoralised people, begging in the towns, pilfering and prone to drunkenness, when their evangelisation was begun by the Pentecostalists of the Parana cities. The Toba adopted the beliefs and practices of Pentecostalists, but did not altogether abandon their own religious practices, which were without too much difficulty adjusted to Pentecostal styles. The Pentecostal churches refused to support the Toba Pentecostal churches when the latter sought recognition from the government, because of the persisting pagan practices of the Toba. Toba syncretism of the new Pentecostalism and traditional shamanism persisted, and with the aid of Mennonite missionaries who lived among them (but who had had no success in promulgating their own austere religious code), the Toba registered their churches – which now number forty – as the *Iglesia Evangélica Unida,* in which singing, dancing and the search for the power which descends are the conspicuous activities.

The complex history of Pentecostal influence in Nigeria cannot be more than mentioned here, but as a result of the evangelical activities of various denominations, the conversion experience was a well-known phenomenon, widely sought among Christian Nigerians before Pentecostalism was disseminated. Nigerian traditional religion had been preoccupied with healing and with the elimination of witches, and when the Pentecostalist teachings arrived, during the First World War, Nigerians quickly assimilated the emotional expression and the ecstatic utterance. The Babalola Revival in Yorubaland was one consequence of the new teachings of holiness and Pentecost. Eventually the Nigerians followed native leaders. The churches that arose, particularly the various branches of the Cherubim and Seraphim, and the Aladura Church of the Lord, all emphasised the power of the Spirit, and the prospect of being healed, receiving guidance, and experiencing the power of the Spirit. These sects have all adopted practices alien to American and European Pentecostalists. The emotionalism of their services is more intense than anything that can usually be met with in Europe or – the backwoods of Tennessee and the other border states perhaps excepted – in the United States. They represent a cross-fertilisation by the Pentecostal movement of indigenous thaumaturgical practice, even if the latter remains their dominant preoccupation.

The Pentecostal style

Whether particular congregations are organised into one of the bigger sects, or whether they are entirely independent, there is a distinctive style about Pentecostal communities. In general Pentecostalists are relatively simple people, with unsophisticated conceptions of doctrine and church government. In the Elim movement, it is only pastors who are regulated in terms of doctrinal belief: the lay members are mainly concerned about their experiences of the Spirit. Some sects have sought to impose conscientious objection upon members, as an earnest of their commitment, but this has never been wholly successful. Pentecostalists are not people of intense conscientious concern for ethical issues, and few have had the solid conviction needed to press a claim for exemption from military service. Many who are drawn in are emotionally volatile, and revivalism has brought in many who have not stayed once the initial excitement was over. Of those who do become regular members, the gratifications of tongues-speaking, prophecy and emotionally intense meetings often appear to be of more significance than the Christian life. Despite the importance attached to the Holy Ghost, Pentecostal sects are, in their general evangelical commitment, essentially Jesucentric. It is Jesus whose name is called out in the meetings and some Pentecostal sects (especially some Negro and West Indian sects, including those found in Britain) baptise in the name of Jesus, rather than of the Trinity. Jesus becomes an important symbol of emotional attachment for many Pentecostalists, in a way typical for other conversionist sects.

It is an indication of these preoccupations that permits Pentecostalism to follow such divergent ecclesiastical patterns – from the congregationalist polity found in Swedish Pentecostalism, and, in a more muted way, in the Assemblies of God organisations in various countries, to the centralised organisation of Elim, the 'Pentecostally-legitimated' hierarchy of the Apostolic Church, and the episcopal structure of the Pentecostal Holiness Church in the United States. Almost all Pentecostal movements have evolved a professional ministry, and this fact also reflects the relatively limited capabilities of the lay following, and their need, especially where they have been converted in revivals, for continuing leadership if they are to persist. Yet the Pentecostal movement, like all sectarian movements, has a considerable ideological inheritance of hostility towards the clergy and towards ecclesiastical organisation. It is one of the ironies of Pentecostal sects that they have been steadily obliged to adopt those features of the older churches against which much of their early polemic was mounted. They remain of course anti-sacramentalist and anti-sacerdotal, but all the larger movements have evolved elaborate agencies to promote missioning, Bible colleges and the publication of literature. The lay ideology obliges the typical Pentecostal minister to play a careful role with a flock that needs a leader, but which is theoretically committed to the priesthood of all believers and the free operation to all of the Holy Spirit. The monopoly of power positions by the ministry has brought into being some lay organisations in Pentecostalism, such as the *Full Gospel Business Men's Fellowship International,* for at least the more competent lay members of Pentecostal churches. This movement has acquired an interdenominational character, and some of those who have experienced sudden outbursts into unknown tongues in orthodox church services have become associated with it. This development of neo-Pentecostalism – a phenomenon that has gathered momentum in the United States, Britain, New Zealand and in some countries in continental Europe – transcends (at least for the present) the specifically sectarian forms to which the earlier manifestations of Pentecostal utterance gave rise between 1900 and 1950.

Conversionist sects have a history in Christendom that goes back only to the time when Zinzendorf inspired the Moravian Brethren with his ideas on piety and the loving nature of God in 1730. Revolutionist sects have a much longer history in Christendom, from the time when the followers of the dead Jesus looked eagerly for his second advent as the Jews looked for their messiah. Although advent and millennium are closely associated ideas in Christianity, it is only when they are combined to emphasise the advent as a pre-millennial event that they can give rise to revolutionist sects – sects that look forward to the overturn of the existing dispensation.

Pre-millennial adventism itself has been an orthodox, if unstressed, article of faith of the principal churches of Christendom. Until the development of modernist ideas, the second coming of Christ was a belief required of Christians. Until Augustine provided a spiritual interpretation of the church as the kingdom of heaven where the saints would reign, many early Christians expected Christ's early advent. As the church became established, and as its hierarchy became men of influence in the world, and its chief laymen wealthy and powerful, so the appeal of the advent receded. Scriptural interpretation became spiritualised, and Greek concepts of souls migrating to heaven displaced Jewish ideas of resurrection and transformation of the world. But the scriptures affirmed Christ's second coming, and in periods of social unrest the church found these biblical ideas regaining currency. Their extreme expression was almost always sectarian, in consequence if not in origin. But orthodox theologians such as Hus and Luther accepted them. They gained wide currency in Britain from the writings of Joseph Mede, a seventeenth-century scholar whose works attracted the divines of Cromwellian England. Scientists such as Sir Isaac Newton and Joseph Priestley (the discoverer of oxygen and a pioneer of Unitarianism) were convinced adventists, and so was Timothy Dwight, President of Yale University, who preached frequently between 1781 and 1812 to show how the prophecies of the book of Revelations were even then being worked out in world politics. His views, in which the Papacy was characterised as the Beast, were widely shared among Presbyterians and Congregationalists in the United States.

The difference between the beliefs of orthodox Protestants and those of revolutionist sectarians lies in the prominence accorded to the millennial hope. Christian sects of a fundamentalist kind have probably all believed in the second advent, but only for some has this been the central and dominant article of faith. For these sects the transformation is always expected to be sudden and soon, and thus the proclamation of the truth has always been a matter of urgency. Such sects in earlier periods of history were always ill-organised and unstable. Those drawn in probably had little capacity for sustained commitment – the attraction of the millennium was enhanced by its nearness in time. The followers of Thomas Münzer in the early days of the Reformation, and those of Thomas Venner, who were known as the Fifth Monarchy men in the days of the Commonwealth in England, certainly constituted millennial movements, but they were not persisting sects. The circumstances for enduring revolutionist sects came only with the modern period.

Since the twelfth century there has not been a period of European history without new millennial movements, but most of the persisting revolutionist sects have arisen since the end of the Napoleonic wars. There are two reasons for their relatively recent provenance. First, the expectation of social transformation is not easily sustained over a long period, when the awaited advent fails to occur. Consequently, revolutionist sects are often of relatively brief duration, or, in becoming institutionalised, undergo a change in their response to the world. Secondly, with the exception of those few sects that discovered effective means of insulating themselves from the wider society, such as the Waldensians and the Amish, sects arising in earlier periods rarely attained sufficient stability of organisation to endure over centuries.

The Napoleonic wars gave rise to a great deal of speculation of an apocalyptic kind, especially among Protestants. World disorder, the emergence of a few major *dramatis personae* on the global stage, and the improved means of communication that led to increased knowledge of international politics, induced many to search the scriptures for guidance on the portent of the times. Numerology and prophetic exegesis (drawing especially on the books of Daniel, Ezekiel and Revelation), were widely employed in the search for a pattern in history. The whole world seemed to be embraced by one pattern of disorder, the like of which had not been known before, and many saw revealed in this the hand of the Devil at work in men's affairs, and prospect of the struggle for the world at the battle of Armageddon between God and Satan. When scientists like Newton, Priestley and Faraday could speculate along these lines, it was evident that many less secularised men would also be attracted to the outworking of prophecy.

Many local prophets have arisen in troubled times, claiming to be heralds of a new age, but only rarely had such figures the capacity to bring into being an enduring movement, and this was more likely in places where there was something of a tradition of an 'open Bible' that men could read for themselves. It was largely in Protestant countries that persisting millennial sects arose. But briefer movements have been numerous: sometimes they espoused semi-political goals; at other times, they bordered on the fantastic. The Camisards of the early eighteenth century in France were one such.

An extraordinary outburst was the movement of Davide Lazzaretti, the self-styled messiah of Monte Amiata in the extreme south east of Tuscany, who began preaching a new dispensation in the late 1860s, a time of great political and social upheaval in Italy. Lazzaretti foresaw the descent of a great reformer from the mountains, who with a company of warriors – the militia of the Holy Ghost – was to reform the laws and the civil government, and liberate the people. He began to collect his followers together into communist colonies. Undoubtedly, his vision was largely of a political kind, but he couched his message in religious terms: after the existing dispensation, which he designated the Kingdom of Grace, there was to occur a Kingdom of Justice, the last great age of the world. In 1878, on the death of Pope Pius IX, Lazzaretti declared himself to be the new messiah, and he announced that he would descend from the mountain, to set up the Republic of God. Thousands came to see his arrival, and undoubtedly many believed that some great transformation was to occur. But Lazzaretti's hymn-singing followers were met by the military as they approached Arcidosso, and in a few moments the prophet was killed and his chief followers were arrested and subsequently brought to trial.

America and the millennial dream

Adventist speculation became especially rife in the United States in the nineteenth century. In the uncertain conditions of a new country, literal biblicism was a substitute for the standards of order that had been imposed in England by a settled church, monarchy, aristocracy, gentry and their magistracy and government. Needing as had the Puritans before them, a model for social organisation, they, too, identified themselves as a covenant people. With the Bible as the basis for interpreting their destiny they were, in troubled times, easily led to millennial speculations. In the up-country areas of a society undergoing rapid change, and still uncertain of itself as a new nation which had dared to challenge the mystique of traditional theories of power and legitimacy, the search for security and re-assurance was an understandable phenomenon. The most authoritative source of such reassurance was the Bible. But the Bible itself was full of promises and prophecies that needed interpretation.

Adventism had a long pedigree in Europe, especially among artisans and peasant classes, but in America its attraction in the early nineteenth century was not specifically as a vehicle of class contention. The military revolutionism that had often affected millennial hopes in continental Europe was absent. Millennial hopes had more to do with the destiny of the American people who had a self-conscious sense of themselves as engaged in a great pilgrimage, than with a class struggle in which adventism was unwittingly used as a weapon by some of the dispossessed. Exaggerated patriotism was frequently evident in the search for salvation of American adventists, and there was no doubt that salvation was to be locally discovered, or that God's plan for the advent was to be locally enacted.

The recurrent revivals that were promoted in rural districts stimulated widespread religious speculation, and the 'signs of the times' were always such that they could be interpreted as indications of the approaching end of this dispensation. Nowhere was this religious ferment greater than in up-state New York and neighbouring Vermont, a region of cultural retardation, in which half-knowledge, rumour, reforming crusades and revivals were the main stuff of culture, and which became known as the 'burned-over district'. Here Joseph Smith, the founder of Mormonism, indulged in youthful fantasies of buried treasure, and in the 1820s received the golden plates on which was written the Book of Mormon. Here Finney became active with revivalism which brought the sinful to the 'anxious seat' where they were subjected to the full impact of evangelical exhortation. Of particular importance for the history of modern sectarianism, not only in the United States but throughout the world, were the writings and subsequent preaching of William Miller, a farmer, who by about 1818 had convinced himself that the date of the second advent could be deduced from the scriptures. With reasoning very similar to that employed by Henry Archer in seventeenth-century England, though with different conclusions as to dates, Miller calculated that the advent of Christ would occur between 21 March 1843 and 21 March 1844. Miller did not give public expression to his views until 1831. Up-state New York was ready to hear him, and within a little time his preaching was in great demand in Baptist, Presbyterian and other churches in New England.

Joshua Himes, minister of a Baptist chapel in Boston, promoted lectures, and, as the predicted date neared, several hundred itinerant preachers were engaged to expound the prophecy of the time of doom. Two special periodicals were launched, and Miller himself gave three hundred lectures in the space of six months. Even the thoroughly orthodox were prepared to interpret events as relating to the coming kingdom of God, particularly the appearance of a

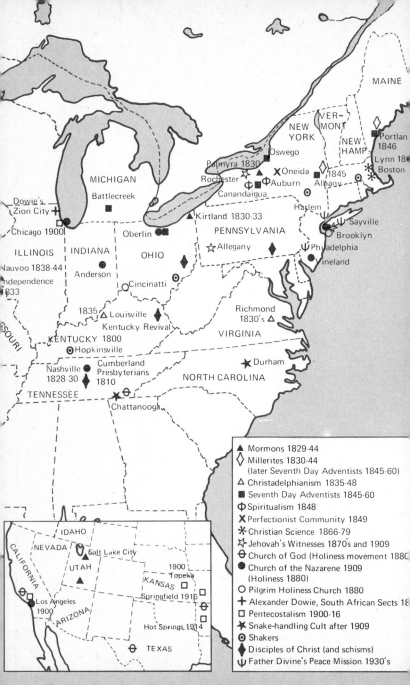

MAINE

VER-
MONT

NEW
YORK

NEW
HAMP

◇ Portlan
■ 1846

Lynn 18
✳ Boston

Oswego

Palmyra 1830
Rochester ☆ ▲ ◇ Oneida
Φ Auburn
Canandaigua

◇ 1845
Albany

MICHIGAN

Battlecreek

Dowie's
Zion City ✚
□
Chicago 1900

Oberlin ● ■

Harlem ◉

ψ Sayville
○ Brooklyn

Kirtland 1830-33

PENNSYLVANIA

ψ Philadelphia

ILLINOIS   INDIANA   OHIO

Nauvoo 1838-44
Independence
1833

Anderson ●

☆ Allegany

◆

Vineland

Cincinatti ◎

1835 △ Louisville
Kentucky Revival ◆

Richmond
1830's △

MISSOURI

KENTUCKY 1800
◎ Hopkinsville

VIRGINIA

Nashville
1828-30
◆

Cumberland
Presbyterians
1810

NORTH CAROLINA

★ Durham

TENNESSEE

⊖
Chattanooga

IDAHO

NEVADA

CALIFORNIA

UTAH

◉ Salt Lake City

▲

1900
Topeka □

KANSAS

Springfield 1918 □

Los Angeles
1900 ⊖

ARIZONA

Hot Springs 1914 □

TEXAS ⊖

▲ Mormons 1829-44
◇ Millerites 1830-44
   (later Seventh Day Adventists 1845-60)
△ Christadelphianism 1835-48
■ Seventh Day Adventists 1845-60
Φ Spiritualism 1848
✗ Perfectionist Community 1849
✳ Christian Science 1866-79
☆ Jehovah's Witnesses 1870's and 1909
⊖ Church of God (Holiness movement 1880
● Church of the Nazarene 1909
   (Holiness 1880)
○ Pilgrim Holiness Church 1880
✚ Alexander Dowie, South African Sects 18
□ Pentecostalism 1900-16
✶ Snake-handling Cult after 1909
◎ Shakers
◆ Disciples of Christ (and schisms)
ψ Father Divine's Peace Mission 1930's

comet in 1843. The enthusiasm led to some excesses in the tent
meetings that occurred, but in general the adventists were much
more restrained than popular writers have suggested. Certainly, the
adventists were disappointed when the year ran out without the
Lord's coming. When even a postponed date in October 1844, set to
meet the Jewish calendar, failed, many of the fifty to a hundred
thousand who had become advent believers acknowledged their
folly and abandoned their hope.

Inspiration redeems disappointed prophecy

Before the time of their disappointments, Millerites were not a
distinct sect. They were of various denominations, and they had
met relatively little hostility from their fellow religionists. Paradoxically, it was after the failure of the advent that the adventists
became a distinct sect. Their development as a separate body of
believers was relatively slow, and adventist faith alone did not prove
sufficient to unite them as a persisting sect. Other elements and other
prophets were needed. Only revelation was now adequate to explain
the failure of an event so confidently predicted, and to offset the
obloquy that adventists everywhere met in late October 1844.
Some continued for a time to believe in a brief postponement; some
sought to discover new dates; others believed that in some concealed
way the Lord had come in 1844 (a device subsequently used by the
followers of Charles Russell, Jehovah's Witnesses). Miller himself,
although an adventist till his death a few years later, was a spent
force, clinging desperately to the idea of the nearness of the Lord's
return. He disavowed the excesses to which some disappointed
adventists turned, for instance, spiritualism; 'promiscuous lodging
... to raise up spiritual children'; indiscriminate kissing at conferences; and the testing of each other's faith by 'licentious advances'.

The most successful recourse of the adventists was to prophetic
revelation, and some began having visions very soon after the disappointments. Hiram Edson saw a vision of Christ entering the
second apartment of the sanctuary in heaven, where he still had

work to do before coming to earth. That work, elaborated in reference to the Old Testament, was seen as the work of a High Priest's activity on the Day of Atonement. Until 1844, Christ had been engaged in the daily office of a High Priest, resulting in the forgiveness of sin: since then – it came to be held – he has been performing the higher task of blotting out sin. Thus an investigative judgment is now in progress to discover who among the dead are worthy of resurrection, and who among the living are to be translated. The final blotting out will occur just before Christ's return to earth, when sins will all be placed on Satan the scapegoat, who will bear the retributive punishment. Thus Christ atones and Satan will bear away. This theological scheme, based on subsequent revelations, rationalised the failure of the adventual prediction of 1843–4.

Some adventists came to believe that a principal hindrance to the advent had been their failure to maintain the biblical law, of keeping the seventh day as the sabbath. This recourse to the Old Testament was again underwritten by visions. Ellen Harmon (later Ellen Harmon White after her marriage to James White) claimed to possess the spirit of prophecy, and her many visions, confirming those of Edson and others, came to be regarded as inspired counsels from God. Although her writings are not regarded by Seventh Day Adventists as part of the sacred canon, and are not accorded universal application, nonetheless they confirm faith and pronounce their church to be the remnant church which is the subject of biblical prophecy.

The theology of the Seventh Day Adventists is complex: they emphasise free will; they believe that the atonement was not completed on the cross, but continues; they reject the immortality of the soul, emphasising rather the resurrection (or translation) as do other adventist movements, which have little use for the conventional categories of Christian eschatology. They do, however, accept heaven as a sphere of operations, and believe that believers will go there at the time of Armageddon (a battle between non-Christians and Christians) when Satan will be left for a thousand years on the wilderness of earth, whilst the saints rule with Christ in heaven. After the millennium is over, Christ will descend with the saints, punish the wicked, and create a new earth with the New Jerusalem as its centre. A special resurrection will take place for those who have died since 1846 and who accepted the need to keep the seventh day as the sabbath.

Ideological adaptation: the goal of sabbath-keeping

The seventh day sabbath early came to occupy a vital place in the theology of this adventist movement. It excused the failure of prophecy (although other reasons were also advanced) and became a necessary condition for salvation. Those, in the latter days, who fail to keep the seventh day as their sabbath are regarded as being lost, since this is the message of the third Angel of Revelation xiv 6-11. Various dietetic taboos have been added to the requirements made of the faithful, also based on Old Testament injunctions: a Seventh Day Adventist abstains from shellfish, pork, coffee and tea, as well as from alcohol and tobacco. These prohibitions were conceived in some way as a programme of health reform.

Under the vigorous leadership of James White and his wife, Ellen, now credited with the gift of prophecy, the new movement grew. Adventism had been retrieved from the débâcle of disappointed hope, and believers were now provided with highly distinctive teachings for the conduct of their daily lives and their separation from other men. The evangelistic zeal of the Millerites was recaptured for the dissemination of the third angel's message about the sabbath. Believers had now an imperative task to do to prepare for the coming advent, instead of simply passively waiting. Men had to hear sabbatarian truth before the advent could come. This emphasis had the added advantage of giving men the feeling that, although history was prescribed already, they had a part to play in helping the wheels of ordained destiny to turn. Meanwhile the leaders of the movement continued their prophetic exegesis and their search for certainty in identifying political and religious powers with the beasts and other allegorical figures of the prophetic books of Daniel and Revelation. Inevitably, the Pope and the Roman Church were branded as particular enemies of God, but the Protestant United States was also regarded as the second beast. The Adventists believed that the events of the last days were prophesied to include the United States as an important arena.

The Seventh Day Adventists had every justification to enter the mission field, and once they had organised themselves as a movement – which occurred in 1860 – they sent evangelists throughout America, and in the 1870s to other countries. In the twentieth century the movement had spread to Africa, Melanesia, and to all the countries of continental Europe. Its greatest success in Europe has been in Germany, where in the early 1960s, despite some earlier schisms, there were 867 churches, over 43,000 members and over 90,000 adherents. (These figures are for both East and West Germany. 1966 figures are shown on pages 12 and 116.) In Britain there were 151 churches and nearly 8,000 members; in Switzerland 59 churches, 3,300 members and over 6,000 adherents, and in France 65 churches with over 3,000 members and 6,000 adherents. Austria, Italy and Holland all had more than 2,000 members and each had between 4,000 and 5,000 adherents. The movement has remained strongest in America, where it has more than 3,000 churches, over 275,000 members and about four times as many adherents.

The Seventh Day Adventists are an unusual sect in that they combine several distinctive features that are not normally associated. When millennial movements have had their own prophets they have usually been people who have proclaimed themselves as messiahs or as important messianic forerunners: neither Edson nor Mrs White did this. The movement remained conferential in character, and local churches have maintained a degree of congregational autonomy that allows them to preserve a distinctly sectarian *Gemeinschaft* (community) character. Yet as a tithe-paying organisation, they maintain a vigorous centralised headquarters, and this, with their large, well-equipped and efficient publishing organisation, theological schools and colleges, give the movement an appearance much nearer to that of an institutionalised denomination. Sabbath-keeping and the insistent hopes for the millennium are issues that keep Seventh Day Adventists distinct from other believers, as are also their dietetic taboos and their conscientious objection to military service. From Millerite times, many regular ministers of various denominations accepted adventist beliefs, and many of them became prominent in promulgating the doctrine, and in the conferences in which new teachings were adopted. Thus the movement has accepted a professional ministry. In this it differs markedly from other millennial sects: indeed, the combination of a ministry with a belief in a vessel of divine inspiration at a particular stage of a move-ment's development – in the person of Mrs White – is unique.

The diversity of elements in Seventh Day Adventist teaching has facilitated the movement's adaptation to changing social conditions. In its missionary work, it has been able to emphasise practical training and, in association with its preoccupation with health reform, hospital services. Adventist movements, when they remain single-minded, find it difficult to adopt any practical measures that benefit men in their daily concerns, since the coming saviour will wipe away all need for knowledge and for facilities of this kind. In providing themselves with a biblical exegesis to explain why the advent did not come at the expected time, the Seventh Day Adven-tists also, no doubt unwittingly, provided themselves with new orientations that facilitated the process by which the persisting and expanding movement became institutionalised.

The Christadelphians: a stable adventist sect

One of the first men to be stirred by Miller's ideas on the advent was Dr John Thomas, an immigrant to America from England, who abandoned medicine to study scripture and to preach the forth-coming end of the age. Thomas wrote a number of books, expound-ing his own scheme of biblical exegesis. He engaged in debates with Millerites and Mormons, and for a time attached himself to the followers of Barton Stone and Alexander Campbell. He was a

Table 2 Jehovah's Witnesses and Seventh Day Adventists in various Caribbean, Central and South American countries in 1966

	Population (in millions)	Seventh Day Adventists		Jehovah's Witnesses	
		Churches	Members	Congrs.	Publrs.
Argentina	21·0	107	16,225	270	11,475
Bolivia	3·8	42	13,842	20	566
Brazil	85·4	464	112,190	811	37,546
Chile	8·3	72	12,429	93	3,776
Columbia	18·0	99	21,595	101	3,805
Cuba	7·1	81	6,637	—	†
Dominican Rep.	3·8	68	9,264	44	2,040
Haiti	4·5	55	25,840	31	1,088
Jamaica	1·6	327	44,531	155	4,910
Mexico	44·5	243	36,058	1,090	30,261
Panama	1·3	58	5,773	44	1,365
Peru	11·8	115	27,059	63	2,406
Puerto Rico	2·6	103	8,636	70	3,368
Trinidad, Tobago*	1·0	108	12,843	40	2,116
Uruguay	2·5	16	2,653	48	2,212
Venezuela	12·5	44	5,581	78	4,139

† In Cuba Jehovah's Witnesses are subject to harassment from government officials and they no longer report their statistics.

*This entry includes in addition to Trinidad, Tobago, St Vincent and Grenada for each sect.

Table 3 Jehovah's Witnesses and Seventh Day Adventists in various African countries in 1966

	Population (in millions)	Seventh Day Adventists		Jehovah's Witnesses	
		Churches	Members	Congrs.	Publrs.
Angola	5·0	64	19,304	1	88
Congo (Kinshasa)	16·4	137	16,916	58	4,777
Ghana	7·5	61	11,217	264	8,841
Ivory Coast	7·0	7	374	4	141
Kenya	9·7	281	54,195	3	258
Liberia	1·5	14	2,396	8	328
Malawi and Zambia†	7·6	263	38,276	1,022	44,375
Mozambique	6·8	43	6,448	19	1,150
Nigeria	57·8	154	20,267	851	39,751
Rhodesia	3·2	138	26,883	338	9,438
Rwanda and Burundi	5·5	411	76,872	—	11
Sierra Leone	2·2	19	2,913	24	449
South Africa*	21·2	283	20,563	556	19,470
Tanzania	9·8	112	19,883	27	783
Uganda	7·8	60	7,107	1	37

† Malawi and Zambia are combined in this table because the statistics for the Seventh Day Adventists are not separated country by country.

* South Africa includes Lesotho and Swaziland, S.W. Africa, St. Helena and Ascension. Witnesses do not distinguish between white and Bantu adherents: among the Seventh Day Adventists congregations are organised separately. The respective proportions are 11,472 white and coloured members in 136 congregations; and 9,091 Bantu members in 147 congregations.

contentious man, however, and could not easily fall in with the ideas of others. In the 1830s he began to preach, in particular on the obligation of all believers to be baptised, but more especially that baptism could be effective only when men completely understood the truth about God and salvation. His differences with Campbell grew and eventually he came to the point of insisting that the central message of the scriptures was the hope of the kingdom that would come with the second advent of Christ. That event, he believed, was very soon to take place. Abjuring previous errors, he had himself re-baptised and refused fellowship to any who dissented from his teachings. Men were to repent their sins, live soberly, and look for the glorious reappearance of Christ, whereafter the earth would be made new. In particular, Thomas rejected the concepts of soul, heaven and hell, and, although not unitarian, nonetheless fiercely rejected the doctrine of the Trinity.

Thomas regarded the Bible as inerrant and his own commentary as merely that of a serious student. He denied having any special inspiration, and always rejected the idea that he was a prophet – or a pope. Even the idea of guidance of the Holy Spirit was rejected: the word of God, as recorded in the Bible, was the only way in which God spoke to man in that age. Thomas and his followers, who eventually called themselves Christadelphians, rejected the idea that simple faith was sufficient for salvation: believers had to understand the truth, and be baptised when their understanding was complete. Thereafter they had to live according to the commands of Christ. Salvation was not easy, and certainly it was not to be got by a decision to 'accept the saviour' taken in the emotionalism of a revival campaign. Pagans, imbeciles, and those who died as children had no chance of resurrection, and resurrection was the only way of salvation, since the dead were completely dead, with no part of them – since they had no soul – continuing to live. In consequence, only Christadelphians could be saved to eternal life and if they failed to live the truth, not all of them would be saved.

One very significant aspect of Christadelphian belief was that the promises of the scriptures were understood to relate in the first

John Thomas (1805–71) founder
of the Christadelphians in
the United States in the 1840s.

instance to the Jews, and only subsequently to those who accepted
Christ's later offer to become joint-heirs with him, and with believing
Jews. Christadelphians are thus those who have voluntarily chosen
to become Jews. They have therefore done better than those Jews
who were given the law and yet failed to keep it, to whom the
promise of the kingdom of God was originally made and to whom
God will honour his promises. On just what conditions Jews will be
subjects of the kingdom is somewhat unclear, but the early Christadelphians in particular followed the fortunes of the Jews very closely;
they called their meeting houses synagogues for a time, donated
funds, poor as they were, to help Jews in Palestine, and from an early
date did all they could to help Jews to return there. At one time,
they had the help, in distributing goods to Palestinian Jews, of that
curious religious enthusiast, Laurence Oliphant, one-time intimate
of the Prince of Wales (later Edward VII), member of Parliament, and
correspondent of *The Times,* although he never included Christadelphian ideas in the curious adventist beliefs he adopted.

Thomas returned periodically from Richmond, Virginia to

Britain, where he had rather greater success than in America. Some Millerites and Campbellites took up his teachings, and Christadelphian 'ecclesias' sprang up in many of the larger cities, particularly in Birmingham, where metal workers and nailers and other poor workmen were drawn to this hard-headed adventism. Converts were not accepted lightly, and to become a Christadelphian meant serious study of the Bible, examination by local leading brethren in essential doctrines, and commitment to lead a scrupulous life, avoiding, in particular, association with those outside the fellowship. The social teachings of the sect were based closely on scripture. Thus alcohol was not prohibited absolutely, but excess was strongly proscribed; frequenting ungodly people, or visiting taverns would certainly have been a cause for excommunication. Christadelphians were not opposed to war, and although they maintained conscientious objection to military service, Dr Thomas rejected leagues for peace, since wars among the nations, the 'sin-powers', were clearly part of the divine plan.

The Millerite enthusiasm had not really reached Britain on any considerable scale, and, in consequence, there had been no widespread disillusionment with adventism. This may be one cause of the greater success of the Christadelphians in Britain than in America. The Christadelphians expected the advent very soon, and at times, for instance in 1866, some brethren became very agitated about its imminence, but some freedom was allowed to members to work out the details of prophetic exegesis, particularly in application to contemporary political events, even though date-setting was nearly always resisted.

Informal leadership and schism

Christadelphian ecclesias have remained essentially congregational. Professional clergy have always been regarded as a corruption of true Christianity by them and no ministry has developed. Their democratic assemblies reject all formal organisation, presidents or committees. In the modern world, and particularly when treating with governments on such matters as military service, this rejection of all formal leadership has strained the resources of the movement. Inevitably, strong informal leaders have emerged, particularly from the principal Birmingham ecclesia, which – partly because the most important of the movement's periodicals has always been edited and published there – has attained a certain status, at least of *primus inter pares,* among the ecclesias. But informal leadership and purely doctrinal tests of orthodoxy are poor defences against division, and so the Christadelphians underwent, particularly in the nineteenth century, a series of bitter schisms. Excommunication of members and of one ecclesia by another became a common pattern in the attempt to maintain purity of doctrine and association. Whilst undoubtedly some schisms were at least partly a consequence of struggles for informal influence between leading brethren, there was always a strong concern for obedience to the word of God which led to over-scrupulousness, to purging evil men who arose in the fellowship, and hence to divisiveness.

The Christadelphians maintain an impressive ethic. They have remained well segregated, and have become a largely self-recruiting sect, although they have engaged in evangelism in obedience to scripture. The movement has more members in Britain than elsewhere, where they number between 20,000 and 30,000 now that the principal schismatic wings have effected a reunion. There are several thousand Christadelphians in other English-speaking countries, and a few congregations meet in Germany, particularly in Württemberg and Berlin, and there have been (and there may still be) a few Christadelphians in Norway.

Jehovah's Witnesses:
a case of organisational transformation

The north-eastern United States were still susceptible to adventist ideas in the 1870s, when Charles Taze Russell, the son of a successful small draper in Allegany, near Pittsburgh, Pennsylvania, first picked up his knowledge of adventism at a local meeting in 1870. Like

Miller before him, Russell sought to work out from scripture God's plan for mankind. He concluded that Miller had erred in fixing 1844 as the date of the end of the age, and he himself adopted 1874 as the time of Christ's invisible return to earth. (Subsequently Russell's followers have dropped the emphasis on 1874, and have fixed on 1914, a year that Russell discerned as significant, as the date marking the end of Gentile times.) By 1881, when Russell had gathered a growing following of at least thirty congregations, he set up Zion's Watchtower Tract Society (later to become the Watchtower Bible and Tract Society). He wrote extensive commentaries on the scriptures to prove that salvation was only for those who obeyed Jehovah, and that the principal purpose of all creation was the vindication of Jehovah's name and word.

Russell's writing, his periodicals and his world travels, brought into being an international movement. A branch was opened in London in 1900, in 1903 in Barmen-Elberfeld, Germany – ever a centre of sectarianism – and in Australia in the following year. The movement gained momentum as 1914 approached, but when that year passed without any visible sign of Christ's appearing, the movement suffered some reverses. In 1916 it distributed only half the quantity of literature it had disseminated in 1914, and in that same year Russell died.

A struggle for leadership of the movement occurred at this juncture, and a number of groups, especially in America and Germany (some of which still persist), split off from the parent body when Joseph Rutherford, a Missouri lawyer, known as 'Judge Rutherford' from his occasional service as a 'Special Judge' in the Eighth Judicial Circuit Court, became president of the society. Until his death in 1942, Rutherford dominated the movement and gave it a new direction, writing dozens of books and pamphlets and, in the earlier years of his presidency, lecturing widely. Towards the end of his life he became more remote, and led the movement to the type of semi-anonymous leadership that was continued under its third president, Nathan Knorr. The movement changed: from consisting of more or less democratically organised local assemblies of Bible students, it came to consist of centrally controlled branches of the international executive headquarters of a publishing concern. The new style of organisation was regarded as a theocracy, but the religious character of meetings became less significant than the organisation of door-to-door salesmanship and evangelisation.

A growing flood of literature over the years steadily saw Pastor Russell's works superseded by those of Rutherford. Sometimes there were explicit rejections of Russell's ideas – for example the rejection of the prophecies that were based on the Great Pyramid (a favourite supplementary basis of prophecy with various adventist groups) – but the disruption caused by such abrupt changes led to a more gradual policy of simply letting older works go out of print, and emphasising the importance of the latest works on which Bible study was to be based. Since Rutherford's death much the same fate has overtaken his copious writings as new and now anonymous works are distributed from the movement's Brooklyn (New York) headquarters. The members of the movement are, of course, a guaranteed market for new works but in any case publishing soon came to be a dominant organisational goal of the movement. It became the particular duty of Witnesses to sell the movement's literature to others, to 'publish' the good news. 'Divine service' for Jehovah's Witnesses is in selling the movement's periodicals, *Watchtower* and *Awake,* and conducting Bible studies with potential converts. For this reason, they are left free on Sunday mornings, when other Christians are worshipping, and are expected to canvass from door-to-door. The society itself is seen by its Witnesses as God-inspired, as the custodian of the Divine plan, and to emphasise this they deny that they are members of a human organisation, and even use their own title (adopted first in 1931) without a capital 'W' – they are merely the people witnessing to Jehovah. They keep no statistics of membership, but only of 'publishers' – since the publishing of the word is just an ancillary human activity for which human organisation is necessary until the present dispensation is superseded. Thus they maintain dual organisations: a nominal and 'theocratic' association of Bible students, free from human government, and a

rational bureaucratically organised publishing system in which all Bible students should serve as voluntary distributors as part of the work essential to realise God's plan.

Witness theology had to undergo some change after 1914 if the confident predictions for that year were to be explained away. Their response has been to go on asserting that the kingdom of God did begin in 1914, but that this kingdom is a heavenly kingdom. Christ began his reign then, and took up some of the 'anointed class' (the 144,000 of Revelation) to rule with him, but their resurrection was in heaven and was spiritual, hence not evident on earth. In 1918, at the time of all the schisms in the movement, Christ was cleansing the temple (a favourite type of sectarian symbolic allusion to events actually occurring among themselves). Not all of the 144,000 have as yet died, however: some remain on earth, and until at least some of these are translated to the heavenly sphere there is an interim, in which the world is increasingly experiencing the activities of Satan. Christ is at work judging the nations, and the basis for this judgment is the attitude of nations towards the kingdom message and its bearers, that is, Jehovah's Witnesses. Those who have rejected the message and persecuted the messengers are the goats upon whom judgment will be executed at Armageddon – the great war to come, in which the churches, the United Nations, and devils and demons will fight against Jehovah's Witnesses, Jesus Christ and the angelic hosts. Millions will die, indeed everyone who has opposed Jehovah. Thereafter a new heaven with the 144,000 will appear, and a new earth peopled by others loyal to Jehovah and by the resurrected dead (although it is not altogether clear just who among the dead will qualify – certainly not those taking part in Armageddon). A further judgment at the end of the millennium will test the good done by those who previously had no chance to hear the message of God.

The changing prospects of salvation

Some changes of emphasis have occurred in this eschatological scheme since Russell's day. Russell allowed that some spiritually begotten 'other sheep' would be saved, but these have become less clearly indicated in recent years. Two distinct classes of saved persons are, however, recognised: the 'anointed class', sometimes called 'God's woman', whose destiny is heaven, and others, 'Jonadabs', so called in reference to the companion of King Jehu (2 Kings 10:15-28) or 'other sheep', who, as faithful witnesses, will also inherit life in the new earth. The 'anointed class' are an only slightly differentiated élite within the body of Jehovah's Witnesses. Acting apparently on their own self-knowledge and assurance, they alone are permitted to participate in the memorials of a communion service that Jehovah's Witnesses celebrate annually. Others attend but do not partake of the emblems. It would appear that this class has been diminishing in recent years. In 1951, of over 623,000 at communion service, some 21,619 partook of the meal; in 1961, 13,284 partook of the emblems from a total attendance at the annual service of more than one and a half millions. In 1965, only 11,550 partook from among 1,933,000; and in 1966, only 11,179 from among 1,971,000. This decline may reflect the increasing expectation that the class is almost all gathered, and that therefore little remains to delay Armageddon.

Informally, some Witnesses strongly believe that 1975 will be the time of its occurrence. The movement does not now officially commit itself to dates since these have proved embarrassing in the past. Soon after Rutherford's assumption of presidency, 1925 was expected to be the year of doom, and in 1921 Rutherford coined his celebrated promise, 'Millions now living will never die'. Russell had held that after the time of the harvest in the year 1918 the door to immortality would close, but this idea was quickly superseded. In 1932, Rutherford declared that the end was only a short time away, 'much less than the length of a generation'.

The Watchtower movement has produced a translation of the Bible, which favours its own exegesis. Complete obedience to God's will, and belief in his word, are conditions for immortality, and in effect this means obedience to the movement. Obedience is most fully manifested in loyal attendance at the catechistic sessions held at the local Kingdom Hall, and in doing one's full stint as a 'publisher' of the good news. Some Witnesses, known as pioneers, work full time as publishers, but there is a strong emphasis on the priesthood of all believers, and, since ministers of religion in many countries are exempted from military conscription, Witnesses have tried to obtain exemption from military service by claiming that all Witnesses are ministers. Many were successful in this claim in the United States during the Second World War, although about 3,000 others were imprisoned; the plea failed when tested in a Scottish court of law during the period of military conscription in Britain. Witnesses reject allegiance to nation-states, since this interferes with obedience to God, on which salvation depends. They claim to be a nation apart. They are not pacifists, however, and if called upon will fight for the returning Christ.

This claim to a distinctive allegiance, with no obligation to the nations in which they live, has repeatedly brought Witnesses into conflict with the authorities. In the United States, where Witnesses refused to salute the national flag in schools in defiance of normal custom, they experienced some persecution during the war of 1941–5, until the Supreme Court outlawed compulsory flag-saluting.

The movement was proscribed in Australia, Canada and New Zealand in the war years, and questions about their activity were asked in the British House of Commons, although they were never banned. They have encountered difficulty with the authorities in many countries, recently in both Greece and Portugal. They are proscribed in eastern Europe with other American sects, and in 1968 they were prohibited in Malawi, as they had been in the United Arab Republic in 1960.

Jehovah's Witnesses are widely known to the general public from their door-to-door selling of the *Watchtower,* and their refusal, on the strength of particular biblical texts, to accept blood transfusions. Their other social involvement is minimal, and this is so, less because of injunctions to keep separate from the world, than because the good Witness is kept busy at Kingdom Hall and in publicising the movement. The theatre is not banned, but Witnesses do not go there; smoking is not prohibited, but is disliked; drinking is permitted, but excess is frowned upon; dancing is not proscribed, but dancing that might awaken sexual desire is held to be improper. The society does not particularly encourage its members to marry: its emphasis is rather on engaging in useful work for God's kingdom. It is not clear what professions a Witness might find irreconcilable with his faith. Mickey Spillane, the thriller writer, became a Witness some years ago; surprisingly, he went on writing in much the same vein.

The Witnesses have grown perhaps more rapidly than any other individual Christian sect in the last thirty years. Rutherford sought to make the movement something of a mass movement by his emphasis on public testimony. The movement has no statistics of members but its carefully culled statistics for 'publishers' give a clear picture of the numbers active in the movement. In 1966, they numbered more than a million (although nearly 2,000,000 attended the annual communion services). Nearly thirty per cent of this total, some 305,000, were in the United States of America. West Germany had the second largest number, with nearly 76,000; Britain had almost 50,000; Canada, 39,000; Brazil, 33,000; Mexico, 29,000;

Table 4 Jehovah's Witnesses and Seventh Day Adventists in various countries in South East Asia and the South Seas in 1966

	Population (in millions)	Seventh Day Adventists		Jehovah's Witnesses	
		Churches	Members	Congrs.	Publrs
Indonesia	115·7	455	34,930	54	1,232
Japan	100·6	69	6,558	157	4,112
Korea	20·2	240	30,787	193	5,602
Philippines	33·4	1,124	134,932	1,233	33,787
New Guinea, Melanesia, Polynesia	2·3	431	41,932	46	1,689
Taiwan, Hong Kong Macao	17·0	40	8,050	50	1,276

Table 5 Seventh Day Adventists behind the Iron Curtain in 1966

	Population (in millions)	Seventh Day Adventists	
		Churches	Members
Bulgaria	8·1	70	2,803
Czechoslovakia	14·1	50	8,733
East Germany	18·4	343	12,842
Hungary	10·1	153	5,800
Poland	32·0	68	3,810
Romania	19·0	511	34,069
USSR	200·2	834	40,000
Yugoslavia	19·6	251	9,888

France, 21,000; South Africa, 18,000; Australia, 16,000; Holland 13,000, and Italy, Greece, Finland, Denmark and Sweden, all within a few hundreds of 10,000. There are nearly 4,000 publishers in Spain and in Norway, and 2,500 in Portugal. The highest proportion of Witnesses to total population is, however, in Zambia, where they number nearly one per cent. A sizeable proportion of the total population is thus committed, in this particular new nation, to reject any sort of allegiance to the state.

7 Introversionists

Although all sects separate from the orthodox and, at least in some respects, from the wider society, introversionist sects make this pattern of action their overriding concern, the issue on which salvation is to be realised. Being in the safety of the community becomes the symbol, and sometimes more than merely the symbol, of being in the safety of God. The individual feels safe in the fraternity, and thus the fraternity is the agency of the saving Christ. Individual holiness depends on community holiness; the community itself provides the reference for individual behaviour. It becomes the object of adoration, being at once an objective entity, and a subjective experience. It presents the individual with a mystery that is awe-inspiring.

It is precisely this 'mystery' that sociologists have wrestled with in explaining the relations of the individual and society, and the basis of moral conscience and social norms. Society is the objective reference point from which the individual acquires his comprehension, values and purposes. It is the dependence of man on his society that allowed Emile Durkheim, the French sociologist, to suggest that what men really worship in worshipping God is the society itself:[6] in the modern era, in ceasing to worship God, men also manifest their disbelief in the superior authority embodied in society. They reject the idea that they are dependent on it, as their lives and their standards become increasingly 'privatised', and their public performances increasingly dictated by their specialised roles. In their cynicism modern men continue a curiously ambivalent and often mentally disturbing dialogue with themselves, by recognising that roles are dependent on shared expectations, and yet by also 'seeing through' the relationship and becoming cynical about the motivations of other role-performers.

The introversionist sect perpetuates a condition of pristine innocence in these respects. As a gathered community, even if not vicinally segregated from the world, individuals deal with each other, not as role performers, but as total persons. The community retains the strong sense of its own sacredness, and its members have a powerful apprehension of community sanctity. In separating from the world, they make the community into all that they have. Once such a community is established, and once its members are socialised to life within it, their covenant with God to abandon the world for him and for salvation becomes a social reality. Men then treat each other as ends, as sacred objects: instrumental ends are clearly subordinated to the sacred purpose of the community's separateness, independence and insulated sanctity. The life of the community focusses on, but is necessarily not completely engaged in, religious exercises and it is in these that the individual experiences and realises its transcendent holiness. Often introversionist sects expect this holiness to be manifested in the presence of the Holy Spirit among them. It becomes their unique possession, confirming to the community its sanctity, and making the individual aware of the saving power that exists within it.

The social conditions of sectarian withdrawal

Many introversionist sects isolate themselves, not only socially, but vicinally, by establishing colonies of their own. Such colony-building has not been possible in every period of history, nor in every society. In feudal Europe such withdrawal would have been difficult, even had sectarians possessed the imagination, the organising and managing abilities, as well as the lasting convictions that colony-building required. At that time too, monasticism, within some obvious limits, was an alternative outlet for this particular response to the world. A degree of tolerance and the availability of land were important facilitating circumstances for the introversionist sect to come into being as a colony. In general, such tolerance was rare before the eighteenth century, and land was generally available only when some feudal nobleman of clement disposition permitted sectarians to settle on his estates. Such cases occurred, notably in the early history of the Hutterian Brethren, but they were uncommon, uncertain and precarious.

In the eighteenth century, when the frontiers of America and Russia were expanding, large new areas became available for settle-

A Doukhobor woman begins to strip as she watches the destruction of Doukhobor farms. Arson, bombing of their own property and public displays of nudity were common forms of protest among the extreme groups of Doukhobors in Canada in the 1940s and '50s against the treatment of the sect by the public authorities.

ment and this provided places where men of conscience could escape the evils of the world. It was then that communally organised, vicinally segregated introversionist sects became common. The Hutterians, the Rappites, the Amana Society, the Doukhobors and the Amish Mennonites are among the best known. Some of these sects were communitarian, following a form of more or less primitive communism in their colony organisation. Not all of them were: the Amish, the Doukhobors and, except as a matter of temporary expediency, the colony-building Mennonites in Brazil, Paraguay and Mexico, have never been strictly communitarian. Even colonies that are communitarian may not be so from original religious convictions. The Hutterians acquired their communitarian ideas early and they became religiously sanctioned. There is always a tendency for particular, expedient social arrangements to be legitimised in religious terms. Thus the Amana Society, after moving from Germany to Iowa, adopted communitarian arrangements that were later underwritten by messages received by the leader from the Holy Ghost. But not all communist or colony-building sects have been introversionist: some have been of the utopian type.

Whilst many of the most conspicuous introversionist sects have been colony-building, other introversionist groups have relied on other means of insulating themselves from the wider society. Strict injunctions against associating with outsiders may be reinforced by strong prescriptions about dress and deportment. Speech habits in well-insulated groups tend to become distinctive, and in time, such patterns of speech may tend to acquire a sanctity of their own, not only serving to mark off the faithful from others (since in sects of this kind, which tend to be small, the faithful are generally known personally), but becoming a prescribed language for the truly saved. The English Quakers had, until the 1860s, what they called 'peculiarities', distinctive habits of every-day speech (the retention of the familiar form 'thou', which had otherwise passed from use in all but dialect speech, poetry and prayer) and of dress (plain garments and broad hats). Years of debate occurred among the leading Quakers before the 'peculiarities' were abandoned.[7]

Such sects make sacred all the distinctive practices of their daily lives. Different language from that of the surrounding society is a preservative of sectarian life of particular efficacy. Such it was for the German-speaking Mennonites and Hutterians in Russia; for the Mennonites in Brazil; the German-speaking Amana Society and Rappites in America, and for the Russian-speaking Doukhobors in Canada.

Introversionist sects seek to remain 'unspotted from the world'. They are strictly endogamous, and those who marry out are usually expelled – a pattern common in revolutionist and conversionist sects (although in the latter case 'saved' persons in other sectarian groups may be accepted). Introversionists frequently seek to avoid the regulations of the modern state, and, where they can, they establish their own educational agencies and welfare services, and sometimes even their own medical facilities, although this presents difficulties (such sects are rarely opposed to medicine on religious grounds). In particular, they reject even formal association with worldly men in any type of organisation including trade unions and professional associations. The introversionist sect seeks to confine social relations within its boundaries. The dessication of role-playing and the compromises that this entails with total commitment to a pure way of life are avoided so that members may define themselves in relation only to the religious community. Evangelisation is not an important concern: converts may not be very readily accepted, and may, despite the theory of voluntary adherence, never attain quite the status of those whose parents were members (this occurred markedly with eighteenth-century English Quakers). Evangelistic activity, indeed, may seem to be a particular wile of the devil, to lure the faithful out into the wider world where they may be exposed to alien influences.

It will be seen that many aspects of the introversionist sect are intensifications of positions adopted by other types of sect. It has achieved far greater insulation than the other types of sect, and it has defined its boundaries more closely. It has achieved a stability that, until the mid-nineteenth century, was rare among revolutionist sects (by which time they could employ the modes of rational organisation increasingly developed in the wider society). It has done so by taking the small community with primary face-to-face relations as its model. This particular quality of the introversionist sect arises because in many cases – though by no means all – the introversionist response is a secondary response. An adventist movement, disappointed in the non-occurrence of the advent, may have gradually settled down to a separated and insulated way of life. A conversionist sect, having lost its evangelistic fervour, may gradually come to be concerned more with the deepening of the spiritual life than with its further spread: this occurred in some Holiness sects. We shall later turn to the dynamic aspects of sectarianism, and of mutations of response.

The Hutterian Brethren: a migrating sect

The Anabaptist movement began in Zürich in 1525 in opposition to the town council and to Zwingli when a former Roman Catholic priest, George Blaurock, was baptised at the hands of Conrad Grebel. Adult baptism quickly became the symbolic act of a diffuse and ill-defined movement in Switzerland, Austria and Germany. It appealed strongly to peasants, and many were re-baptised without particular regard to the beliefs they held, thus giving rise to bizarre antinomian consequences, one of which was the reign of terror at Münster (see chapter 1). Other Anabaptists preached repentance of sin, and although they were thoroughly radical, and vigorous evangelists, they were in general a pacific group. Troubled by the outbursts of antinomian licence that sometimes occurred among new converts, and by the spiritualistic tendencies and more vigorous millenarianism of the South German Anabaptists, some Swiss Brethren formulated a confession of seven articles at Schleitheim early in 1527. To define their community they decided to excommunicate wrong-doers, and vigorously rejected the use of arms even for self-defence. They also instituted an office of pastor among themselves to read scriptures, admonish, teach and warn.

Some Anabaptists rejected state power entirely. Others, such as Balthasar Hubmaier, believed the use of the sword to be justified in certain circumstances. Hubmaier wrote and preached widely, and converted Leonhard von Liechtenstein of Nicolsburg in Moravia, whose estate subsequently became a refuge for Anabaptists, who were everywhere being persecuted by the Catholic, Lutheran or Zwinglian authorities. An extreme pacifist group of Anabaptists who rejected the use of arms was led by Jacob Wiedemann. Leonhard of Liechtenstein reluctantly asked this group to leave his lands, but later relented: the Anabaptists went, however, giving as their reason that they could not stay since the count had resisted *by force* the special commissioner of the Margrave of Moravia who had been sent to persecute them. At Austerlitz, where they received aristo-cratic protection from the Von Kaunitz family, this group of sectar-ians, joined by others from the Tyrol, set up a communistic form of group government. Jacob Huter (or Hutter), a Tyrolean Anabaptist pastor, was, from 1533-6, leader of the still amorphous and un-settled community which soon came to be known by his name. The Brethren were thus pacifist, communitarian and – after a period of dissention and difficulties – a united community. In 1540 Peter Riedemann produced his *Rechenschaft* which became the charter document for the Hutterians in their wanderings in the four centuries that followed. Riedemann set forth the communitarian practice of the Brethren as the realisation of pristine Christianity.

The prosperity of the Hutterian communities in Moravia, their later persecution by the Catholics and their subsequent wanderings in Slovakia, Transylvania and Russia are a well-chronicled history. At times they virtually abandoned their communal organisation, and many were scattered. In the 1860s, when the Russian govern-ment threatened the Hutterians, who had at that time been in Russia for almost a century, with compulsory military service and compulsory education in Russian for their children, they decided to migrate to North America, and settled, in 1874, in Dakota Terri-tory. About half of the seven hundred who made the move settled in three communities (the groups took the names of their leaders and three slightly different traditions have grown up among the Schmiedeleut', Dariusleut' and Lehrerleut'). In the years that followed, the Hutterians flourished segregated from the world, but the First World War brought considerable local hostility towards these German-speaking settlers: their communism was distrusted by local farmers, and their pacifism seemed to be a poor return to the country that had taken them in. Twentieth-century persecution was by the law rather than by the sword, and under threat of compulsory legal dissolution all but one colony of Hutterians fled to Canada in 1918. The Canadian government promised these highly efficient farmers, whom the country then needed, freedom of worship, exemption from military service, freedom to live as commonwealths, and freedom to set up their own schools. Between 1918 and 1922 the Hutterians established nine colonies in Manitoba and fourteen in Alberta, and since that time they have spread elsewhere, particularly to Saskatchewan. Some colonies have been re-established in South Dakota, and new ones settled in Washington state, Montana and North Dakota. Some harassment has been experienced in Canada, where farmers induced legislation to prevent the rapidly-growing communities in Alberta from buying too much land in any one area. By 1965 the Hutterians had increased to about 12,500 in Canada and over 5,000 in the United States.

Sect as community

The Hutterians are unique among sects in having maintained, with only brief breaks in continuity, a communitarian way of life for nearly four and a half centuries. There is then, a strong sense in which salvation, at least as experienced in this world, is in the bosom of the community. They believe that only those who follow the communal way of life, accepting communality of goods, *Gütergemeinschaft*, and the bonds of love found in such fraternities, are properly Christian. The Hutterians manage to maintain an almost completely segregated way of life. Humility, simplicity of life, the service of God in their daily concerns and in their community's operation are their dominant characteristics. They have no distinctive church organisation – the community and the congregation are co-terminous entities, and terms for church and community are used interchangeably in their articles of association. Adult baptism is the mark of admission to the community, and of submission to it. Submission involves refusing to bear arms (in the First World War every Hutterian was a conscientious objector, and in the second only a very few – and those not baptised members of the community – served in the armed forces). They naturally refuse all political office (a difficulty in some prairie communities where the Hutterians have become a very large proportion of the electorate). They refuse to pay taxes raised for purposes of war, or to take an oath. In all, they practise an extensive form of non-resistance (*Wehrlosigkeit*) and their spiritual ideal is *Gelassenheit* – the abandonment of the world, and of their rights in it, and the maintenance of calm composure, confidence in God's love, and the knowledge that all may be left to him. All this is justified by reference to the Bible, and is elaborated in the authoritative commentary of Peter Riedemann.

The Hutterian communities are self-contained, almost cloister-like, societies. Things from the outside world do not enter, and the ways of the world are not known. Whilst Hutterians marry and have individual households they have, at times, practised communal upbringing of children. They dine in common (sexes segregated) and in silence. Their daily life is that of the farmer, and they have adapted themselves to the farming conditions of the various countries in which they have settled. In the Canadian prairies they have sometimes proved more efficient farmers than their neighbours, due to the advantage of relatively large-scale communal operation. They can use capital equipment more extensively and they enjoy economies of scale in choice of production methods.

Hutterians now have one of the most impressive rates of population growth in the world. This has meant that there has been very little surplus for luxury – to which they are in any case opposed – and the advantages of mechanisation have been used less to provide a higher standard of living, than to support population increase. Once a community reaches about one hundred and fifty people, thought is taken to establish a new colony by dividing the existing one. Thus from birth to division, a colony's life is now about twenty years. In that time, a colony has increased its income to a point where it can support financially the process of fissure by the purchase of new land for those members who will become pioneers. The Hutterians have thus not invested in finance in the world, but in land and in people, and most of all in their own social values. In many colonies, some jobs have been kept as labour-intensive work (for example the painting of buildings, which is largely done by women) and this in almost conscious awareness that such work is necessary to sustain the commitment of members, and to keep them from prolonged and enforced idleness, which might lead to a demand for entertainment and the temptations of the outside world.

Each colony is presided over by a minister, who is elected in three stages, first by community nomination of candidates, secondly by a general vote of the community and of visiting ministers from other colonies (to eliminate candidates with little support) and thirdly and finally by lot. He is the moral exemplar to the whole community, and he is set a little, but only a little, apart. Next to him is the household steward, who looks after the material organisation of the colony, and associated with these two are the elders. Although the colony is run like an extended family, there is necessarily a degree of specialisation in a complex farming organisation. Each department of activity has its elected head, and younger men are assigned to tasks (although they have some choice). In their worship, dining and general community life, however, these divisions are entirely without distinctions of social status: there are no classes in a Hutterian community, and this, of course, is typical of a face-to-face group, since the very concept of 'class' is an abstraction that arises only when the contours of the real, known world cannot be grasped by immediate empirical apprehension of persons and situations.

The everyday speech of the Hutterians is a Tyrolean dialect, but they worship in German and use English, which they have acquired, when necessary. They admit public schools to their colonies in

Canada, but they also have German schools for their children. They are not interested in education beyond the primary level, except for the study of their own religious works, and they have not been stampeded by the high evaluation of education in the outside world. Wisely, they have seen that for their way of life, and their social values, the education of the world has no meaning. They have their own education system, and in its strong moral emphasis, in the apparent happiness it produces, and in its adjustment to Hutterian life it is superior to education outside. Although psychiatrists are generally unwilling to admit that anyone is completely mentally healthy, those who have studied Hutterians admit that whatever their problems they give rise to few symptoms of mental ill-health, and that they 'come off rather well in comparison with other people'. Relatively few Hutterians leave the colonies. Those who do are usually boys who do so before they are baptised, and hence before they are full members. Even outside, they usually continue to be Hutterians in belief, and to maintain some degree of dissociation from the world, but the real Hutterian can live only in the community, and most of those who leave do in fact return and settle down to the religious life to which they have been brought up.

The Old Order Amish: 'the ban' as an insulatory device

Another group that maintains its insulation from the wider society by vicinal segregation and by the use of its own language is the Old Order Amish. But this most conservative branch of the Mennonites is not communitarian – property is not held in common. There are many different communities of Amish, following slightly different patterns of life, and with differing degrees of insulation from the wider society. Thus, they are a less clearly defined sect than the Hutterians. Sect and community, whilst nominally co-terminus, have not quite so precisely reinforced each other. The religious ethic underwrites very strongly a distinctive, conservative and segregated way of life, but as an instrument of social control it has not so effectively prevented young men from leaving, or alien ideas from

affecting some communities. But here too custom has become sacred, and any sort of change is seen primarily as a threat to religion.

The Amish were a branch of the Mennonites, those Dutch and Swiss Anabaptists who, after the débâcle at Münster, came to accept the more disciplined sectarianism formulated by Menno Simons, a former Roman Catholic priest. Impressed by the heroism of Anabaptist martyrs in Holland, Simons espoused adult baptism as the means by which the Christian believer might be liberated from personal sins. He rallied the dispersed sectarians, and provided rules for an orderly way of life. In particular, he established the typical sectarian device of the ban – the rejection of all who threatened the purity of doctrine and of the fellowship. Those who were wayward were to be admonished and eventually banned from the society and shunned, until repenting and being solemnly re-admitted. It was on the interpretation of these issues – and excommunication is a typical issue on which sects experience schism – that, in the 1690s, Jacob Ammann divided the Swiss descendants of the early Mennonites. Insisting on a more rigorously applied ban, and more rigorous shunning of those not in the community, Ammann's followers, mainly in the canton of Bern in Switzerland and in Alsace, became known as the Amish Mennonites. They refused to eat with those outside the community, and, like the Exclusive Party among the Plymouth Brethren in the nineteenth and twentieth centuries, demanded that if a husband or wife were excommunicated, relations between them should cease.

The strictly enforced *Meidung* or shunning became the basis for Amish sectarianism: opponents said that Ammann had made *Meidung* more important than salvation, but the characteristic of the introversionist sect is essentially that purity in the community becomes the basis for salvation, and for purity to prevail, exclusion of the impure, as a type of religious hygiene, becomes essential. The Amish quickly came to emphasise their distinctiveness by adopting conservative forms of dress, notably in their use of hooks-and-eyes in opposition to the newer invention of buttons. Operation of the ban and exclusion from the world were not always easy, even in the agricultural areas of Switzerland and Alsace. Such difficulties, and the need to establish self-help and avoid persecution and interference, induced migrations of the Amish within Europe and more especially to North America. Although the Amish settled in Hesse, Ingolstadt, Regensburg and Munich, and near Groningen in Holland, and persisted into the twentieth century at Ixheim (near Zweibrücken in the Palatinate), in the Saar and in neighbouring Lorraine and Alsace, these groups have steadily returned to the general Mennonite fold. No Amish Mennonites now continue in Europe. Only those who migrated to the United States, and there found vicinal isolation, have maintained their distinctive way of life, even though many divergent groups have emerged among them manifesting rather different degrees of adaptation and acculturation.

In the United States, the Amish found segregated communities easy to establish. Despite the steady encroachment of twentieth-century urban development around some of their farming locations, they have grown in numbers: in the early 1960s, it was estimated that there were about 44,000 of them, settled principally in Lancaster and adjacent countries in Pennsylvania, around Holmes county, in Ohio, and in Delaware, Iowa, Indiana and Michigan. Perhaps because they lacked the rather closer confinement of Hutterian communitarian organisation, the Amish have stressed more fully than Hutterians the importance of rigorously conservative attitudes to dress, speech and material goods, as ways of marking themselves off from the wider society. They make no use of modern motor transport or tractors, but continue to use their 'high buggies' drawn by horses, and relatively rudimentary techniques of farming. However, they have accepted the use of electricity for farming and essential purposes, though not in their homes.

Religion is totally pervasive, not simply a compartmentalised activity. It dictates Amish values and the Amish way of life. The central truths of the Amish faith are non-resistance, avoidance of the world, refusal to be 'conformed to this world', self-denial, obedience to the church and the truth, and the acceptance of Christ as moral exemplar. They reject both Calvinist predestination, in common with other Mennonites, and the Wesleyan doctrine of assurance of salvation. Only at the day of judgment can the believer learn whether he has been saved, and until then his duty, as a pilgrim and stranger in the land of the Gentiles (the rest of Christendom) is obedience, and avoidance of the world, for only thus can he enjoy 'living hope'. Again, it is the community that becomes the only possible context in which a man might hope for salvation. The Amish reject many specific appurtenances of civilisation, particularly decoration, ceremony, all worldly amusements (including cards and party games), musical instruments, large mirrors, photographs, parting the hair for men, or curling and waving it for women. They reject insurance and refuse to accept government subsidies in their farming activities or welfare benefits. But the Amish community has some internal differences on these matters, and some communities have come to permit the use of specific things such as motor-cars. Strictness is sometimes symbolised in the width of the brim of the traditional hat worn by members of the sect.

Although the Amish have bishops and ministers, who are the principal authorities in the districts and churches in which they operate, Amish community life is largely subject to the decisions of the baptised members (all adult men and women). Ministers, although they work full-time in these roles, are scarcely recognisable as a 'professional clergy', since there is no specific training for office, and each district ordains its own deacon, preacher and bishop. There is a mixture of patriarchy and democracy among the Amish, and this reflects the peasant life-style that they have perpetuated. For the sociologist, the Amish present a veritable laboratory of an otherwise vanished peasant life. There are few courtesies, little distinction of polite and familiar language, no squeamishness about the crude or the bawdy, and a distrust of the specific commitment to be 'good' as this is understood by evangelical Christians. They stand much closer to nature even than do other farmers, and among them religion and morality lack many features thought by many Christians to be part of their intrinsic nature. Religious organisation is so completely entrenched in the community that geographic propinquity is a strong element in its operation: the formal bureaucratic conception of an organisation, familiar to most modern sects, is entirely lacking.

The Rappites: inspiration and introversion

Sociological categories do not stem directly from particular theological positions, nor from particular sets of historical circumstances. Sociological similarities exist among groups with quite different historical and theological origins. Stemming from a theological background quite different from that of the Anabaptist Hutterians and the Anabaptist-Mennonite Amish, were the Rappites, the followers of a self-proclaimed prophet in the late eighteenth century, George Rapp, of Iptingen, near Maulbronn, Württemberg. Rapp was a Lutheran, but underwent conversion to a more pious way of life, and, after feeling that Jesus shone in his heart, absented himself from church, and told the church authorities that he felt that nothing counted but being small and pure, remaining in quiet solitude, meeting with true and upright souls in a serious spirit despite the enmity of the world. These separatists came to believe in the inward communion with God (Rapp and some of his followers spoke of revelation from God on particular matters) and on inward, rather than water, baptism. *They* were no longer under the law, though other men might still need 'external religion'. The Rappites declared themselves as not concerned to win over those who lived within the general religious dispensation, but only to restore among themselves the guidance of the Holy Spirit. This is a hall-mark of the introversionist sect. Typically, too, the Rappites accepted the need for civil government – they were not looking forward to its overturn, even though they accepted the general ideas of the second advent of Christ and the inevitable ultimate end of the world as they knew it. Rapp thought that the advent would occur in his lifetime, and speculated on the outworking of prophecy in the events occurring in the Napoleonic Wars. Rappites did, however, reject military service because they had withdrawn from the things of the world.

As Rapp's following in the various neighbouring villages grew, the considerable tolerance of the Württemberg authorities became strained, and Rapp went to America to explore the possibilities of migrating there. In 1804 Rapp's followers, numbering between 450 and 550, led by his adopted son, Friederich Rapp, settled in America. In acquiring their land for settlement, the Harmony Society, as they were now styled, made evident their intention to practise a communitarian way of life. Their other distinguishing characteristic – a strong preference for celibacy, which had already been canvassed among the more convinced among them in Württemberg – was also soon asserted openly. Communitarianism established the identity of *Kirche* and *Gemeinde*, and the terms were used interchangeably in Rappite documents. Rules of association were minimal, since they were to live the life exemplified by Christ until the advent came. The Rappites differed from ecstatic millennarians in being dedicated to a life of work and orderly conduct: although they lived in certainty of the advent, the key to their way of life was the pattern of order that they established in their withdrawn colony, and not the expectation of the world's end.

The Harmonists were prodigious workers. They constructed their first colony on the Connoquenessing creek in Pennsylvania, in 1804–9, with houses, mills, barns, an inn, a fulling mill, a tanery, a brewery and the all-important meeting-house. Here they and later migrant Rappites were able to insulate themselves from the world, as a community of some eight hundred people that was virtually self-contained and self-sufficient. But the Harmonists were not sufficiently insulated here, and perhaps also their capacity for hard work was not adequately satisfied in a completed community, so that, in 1814, they offered their colony for sale, and moved on to a new site on the Wabash river, near Vincennes, Indiana. They played an important part in the life of frontier America, becoming 'the wonder of the West', for such was the contrast of Rappite order, security, good-living and civilisation with normal frontier conditions. The community still grew somewhat from natural increase since marriage had not entirely ceased, even though there was strong encouragement for all to abandon 'fleshly intercourse'. The Harmonists were not interested in having their form of society imitated by others: they were neither missionaries nor reformers, and although they sold their second colony to Robert Owen, the socialist idealist, they were not surprised that his community was a failure. Owen's followers lacked the religious commitment that the Rappites knew to be the indispensable premise on which to build a community.

The Rappites moved in 1824 to a site near Pittsburgh, and began building their third home, Economy. Their religious fervour persisted in its undemonstrative way, for Rapp, who ruled his community in almost dictatorial fashion, had only disdain for the conversionist enthusiasm, such as that of the Methodists. Rapp declared that God was *in* the Brethren, and this was a typical introversionist utterance: holiness is only in the community. The third home, the divine Economy, symbolised their advanced state in holiness: celibacy was now virtually the rule by which they overcame that bestiality which had occasioned the fall of Adam. The community was now the bride awaiting the bridegroom at the fast approaching advent. How at this moment a mountebank styling himself as Count Leon, Archduke Maximilian von Este and claiming to be the 'Anointed One' of Judah, arrived at Economy and nearly destroyed the community, cannot here be told. The solid effort and devoted life of the Rappites was almost undone by their gullible acceptance of this claimant to Christ's title. Thereafter, reduced by seccession, they closed their ranks and saw themselves as purged and too advanced to admit any new members. They continued after George Rapp's death in 1847 as a wealthy community that steadily abandoned communal work for communal investments, its remaining dwindling fellowship continuing to seek that state of preparedness for Christ's return, when all their property should be laid at his feet. In the event it was distributed to such descendants as there were of the now defunct community in the early twentieth century.

Introversionists in the wider society

Although introversionist sects are easily drawn to methods of ensuring community holiness by withdrawal into colonies, this has not been a possibility, nor even an ideological ideal for all of them. For example, the English Quakers, who became increasingly introversionist in the eighteenth century, and the Exclusive Brethren who have undergone this change from the 1880s to the present day, have remained within the wider society, withdrawing from it mentally, socially and politically, although still involved in the world's economic activities. The characteristic insulating devices of speech, dress, avoidance, endogamy and prohibited professions are employed by these sects to emphasise their own purity. The sect community becomes the only place where truth can be heard and where salvation can be attained, and the strong feeling of distinctiveness is manifested to the world by exemplary styles of conduct and integrity. Introversionist sectarians are often respected for their probity, whilst being disliked for their closeness, and sometimes for their shrewdness. Necessarily, they conduct relationships with outsiders in a spirit of calculation, relentlessly employing the world's own highly instrumental criteria of rational conduct, but without the intermixing of affective attitudes which often mitigate the role relationships of worldlings among themselves – since the sectarian confines his affective relationships to his own sect.

The sect known as the Exclusive Brethren (Darbisten in Germany, Switzerland and France) are a branch that separated in the 1840s from the Plymouth Brethren who came into being in the late 1820s in Dublin, and who acquired their name from outsiders who experienced the evangelistic activities of the Plymouth meeting of the movement in the 1830s. The early Brethren were literal biblicists, who arose in strong opposition to the ecclesiastical organisation and authority-structure of the Church of England. Their early ideal was of a community unbounded by formalities, sharing a common Christian life, and this, rather than either doctrinal tests or organisational membership, was intended to define the sect. But the Brethren quickly experienced difficulties. What were the beliefs essential for a Christian? Accusing other leaders of unscriptural teaching one of the pioneers of Brethrenism, John Nelson Darby, a former Anglican clergyman, began to insist on the purity of doctrine in the fellowship. He led a schism in the 1840s, and from the evangelistic nondenominational movement – the Plymouth (or Open) Brethren – emerged a schismatic boundary-conscious sect, the Exclusive Brethren. Open Brethren admitted any convinced Christians to their table to break bread in fellowship; Exclusives insisted that only *proven* Christians be admitted. The definition of who were Christians steadily became narrower, over the course of the years, and the Exclusive Brethren became a community sharply differentiated from other Christians.

To exercise doctrinal tests, however, required agencies by which orthodoxy might be distinguished from heresy, and under Darby's strong leadership, the sect came to establish tribunals known as 'care meetings' which admitted worthy candidates, and expelled those guilty of false doctrine or of conduct unbecoming for a 'saint'. No formal system of authority was instituted, and the sect has always had difficulty in ensuring that the decisions made by the Brethren in one town would be known and accepted by those in another. Lack of communication and the absence of any formally recognised central authority tended to cause the meeting of Brethren in one town to decide differently on a given case from the congregation in another place. The concern for purity of association was so pressed, that no meeting would knowingly permit a person excommunicated by another meeting to share their breaking of bread ceremony: to do so even in ignorance would be to become contaminated, sometimes without prospect of disinfection.

Salvation only in the sect

Such rigour quickly led the movement to assert that purity was a characteristic intrinsic to the community, rather than of any particular style of conduct (although their own standards remained high, and there was never any antinomian excess). Thus the more sectarian-minded, seeking to avoid the taint of the world, reduced the commitment to evangelism (although Darby himself had in his early days been a great evangelist, bringing 'the truth' to many in the communities of the French and Swiss Alps). In obedience to Christ's commands, the preaching of the gospel has never entirely ceased, and non-members are still admitted to one of the sect's Sunday services. Deepening of the spiritual life of the community mattered more than the evangelisation of the world. The dross must be purged, and the community must maintain its life without spot or blemish, virtually as the Church of God on earth. Thus the Exclusive Brethren came to see themselves as having less and less common cause with other Christians. Their own theological development became unique and distinctive with Darby's own theory of the millennium, known as 'dispensationalism'.

This theology rejected the Christian idea that God's promises to Israel were to the Church: they were to the Jews. Thus, the earth will be offered to the Jews at the second advent, but before this the Church and the saints will be caught up to reign with Christ in heaven. It is asserted that already the Church sits in heavenly places and needs only to be brought to heaven in the physical sense. This teaching implies, then, that the community (for Exclusive

Brethren almost identify their own sect with the Church) is already heaven, already the place of salvation. Whilst it is not absolutely denied that a saint could exist outside the Church (outside their own fellowship) the possibility is scarcely entertained. The sect must be apart from the world: only in the sect can the believer experience salvation. Exclusives acknowledge that Christ saves men *objectively*, but they hold that, *in practice,* men are aware of salvation only in the assembly. Only among the Brethren, it is asserted, is the Holy Spirit free to act, and this is the power that exists in their meetings.

Exclusive theology is intensely separatist in its implications, constituting a thorough expression of an extreme introversionist position, although Brethren live among other men. Their social ethic demands rigorous separation from the wider society in almost all activities and these demands have become steadily stronger in recent years. Today, Exclusives are almost suspicious of the stranger attending one of their few meetings that are open to non-Brethren. They do little to propagate their faith. Whilst in the past they permitted their children to go to universities, now they insist that there should be no association with unbelievers, and membership of a students' union (compulsory in British universities) is not tolerated for a 'saint'. Brethren reject membership of trades unions or professional associations, and many of them have had to choose between their careers and their religion. They refuse to occupy a house in which any who are not Brethren use the same front-door as themselves; recently they have refused to eat food cooked by non-Brethren. A member of the sect who is excommunicated is not only barred from the all-important breaking-of-bread ceremony, but is excluded from the homes of all other Brethren, including that of his own family. Schoolchildren are not permitted to play games or participate in extra-curricula activities with school-fellows. All associations are with the members of the sect: an Exclusive has no friends outside the sect, and no outside associations except those that are strictly necessary for business.

Many introversionist sects claim special inspirational guidance of the Holy Spirit, which becomes the unique possession of the community and is the particular basis of their claim to be a people apart. Such sects are strongly opposed, in the general Protestant tradition, to iconography, and yet they need some external entity that they uniquely possess, and by which they are possessed. The Holy Spirit, evanescent, felt if not seen, fulfils the same function as a totemic animal does for some simple societies. Unlike the Quakers and the Amana Society, the Exclusive Brethren do not claim specific inspiration and guidance, but they do believe that their assemblies alone provide a dwelling for the Holy Spirit, whose presence is felt. Salvation is assured for the Brethren, but is continually realised anew in the meetings, which are themselves a 'heavenly' experience.

Power and prestige and the rejection of 'human organisation'

The model of the introversionist sect is essentially that of the community: primary relationships are 'right relationships'. Only in the *Gemeinschaft* can true holiness and divine 'social control' operate. Unless the sect is a vicinally segregated and self-contained community, however, certain types of authority problem arise. The older introversionist sects, such as the Hutterians and the Amish, had their ministerial class – full-time but scarcely professional. But in those introversionist groups that have remained in the wider society, and in which no such separated class has evolved, there has always been difficulty about leadership. The Exclusive Brethren have always denied all formal leadership, since the sect arose in the strongest antagonism to clerical authority. Yet, where formal leadership is denied, informal leadership sometimes develops, giving rise to particular problems because the distribution of power is unlegitimated. Strong individuals may in effect become, as Darby became among the Exclusives, the arbiters of community decisions. But even Darby was challenged, and several close associates separated from him towards the end of his life. When in such groups no one strong leader inherits informal power, delicate struggles ensue, sometimes leading to schism. This has been the case with the

Exclusive Brethren, of which at least eight separate branches have been in existence at different times. Although the greatest number of Brethren in Britain remained in the fellowship of the successive leaders, following Darby down to James Taylor Sr, and James Taylor Jr, the majority of assemblies in the West Indies, and in Germany (Elberfeld and in Württemberg) and in Switzerland, have followed in a schismatic line of succession. No leader among the Exclusives has been wholly sure of his authority, and has always formally denied having it. In practice, however, many Brethren have been motivated by a continual search for the prestige to be gained by 'opening up' new lines of ministry, but in the pursuit of which they have risked propounding unacceptable teachings, for which the consequence is at the least to lose face, and perhaps to be expelled for heresy.

Sects with the imprint of secularity

Whilst conversionist, revolutionist and introversionist sects all espouse radically different values from those of the wider society, manipulationist sects are much more congenial to the prevailing secular culture. What they provide for their votaries is less an alternative set of values for life, than the semi-esoteric means to the ends that are general to society. Whereas introversionist sects (and, in lesser measure, conversionist sects) represent communities of love, with a high premium on affective values, group cohesiveness and primary relationships, manipulationist sects represent almost the opposite. They are much more instrumental in their concerns: the community is not an end in itself. The meeting of the manipulationist group is not the congregating of a community, but the gathering of an association of like-minded and like-instructed people, who use a common method in coping with the world. The manipulationists have found a method by which to achieve salvation, but salvation is largely seen as the ability to realise the good things of the world, and particularly long life, health, happiness and a sense of superiority or even of triumph. The sect provides short-cuts to attain these ends. These values are sometimes expressed in terms scarcely religious, although such sects have often presented their teachings in metaphysical language. Manipulationist sects are secularised sects, for which only the *means* to salvation are religious: the *goals* are largely those of secular hedonism.

Sects emphasising special knowledge of this kind, a *gnosis* that gives the diligent believer mastery to manipulate the world, arise only in particular historical periods and social circumstances. They are most evident in metropolitan centres, where relationships are impersonal and dominated by role-performances. The people who belong to the manipulationist sects regard themselves as sophisticates. Their sectarian adherence is, for them, the superior means of coping intellectually with the complexities of involvement in a social system and a way of life that can be comprehended only in abstract terms. They are acquainted, usually, with other systems of religious belief and worship, and they know that there is a baffling variety of cults: what they accept, they justify intellectually and pragmatically. The manipulationist sect tends to present its message in abstract terms, in literature rather than by means of emotional expression, and its adherents are those who can be reached through literary channels.

The impersonality of city life is reflected in manipulationist sects. Participation is segmentary, not total. The votaries may not even know each other except as passing acquaintances: there is no expectation that the adherents form a family-like community. The control of members is not exercised by the methods of social control that replicate life-styles in the village (the model for introversionist sects) but by inculcating modes of thought and psychological processes, defined in the teachings of the sect's metaphysical system. The sect is not 'restorative' in seeking to justify the moral virtues of a rural past: rather it celebrates the benefits and the optimism of the future. It lines itself up on the side of progress, and presents itself as the real means of advancement into a brave new world in which the adepts of the system will reap untold benefits as they master its use.

Although many of the manipulationist sects that have grown up in Christendom have continued to use some of the terminology, the practices, and even the organisational styles of Christian churches, such sects are essentially syncretistic, and they differ radically from traditional Christianity in their posture towards the world. Christianity grew up in a society that was largely *gemeinschaftlich*. It idealised the small community, and most sects have drawn heavily from the deep deposit of community sentiment (rooted ultimately in family imagery and symbolism) within the Christian tradition: the churches themselves wrestle continually with the concept of *koinonia* ('community') and even the radical theologians of the modern age use the word reverentially. Christianity is deeply implicated in community organisation. It is not adjusted, as are most of the manipulationist sects, to religion in the impersonal urban world. Its values, and its theological assumptions imply – though they are not realised in practice – an opposition to the instrumentalism of twentieth-century society as sharp as that of introversionist sects. Those manipulationist sects that do borrow Christian forms and terms do so largely because these are the accepted and known forms of religious sociation.

In teaching, these movements are self-consciously syncretistic, adding new interpretations of scripture, or combining new ideas with what they have taken from the Christian repository. Sometimes, as in New Thought sects and Christian Science, the syncretism has been with essentially secular metaphysical philosophical speculation. At other times, it has been the conscious attempt to blend the wisdom of some other system with Christianity, as in the 'suprareligious' system of Theosophy. Commonly, there have been additional scriptures, sometimes put on a par with the Bible, and sometimes superseding it entirely. In more recent times, these attempts to blend the gnosis of the sect with Christian concepts has been more or less abandoned, as in Scientology, for the benefit of blending it with a more prestigious body of knowledge – in this particular case, psychotherapy. Yet even in Scientology, though perhaps only for reasons of expedience, the style of 'church' and the simulation of religious forms has been adopted.

Worship as such has given place to other preoccupations. Worship is an end activity of a community, and is more or less the solemnisation of the community itself. Manipulationist sects have secular ends – education (in the sect's teaching), health and happiness. In such sects the individual does not need to celebrate a love-relation with his fellows in the group, since the group is of very little importance in itself. Rather, he recites blessings, demonstrates his power through knowledge of doctrine, commands prestige, and shows his joy in his mastery of his circumstances.

Increasingly too the styles of educational and therapeutic agencies are adopted by the new manipulationist sects. Most prominent is the nomenclature drawn from education – 'lectures', 'courses', 'teachers', 'practitioners', 'therapists' or 'auditors'. The solemn occasions of the Christian year, and even of periodic rededication of the congregation, are abandoned. The organisational structure of the sect also resembles increasingly the secular agencies of education and health. The leader or founder of such a movement is, today, less easily represented as a charismatic figure. It is more usually asserted that all votaries might approach in some measure the wisdom of the leader by continued study ('study' and not 'saintly dedication'). The prophet thus becomes the guru, assimilating the prestige of highly evaluated activities of the modern world with some sort of arcane wisdom of the past.

Christian Science: an old manipulationist movement

Because manipulationist sects reflect the styles and preoccupations of the secular society in which they arise, it is fairly easy to recognise older and newer movements among them. The older tend to be rather closer to traditional Christianity. The newer have more diffuse points of reference, and their tacit dialogue may be more evidently conducted in the context of oriental ideas (stemming from the popular intrusion into the West of eastern mysticism in the late nineteenth century, or the more specialised cults such as Zen Buddhism in the mid-twentieth); of modern mental therapy, as in the case of Scientology, or of Science Fiction, as in the case of the Aetherius Society. One of the older manipulationist sects most heavily reliant on Christian forms is Christian Science, founded by Mary Baker Eddy in New England in the 1860s and 1870s. The background influences on Christian Science were, most conspicuously: a derived form of Mesmer's animal magnetism, the Unitarian-Universalist theology of optimistic universal benelovence current in New England, embracing a strong faith in progress, and the contemporary preoccupation with the search for quick and unorthodox methods of healing. They may have included a garbled version of Hegelianism and incidental ideas disseminated among Spiritualists, Swedenborgians and Shakers – all sects thriving in the area in which Mrs Patterson (as Mrs Eddy was then) claimed to discover the principle of mental healing and Christian Science.

After experiences with Phineas P. Quimby, a local mental healer,

Mary Baker Eddy (1821–1910), founder of Christian Science, as she was in her mid-forties when she first became interested in mental healing.

Mrs Eddy took up his system and taught it. She later amended it and claimed it as her own 'discovery', although she never abandoned the Unitarian Christian tradition of local society. At every point, her system of healing and the metaphysical ideas that supported it looked to the scriptures for confirmation and support. The syncretism is well represented in the title she chose for her church, 'The First Church of Christ, Scientist', and of her book, *Science and Health with Key to the Scriptures*. The Christian Science weekly lesson-sermon, read every day privately by dutiful Christian Scientists, and read publicly as the only form of 'preaching' in Christian Science churches at each service on Sundays, is simply a prescribed selection of extracts from the Bible and from *Science and Health* which, in emphasis of the imitation of educational styles, is called 'our only textbook'. Initially, Mrs Eddy probably did not see the need for a church of her own, but as her healing system was increasingly justified by reference to Christ as a cleanser of lepers, the separate movement she began was necessarily religious. Initially, it was little more than the provision of a lecture by Mrs Eddy in a hired hall, with the general blessing of Christianity in hymns and churchly decorum. What mattered in the early days was the teaching of the Christian Science system of therapy, undertaken in a 'Metaphysical College' in Boston, and disseminated by its graduates to others. Over the years Mrs Eddy rationalised the structure, closed her college and all the branch institutes, and imposed on her followers the discipline of church organisation, in which all Christian Science churches became branches of The Mother Church in Boston, all following precisely the same order of service, with no variation except in choice of hymns.

Mrs Eddy's teaching consisted principally in asserting that God was Mind, and that God alone existed. Man, as God's image, was not a material being but a wholly spiritual one. The material man was no more than a counterfeit of spiritual man, and spiritual man was like God, perfect. Consequently, man could not suffer, sin, be sick or die. These were but the 'false claims' of matter. If man could but realise this (and only his false sense contradicted such divine truth), he would realise his true spiritual being – sinless, healthy and undying. Christian Science prayer was the affirmation of these truths in various forms. This, it was held, was the truth which Jesus Christ had come to earth to propound, but he had not been understood: he had himself said that there were many things that men could not then bear, but which they should learn when the comforter should come. That comforter, the Holy Ghost to most Christians, was declared to be Christian Science. This was the knowledge of 'Mind', which was God, by which all men could be taught to rectify their thinking, and so experience universal good, and demonstrate 'divine Principle'. The system was held to be as logical as mathematics, and, if man could but grasp it, part of the natural order of the universe. This then was salvation: typical of manipulationist sects, salvation is to be had in this world by a mental operation. Little is said of the next, although the implication is that, sooner or later, men must come to the truths propounded in Christian Science.

A distinctive teaching of Christian Science that derived neither from Quimby nor any of the other sources from which Mrs Eddy may have borrowed, concerns *malicious animal magnetism*. M.a.m., as it is commonly abbreviated by Christian Scientists, is evil and false thought, the work of 'mortal mind', sometimes deliberate when an individual engages in mental malpractice, and sometimes more general 'mesmeric' influences. A serious Christian Scientist must do his daily mental work to protect himself from malicious animal magnetism. This mental work consists in repeated assertions that error is powerless and truth and goodness all-pervasive – but it is believed that unless this mental work is done error might *seem* to have power, so afflicting individuals with sickness, sin and death. Advanced Christian Scientists, who take instruction from an approved teacher, are taught most specifically about malicious animal magnetism, and such is the potency that this force might have, that the papers written on the subject by students are subsequently burnt. Towards the end of her life, Mrs Eddy had a constant team of practitioners at prayer, warding off the baleful influence of animal magnetism, which she believed might attack her household, and she instructed Adam Dickey, one of her close associates, that, in the event of her death, he was to declare that she had been 'mentally murdered'.[8] The name, animal magnetism, seems to have arisen from Mrs Eddy's overwhelming need to dissociate her form of mind healing from that of Quimby, which had been derived from a form of mesmerism, and which she came to identify with everything that was contrary to Christian Science.

Organisation, constituency and growth

Mrs Eddy herself was regarded as both prophet and teacher, and by many as 'the woman clothed with the sun', who, as told in the Book of Revelation, would bring forth a man-child (*Science and Health*) to rule over the nations. She closed the door to further developments of her system by setting up a 'board of directors' in Boston to run her movement. Every innovation in the presentation of Christian Science has since been rigorously suppressed, and a considerable number of prominent teachers of the system who have deviated from the strict orthodoxy defined by the Boston headquarters have been suspended and sometimes expelled. Orthodox

148   A Christian Science meeting qualifies as a church (**C** in table) only
       when it has not less than sixteen members, four of whom are members
       of the Mother Church, and one of whom is a registered Christian
       Science practitioner. Many churches are much larger than this
       of course, some with hundreds of members. It is doubtful whether
       many societies (**S** in table) have more than twenty-five members.

teaching is preserved, and in many respects the dead hand of Mrs
Eddy and her decrees (unamended since her death in 1910) still rest
on the movement. The practice of Christian Science healing by
authorised practitioners (all of whom must have had 'instruction'
from an accredited teacher, and who must not follow any other gainful employment) is organised independently of the church structure.
The system of control is very much that of a corporation and the
uneasy dualism of private teaching and healing and public church
services is held together by strong control at the centre.

Christian Science spread rapidly once it was established in Boston,
and Mrs Eddy's book went through many revisions, its early
solecisms being largely eliminated. It attracted, as is typical with
manipulationist sects, a following of reasonably well-to-do people,
with an adequate standard of education to enjoy a religion in which
reading was a primary activity. Christian Scientists attributed the
success of the movement to their healing methods, asserting that
only Christian Science could really heal. Of all the larger sects and
denominations in the United States it became the one with the most
completely urban constituency, and this was probably true of the
other countries to which the movement spread. It always attracted a
higher proportion of women than most other churches, especially
those in higher age groups. The vast majority of the healing practitioners of Christian Science have always been women – perhaps
because women were more fully able to meet the demand that they
should follow no other gainful employment. Practitioners' fees for
their mental work for patients cannot, in many cases, have provided
a regular and adequate income.

Christian Scientists in general have never felt much need to hold
themselves aloof from activities going on in the world. Christian
Scientists have been prominent in politics: a number of American
Senators have been Christian Scientists, and so were Lord and Lady
Astor and Lord Lothian, British Ambassador to Washington in
the early war years. Several prominent theatre and film actors and
actresses have also been among their number. Christian Science
demands that its members abstain from alcohol and tobacco, and

Table 6 Number of Christian Science Churches in various countries at selected dates

	1911		1938		1953		1968	
	C	S	C	S	C	S	C	S
Australia	6	0	24	18	25	24	32	25
Canada	23	12	45	30	47	29	54	34
France	2	0	5	1	5	7	5	9
Germany	3	2	37	42	34†	51†	48†	63†
Gt Britain	28	37	144	134	181	163	189	126
Holland	1	1	2	7	2	9	3	12
New Zealand	1	0	9	9	11	8	11	11
Sweden	0	1	3	2	3	1	4	1
Switzerland	0	2	13	18	14	24	16	21
U. South Africa	1	4	18	9	19	10	23	7
United States	655	510	1,394*	759*	1,624	651	1,821	563

† Figures for West Germany only   * Figures for 1940.

the more scrupulous also refuse tea and coffee. But these taboos are more related to the movement's embargo on drugs and *materia medica* than to any counsel of asceticism.

In America, Christian Science grew rapidly in the period from about 1890 to 1925, and thereafter growth became increasingly uneven. In 1936 there were over a quarter of a million Christian Scientists in the United States, and over 2,000 churches, although their social prominence made many people suppose that they were much more numerous. No official figures have been published since that time, but it is certain that as far as numbers of churches go, Christian Scientists in recent years have grown in numbers only in certain states, particularly in those to which older people retire.

Table 7 Christian Science in the United States

	1911		1926		1940		1953		1968	
	C	S	C	S	C	S	C	S	C	S
Alabama	2	1	4	8	6	8	6	8	7	9
Arizona	3	1	3	9	3	8	6	5	12	4
Arkansas	5	5	10	5	9	8	8	8	11	13
California	52	39	141	95	201	74	255	76	328	56
Colorado	20	15	23	16	24	15	26	14	27	14
Connecticut	10	7	14	12	19	7	26	4	27	6
Delaware	1	0	1	0	1	1	1	2	3	1
D. Columbia	1	0	4	0	4	0	8	0	7	0
Florida	6	4	22	16	31	14	41	13	79	17
Georgia	7	3	7	5	9	5	11	9	15	5
Idaho	5	11	11	11	13	6	12	7	12	6
Illinois	53	38	81	39	100	37	111	26	118	21
Indiana	30	15	46	33	50	29	55	24	56	22
Iowa	34	29	33	25	32	33	30	18	27	12
Kansas	30	20	35	30	37	25	37	18	35	10
Kentucky	3	7	9	6	8	8	11	5	13	5
Louisiana	3	2	7	1	9	6	12	9	14	6
Maine	10	10	9	14	11	16	11	12	11	16
Maryland	2	3	4	2	7	4	15	6	18	5
Massachusetts	38	9	53	16	64	13	69	9	76	6
Michigan	33	27	49	39	57	44	71	37	84	25
Minnesota	14	13	24	18	27	20	27	14	29	10
Mississippi	1	5	4	7	8	4	10	3	8	4
Missouri	22	14	33	22	44	17	48	11	51	15
Montana	8	3	12	8	14	12	14	8	12	6

	1911		1926		1940		1953		1968	
	C	S	C	S	C	S	C	S	C	S
Nebraska	13	15	15	23	20	17	21	10	20	10
Nevada	2	2	1	8	2	6	3	6	3	5
New Hampshire	7	12	9	14	10	12	11	14	17	4
New Jersey	19	5	39	15	55	12	66	7	64	8
New Mexico	1	3	3	6	5	9	8	7	11	7
New York	49	31	105	36	126	34	138	26	139	16
N. Carolina	4	3	10	5	11	9	13	8	16	7
N. Dakota	3	2	6	9	7	5	7	5	5	5
Ohio	34	28	56	32	73	27	83	24	86	20
Oklahoma	11	12	21	16	23	29	31	21	30	17
Oregon	8	15	24	25	32	21	39	20	42	21
Pennsylvania	24	28	46	17	56	24	64	17	64	18
Rhode Island	3	0	5	0	5	1	5	2	6	1
S. Carolina	1	0	3	2	3	2	3	5	5	6
S. Dakota	8	6	8	8	8	11	9	7	9	6
Tennessee	6	1	7	2	9	1	9	2	7	8
Texas	15	17	29	24	40	35	63	34	75	32
Utah	5	1	5	0	0	2	4	1	5	0
Vermont	5	6	6	6	7	7	7	5	7	8
Virginia	2	3	6	6	11	2	11	8	18	8
Washington	16	13	34	42	46	45	57	42	65	30
W. Virginia	3	1	6	3	7	2	8	0	8	0
Wisconsin	25	22	30	40	41	33	45	29	48	21
Wyoming	1	4	3	8	5	9	5	5	5	7

In addition, in 1968 the new state of Alaska had 4 Churches and 1 Society and the new state of Hawaii 2 Churches and 3 Societies.

Thus, although the number of Christian Science churches and societies has increased from 354 to 390 in California in the period from 1956-68, and from sixty-seven to ninety-eight in Florida, in the same period there has been a slight decline in the number of organisations in, among other states, New York (from 166 to 156); in Illinois (from 141 to 139); in Iowa (from forty-seven to thirty-nine) and elsewhere. Growth has continued in other countries, particularly in those where Christian Science was disseminated rather later, although at a diminishing rate.

Decline is even more evident when statistics of Christian Science practitioners are examined. In Britain, there were more than a thousand registered practitioners in 1940, and a steady diminution had brought the number to just over 540 in 1968; in France, where the movement has never had a large following, although there are churches in a few principal cities and holiday resorts, the number of practitioners was thirty-seven before the war, and today is only twenty-five. In Germany, there were more than a hundred practitioners in 1940; at the peak after the war the number rose to almost that figure in the 1950s but has now declined to eighty-four.

Of the seventeen practitioners in Holland, fifteen are women, and of the fifty-five Christian Science healers in Switzerland, forty-eight are women. In both countries the number of practitioners has declined since before the war. These figures, however, give only oblique indications of the decline of the movement. It may be that there are fewer people now who have the private means to practise Christian Science healing as a full-time occupation, but the slowness of the number of organisations to increase in most parts of the world, the very evident decline in Britain, and the stagnation in many parts of the United States suggests that this sect has now passed its peak. Christian Science appeals to the elderly, and in a world increasingly devoted to a youth-culture, it may fail to recruit the rising generation. This may not cause its demise, since it appears that Christian Science has always had a considerable population of relatively transient adherents, who are involved in the system for a few years and then gradually drift away from it again.

New Thought : movements with loose structures

At least some of the sources from which Christian Science arose were also those of the congeries of movements known collectively as New Thought. Phineas P. Quimby, who first practised a type of mesmeric healing with the aid of a medium and who later developed the idea that healing was achieved only by altering the thought of a patient, inspired a number of followers who believed in the power of mind over body. Only Mrs Eddy discovered that she could really make her living by teaching the Quimby system, and only she went on to gather students, give lectures, and establish a church. The other patients and pupils of Quimby were much slower to recognise that the new ideas, the philosophy for living, might be made the substance of sectarian teaching, and disseminated by organised methods. When they did, perhaps because they were later and recognised alternatives to traditional church structure, the organisations that they set up were less like traditional sects or churches.

New Thought ideas have remained more widely diffused than most sect beliefs, and have penetrated more orthodox inspirational religious literature in the United States. In writers like Norman Vincent Peale, and his Catholic counterpart, Fulton Sheen, the exhortation to 'positive thinking' carries the strongest echoes of New Thought.[9] Men are told that by 'right thinking, one's loftiest ideals may be brought into present realisation'. This is the principal message of New Thought, and it is applied specifically to disease. These ideas have never been anchored in a very definite religious tradition, however, and although New Thought adherents legitimate their system in terms of God and the divine Mind, they reject creeds and deny that they belong to a cult or a sect. But some 'schools' of New Thought have, despite this, particular styles and approved terms for their own statement of beliefs. The movement emphasises all the benign elements of Christianity and, following those currents that had led to Unitarianism and Universalism, simply rejects damnation, eternal punishment and hell as expressions of man's groundless fears.

It was at least partly in reaction to the emergence of Christian Science that Quimby's other patients promulgated his teachings. None of them had Mrs Eddy's drive to establish a movement, nor, perhaps, any of her personal charismatic quality. Julius A. Dresser and his son Horatio were largely responsible for revealing the extent to which Christian Science had come from Quimby, and from 1882 the elder Dresser was active in mental healing in Boston. Subsequently the ranks of New Thought teachers grew from disaffected practitioners of Christian Science. Their disaffection, then and since, has been occasioned principally by the rigidity of the Christian Science organisation, and because no new lines of teaching have been permitted. One of these disaffected Christian Scientists, Mrs Emma Hopkins, set herself up as an independent teacher of metaphysics in Chicago, and came to influence and instruct those who later set up the New Thought movements known as Divine Science, Unity and the Church of Religious Science.

Many of the leaders of New Thought schools were women. Divine Science was established by two women teachers of metaphysics in Denver, Colorado, in the late 1880s. First and quite typically – before a church was founded – a college was established to teach the system of philosophy and healing; there followed magazines and then *Daily Studies in Divine Science*. The movement also conducted a correspondence course. Steadily the churches of Divine Science spread, sometimes by absorbing local congregations established by previously independent ministers. The organisation of the movement remained relatively loosely structured until 1957.

At much the same time as the origin of Divine Science, the Unity School of Christianity was founded in Kansas City by 'a real estate operator', Charles Fillmore, and his wife Myrtle. This movement began with the publication of a magazine after the Fillmores had experienced healing by metaphysical means. A group began to meet 'in silent soul communion every night … for all those who are in trouble, sickness or poverty, and who sincerely desire the help of the Good Father'. Correspondence with enquirers led to the establishment of many little groups praying 'in silent unity'. The movement grew and large numbers of workers were eventually employed; a recreational centre, with sports facilities, has been built for them at Unity Village, and a hotel for guests attending courses at the centre. Steadily the movement developed into a regular church, although its output of literature, produced in several languages, has also grown and remained an important activity. The movement's literature includes a journal, *Good Business,* which shows how positive thinking is an asset in business activities. The Fillmore family have remained at the top of the organisation, although with the spread of the movement there has emerged an association of those who are trained and accredited ministers in the movement's churches. The movement has steadily come to acquire its own distinctive structure and system of metaphysics and for a long time it has ceased to be affiliated to International New Thought Alliance, in which most other New Thought groups are united. In many respects Unity is more specifically Christian in its teaching than other New Thought bodies.

Embracing the impersonality of the age, New Thought groups have always used literature as a principal medium of communication and to this they have added the idea of healing treatment *in absentia*, and silent prayer (all of which are also found in Christian Science). The use of radio broadcasting and correspondence courses has also been common. One movement, now defunct, relied entirely on correspondence courses and the circulation of literature by post. This was Psychiana, founded by Frank B. Robinson of Moscow, Idaho. Robinson inserted advertisements in newspapers, under the heading, 'I talked with God', and invited others to write to him to learn how to do the same. His 'mail-order' religion became widely known in the United States, and in the 1930s and 1940s he sold more than a million copies of his correspondence course and other publications. He was opposed to organisation, and did not even seek to put his correspondents in touch with one another. After his death in 1948, Psychiana dwindled away: its transience as a movement reflected the segmentary involvement and ephemeral commitment of the votaries of New Thought.

156

The ideas of the New Thought movement never achieved great acceptance in Britain. About twenty local groups formed an association in the 1950s, but this did not last, and New Thought is principally represented by a few branches of the principal American organisations. France has been equally unreceptive, although a somewhat amorphous group, *Unité Universelle*, exists in Paris, which offers silent spiritual help for those who seek it, and which relies essentially on 'love-offerings'. At Roquebrune-Cap Martin in the south of France, the *Institut de Psychosynthèse Spirituelle* was established by Auguste Joseph Berg, and this movement has associated groups in Marseilles, Paris, Bordeaux, Pau and Perpignan. New Thought literature was translated into German at an early date, and before the war some two hundred groups of the *Neugeist* movement existed in Germany, linked by the periodical *Die Weisse Fahne*. Although suppressed in the Nazi period, the movement re-emerged after the war, and the writings of K.O. Schmidt, its principal exponent, have had wide circulation since then.

Whereas older sects inculcated in their members particular dogmas about God, and regulated minutely their day-to-day activities according to strong moral precepts, the New Thought movement offered its adherents an essentially hedonistic philosophy. Without regular congregations, the movement's control of members was simply to insist on the importance for the individual of regulating his thought. As in other manipulationist sects, even organisational means of binding the individual to the teaching have been minimal: commitment was summoned by constant encouragement to 'progress in the truth', and by promise of benefits to be realised. At its less spiritual levels, New Thought was always capable of becoming a system of short-cuts to success: even one of its most reputable exponents, Elizabeth Towne, was capable of writing, 'Money is *really* as free as air. Take it by knowing that it is yours ...', and it was a commonplace of New Thought literature to suggest that men created wealth, health and happiness by practising mental hygiene. By taking thought, men would manipulate their own circumstances and the world.

Occultism and modern organisation

A distinctive group of manipulationist sects are those that draw their esoteric teachings from occult sources, often from the Orient. Their metaphysical systems are always a complex amalgam of mystical ideas and a full account of them would need to trace their ramifying divisions and schisms. These movements share certain broad characteristics worthy of brief mention. In particular, there is the attraction of the exotic. Once popular knowledge of eastern religion had spread in the nineteenth-century, the idea of mystic wisdom preserved in the religious centres of the East, free from the restrictive tradition of Christianity, began to appeal to many 'seekers' in the west. Many were drifters from one spiritual 'cause' to another; others were those who, for one reason or another, had missed the chance to make their way in the intellectual traditions of the west. Both factors explain why women were often the founders and why so many women became devotees of the new cults, which promised a higher wisdom than was available either in the churches or the universities, and one which would lay bare the real secrets of the universe and of man's destiny. Some cults, such as the Gurdjieff system, remained essentially secret organisations: others, Theosophy being a conspicuous example, were subjects of publicity and were canvassed in the drawing rooms of the well-to-do as a philosophy to embrace all religions.

Theosophy was first propounded by Madame Petrovna Blavatsky, who claimed it as wisdom accumulated by the Masters, an occult brotherhood in Tibet, over thousands of years, and for which she was the chosen and prepared vessel and ambassador. With Colonel H. S. Olcott, she founded the Theosophical Society in 1875 in New York. Madame Blavatsky claimed to have been instructed by the Masters in Tibet, supernormal men possessing physical bodies but normally perceptible only in their 'astral bodies' (the 'astral plane' being a plane of matter less physical than that known to ordinary men, and perceptible by clairvoyance and clairaudience). The Masters were those who taught the truth about man: that divine

life of the Great Being had been obscured by the dense forms of matter, and must be revealed again through evolution, by which man would become perfect. Perfection was to be attained by re-incarnations, but, by serious study of the Theosophical system, man might improve himself, accelerate the evolutionary process and enter the Path of Discipleship, be liberated from the normal law of cause and effect, and so himself attain the occult hierarchy.

Jesus is regarded as a teacher who taught principles contained in all religion that were of course much more ancient than he: with the other Masters, he was merely part of a hierarchy under the Trinity of the Lord of the World, the Lord Buddha and the Mahachohan (the Arm stretched out to the world to do the practical work). Their

Madame Blavatsky, at one time a
practising medium, established the occult
teachings of Theosophy in 1875.

representatives, the Manu and Bodhisattva, transmitted the influence of the Godhead to earth: the Bodhisattva, Lord Maitreya, had
done this in the body of Jesus. Theosophy thus superseded Christianity and offered its students the opportunity to discover the secrets
of the universe. Two of its leaders in the period following Madame
Blavatsky's death in 1891 – Mrs Annie Besant, formerly a prominent free-thinker and early exponent of birth-control in England,
and C. W. Leadbeater – claimed to have been instructed by the
Masters in Tibet, and even produced drawings of the atoms and
molecules then unknown of the chemical elements, hydrogen,
oxygen and nitrogen. Such was the extent to which the esoteric
teachings were believed to enable men to manipulate their world.
(The drawings were of no scientific value.)

Theosophy became a fashionable sect and attracted well-to-do
titled and professional people whilst claiming to be above all
religions. Its greatest influence was in India where the ubiquitous
Mrs Besant drew youthful enthusiasts such as Jawaharlal Nehru
and Krishna Menon, both later to become leaders of independent India (a cause into which Mrs Besant also threw her immense
energies). It had followers in most European cities, among them
Rudolf Steiner, who, however, rejected Mrs Besant's attempt to
school a young Indian boy, Krischnamurti, as the forthcoming
messiah, and took the majority of German Theosophists (about
2,500) into his own Anthroposophical Society in 1912. Steiner
emphasised human instead of divine wisdom, and built his society
on his mystical revelations. Despite pronounced tendencies to
schism, and the many distracting causes that Mrs Besant espoused,
Theosophy has persisted, but without retaining the numbers or the
influence it had in the early years of the century. Mrs Besant's
enthusiasm for Indian nationalism, and Leadbeater's attempt to
add ritualism to Theosophy in becoming a bishop of the Liberal
Catholic Church (the bishops of which claimed, via the Old Catholics
of Holland, the apostolic succession) caused defections. Their
followers also found that the devious courses prescribed by the
Masters to their two principal agents were incredible.

After Madame Blavatsky's death in 1891, C. W. Leadbeater (*far right*) and Mrs Annie Besant (*left*) became prominent leaders of the Theosophical movement. In India they schooled Krishnamurti (*right*) to be the coming messiah, but he later disavowed this role although remaining a religious teacher.

More recent manipulationist sects that draw on eastern practice have generally abandoned the elaborate metaphysical and dogmatic descriptive matter that formed so large a part of Theosophy. Some have been health cults, stressing exercises and diet (as did Theosophy), and others, like Subud, have emphasised the means of eliminating tension and becoming sensitive to beneficial superhuman influences. Various meditation cults, such as that of the Maharishi, have spread, especially to America, drawing their devotees into regular exercises in clearing the mind by the repetition of a *mantra,* or mystic word, diagnosed to suit the personality of the votary. These cults were the successors of more sedate movements, such as Vedanta, which acquired more permanent success after the teachings of Ramakrishna, the Indian self-styled avatar, were disseminated in the United States by Swami Vivekananda at the World Parliament of Religions in 1893. Vedanta has ten centres in the United States, and one each in Britain, France and Argentina.

New problems for metaphysical therapy

As the much less advanced material conditions of eastern countries has been borne in upon westerners, particularly through the need for foreign aid programmes, the spiritual ideals of oriental societies have commanded less appeal. In a world in which material well-being has come to be very strongly emphasised, mystical flights and other planes of existence have become less credible. The circumstances of the more affluent classes now provide less leisure for metaphysical speculation, and a less mystic type of manipulationist sect has emerged. The preoccupation with physical health, evident in Christian Science and the early New Thought cults, has also somewhat receded with the general improvement of living standards, hygiene and medical services. Modern insecurities are of a different kind. In particular, they focus on war and mental health. Even sects that are not to be classified as manipulationist have come increasingly to pick up these preoccupations: thus the Radio Church

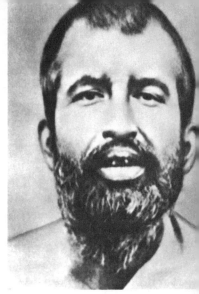

of God, (now called the Worldwide Church of God) founded and run by Herbert Armstrong, and broadcasting widely to America, Britain, Australia and Germany, has couched its essentially millennialist message in terms that emphasise these problems. More recently, their magazine, *Plain Truth,* has concentrated on modern social and psychological problems (such as 'Hippies' and marital relations). At one time their Bible-based prophecies about the future time of doom depicted particularly horrific scenes of war and atomic devastation, although this aspect has now been 'phased out'. The movement now emphasises correspondence courses and study at its three colleges. The manipulationists, with their much more strongly optimistic tone, bring forward mental therapeutic systems, and translate contemporary military developments into events of cosmic importance.

The various societies growing up in Europe and America that are concerned with 'flying saucers' and 'unidentified flying objects' are not always sectarian, but many manifest a speculative and almost religious disposition. One that takes such tendencies further is the Aetherius Society, which seeks to form a brotherhood based on the teachings of the cosmic masters. This British sect offers solutions to those who are curious about cosmic developments by a

Vedanta, the Hindu cult established by Ramakrishna (*left*) was widely
disseminated in the United States by the Swami Vivekananda. One of
the recent leaders of Indian meditation cults who has been active in
proselytising in America is the Maharishi (*far left*). The meditation
cults have had wide, if ephemeral, appeal among the younger generation.

mixture of methods including yoga and the reception of radiations
from particularly chosen spots, where messages from other planets
might be received. The star of Bethlehem is held to have been a
particularly significant 'flying saucer', and Christ a being with a
terrestrial body, endowed with intelligence from another planet.
These ideas are, of course, sometimes associated with millennialist
expectations, in which the space ships are the vessels by which the
initiates will be saved.

Sects in the name of science

Manipulationist sects offer men new knowledge with which to
achieve salvation, but in a modern world with scientifically established facts and theories, such knowledge must necessarily be of a
kind that transcends ordinary empirical science. It deals with the
more remote cosmos, or with the closer confines of the mind about
each of which science has made no final pronouncements. Sometimes these new movements combine the two. A particularly
interesting movement beginning virtually in science fiction and
therapy, and going on to present itself in cosmic terms, is
Scientology. Scientology did not begin as a sect, but as a therapeutic
system: its sectarian character emerged relatively late, when the
therapeutic method was seen to have implications of a cosmic kind,
and when mystical and metaphysical legitimation could be provided
for what had previously been a pseudo-scientific orientation.

Scientology began as Dianetics, at which time it had no religious
character. It was a system of speculative diagnosis of mental illness,
and, by implication, of many other illnesses which were attributed
to psychological rather than biological or bacteriological causes.
Its founder was an American fiction writer, Lafayette Ronald
Hubbard, who published a work on Dianetics in 1948: he elaborated
a theory attributing mental aberrations to pre-natal impressions,
'engrams' received by the embryo in the womb. Hubbard trained
'auditors', who acted as psychotherapists directing a patient's
thought back to earliest impressions, in order to eradicate the

Scientology is a therapeutic system controlled through a church organisation. Shown here is an electro-psychometre, used to diagnose the psychological problems of those who join the movement.

engram from the unconscious mind and so liberate the patients from behaviour caused by the compulsive fears that engrams produced. Engrams had odd similarities to some of the 'causes' of seeming illness in Christian Science (a Christian Scientist experiencing a feeling of 'soreness' might find its cause to be the fact that someone was 'sore at him': so an embryo might pick up an impression that would produce a similar consequence). Whenever, in later life, the engram was re-enlivened by crude association of ideas, so aberrant behaviour or sickness would follow. If all engrams could be eliminated, an individual would become a 'clear', who would have no neuroses or illnesses, and who would have instant recall of all sense-perceptions.

The therapeutic theory underwent some considerable change as Dianetics was merged into the more embracing Scientology, which included a metaphysical theory of knowledge. A theory of reincarnation was added: in the human mind was an immortal element, a Thetan, the scientological equivalent of a transmigrating soul, which was also subject to engrams, not only from the experience of the individual that it occupied at a given time, but from all previous individuals in which it had resided. The therapeutic process – already elaborated into lower stages of development than that of 'clear' – was now extended to the clearing of the engrams of earlier incarnations. The 'unclear' Thetan, like the sinful soul, goes to an equivalent of hell, an unpleasant place in outer space, where it must repent of (or forget) the evil past. The condition of being 'clear' represents human freedom, and this is achieved only after a long process of therapy: the problem of humanity, however, depends on the production of clears, who will be the salvation of the world. In the therapeutic process, the auditor is assisted by a device known as an electro-psychometre, which 'measures' emotional reactions to questions – those producing strong reaction are seen as re-activating the harmful engrams. The sect places heavy emphasis on the art of communication: lack of communicating skill is itself an aspect of man's suffering.

Scientology is taught in institutes; training, and the therapy that

precedes it, are expensive processes. Successful patient-pupils may
themselves be licensed to operate a branch office. Thus, again as in
some earlier manipulationist sects, the esoteric doctrines become
not so much an aid to leading a normal life as a means of making a
new livelihood. The advanced initiates, who are credited with
remarkable powers as 'operating Thetans' with control over matter,
energy, space and time, are drawn very closely into an élite circle,
like 'saints' in a traditional sect, and become the equivalent of a
ministry. It is not clear to what ends scientologists who do become
full-time organisers and therapists, use their 'clear' powers. In San
Francisco, Scientologists were – although most probably not in any
official capacity – the leading organisers in 1967 of the Sexual
Freedom League, which existed to promote completely uninhibited
sexual behaviour. Advanced Scientologists, however, appear to
remain in the movement, and this perhaps is the condition of their

advancement. The movement has attracted unfavourable attention, less for its religious than for its therapeutic theories. It has been banned in the state of Victoria, Australia and has encountered some degree of restriction in Great Britain, where the headquarters were established after the movement found that it risked prosecution in the United States in using the American mails for material and propaganda that might be deemed fraudulent.

The elements found in Scientology, as well as its belated transformation from therapy system to religious sect, are also found in an English movement, initially called The Process (a word widely used in Scientology) and now called The Church of the Final Judgment. With a fashionable west-end address, the leaders of the movement have offered therapy and courses in 'communication', in which techniques essentially similar to those of Scientology are used. The sect has undergone rapid transformation: it has sloughed off its early conventional respectability as a system of psychotherapy and has adopted modish and ephemeral styles of dress, hirsuteness, publicity and literature. Its preoccupations appear to be the occult, magic, hypnosis and telepathy, and freedom in matters of sex, drugs and general morality. It offers a choice of deities – Jehovah, Satan and Lucifer – and of attendant life-styles. Those not in the movement are referred to as 'the grey forces', to indicate their conventionality and the boredom that they apparently induce in the (usually rather young) votaries of this sect. Information on this sect is, however, very limited, because despite the emphasis on human communication its literature is unrevealing and frivolous.

The sects of greatest significance in the western world have been of the conversionist, revolutionist, introversionist and manipulationist types. For different reasons, the remaining three responses have been either rarer or of much less consequence. They represent the extreme forms of religiosity. Thaumaturgical religion is most evident in less-developed societies: it borders on the magical in its concern with spirits. It represents a primitive, almost primeval form of religion. Reformist sects arise only in rather special circumstances when the self-identification of sectarians has become established, but when their specific practices, preoccupations and beliefs have undergone some change, and new spheres of operation have opened up for them as a group. The utopian response depends more radically than any other sectarian position on active and conscious social organisation. It implies the political and economic re-making of the world and the more or less conscious re-structuring of social relationships and the norms of social behaviour. Except in those extreme cases when revolutionist sects have become militant, it comes nearer than any other to being a political and secular response. Its distinctiveness is that the utopia it seeks is based on religious principles.

Thaumaturgical sects: thaumaturgy versus orthodoxy

Demand for personal dispensation from the normal laws of cause and effect, and for miracles and oracles, is a commonplace in primitive religion, in the Lamaist form of Buddhism, in Chinese religion, in India, and at the fringes of the Islamic world. But all the major founded religions, as well as Judaism, have restricted or eliminated thaumaturgical practice. Since thaumaturgy is particular, personal and local, it is always a threat to the powers that priestly classes have sought to monopolise and systematise. Yet this response has revived in every religious tradition, and sometimes it has been accepted and regulated by priestly classes themselves in cults centering on such things as relics, shrines, *baraka* ('holy power'), local saints, etc. Sects that are distinctly thaumaturgical (in contrast to locally established cults, superstitions and remnants of former 'pagan' practice) are of relatively recent provenance. This is so because the appeal of thaumaturgy is in local and immediate benefits, and even in the modern world these interests are only with difficulty shaped into a persisting separatist movement. The medium and the magician have not until recently needed formal organisation, as have movements disseminating distinctive doctrines. In thaumaturgy, votary and leader stand in the relation of practitioner and client, rather than in that of priest and penitent, or (more typical of sectarianism) exhorter and respondent or teacher and student. What has pressed thaumaturgy increasingly into a *sectarian* mould in the modern world has been the need for protection, the desire to acquire prestige beyond local level (increasingly possible with improved physical communication and with mass-media); and the benefit to all practitioners from joint sponsorship of propaganda.

Thaumaturgical sects are much more concerned with perceived experience than with theoretical formulations, whether dogmatic or metaphysical. Their votaries, whilst by no means always uneducated and uncultured, are predominantly interested in first-hand manifestations which give security and reassurance. Thaumaturgy offers comfort in a more pragmatic way than any other religious system: it cures illnesses, placates spirits, assuages the griefs of bereavement, and reassures the individual of his eternal destiny and that of his kin. All this it does by 'proofs' rather than by faith. Particular thaumaturgical practices vary from one society to another, according to the preoccupations of the culture. In Africa the concern is to smell out witches – who may often be precisely those individuals in the social system whose activities (old men in some societies), or whose redundancy (often old women) create tensions.* In other societies, where there is a high degree of insecurity – in Singapore for example – luck may be the stock in trade of the thaumaturge. In the hedonistic societies of the modern west, where death has become a subject of great anxiety and where – with the decline of socially-

*See *Witchcraft* by Lucy Mair, World University Library.

sanctioned mourning practices – bereavement has become acutely embarrassing, the chief concern of thaumaturgical sects has been reassurance that death is only a transposition of the ego from one plane to another.

Spiritualism and Christianity

Spiritualism in America and western Europe, now organised in a number of movements, is based essentially on the idea that the dead pass as spirits into another world from where they seek to communicate with and to help their 'loved ones' on earth. In its popular form, it draws on the ideas of heaven widely disseminated among literal-minded Christians. Indeed, Spiritualists have often asserted that spirit communication proves the existence of heaven. Belief in spirits has always been part of Christian orthodoxy, but in periods when Christianity was a powerful agency of social control spirits tended to be identified with evil. In the nineteenth century, when increasing emphasis was placed on a God of love, the way was opened to reinterpret the spirits of the dead as essentially benevolent. This would appear to have been an important development in the popularisation of spiritualism: it provided a basis for thaumaturgical religion more compelling than the belief that the spirits of the dead needed to be placated, an idea which is found in spiritualist beliefs of less-developed peoples.

Western Spiritualism was first expounded in the prolific writings of Emanuel Swedenborg, the Swedish mystic, who claimed to have communication with the spirits, but its popular manifestation is more properly dated from the 'spirit rappings' heard (and, as they later confessed, produced) by two sisters, Kate and Margaret Fox, at Hydesville, N.Y. Once rappings became transformed into spirit communication, popular imagination was captured. Andrew Jackson Davis, a shoemaker, who was much influenced by Swedenborg, had already proclaimed himself a vessel in receipt of revelation, and was an early convert. In England, many people including Anglican bishops, Sir Arthur Conan Doyle the novelist, and Sir

Sectarian influences in South America

South America has been extremely receptive to all kinds of sectarian influences from the United States, Europe and Africa.

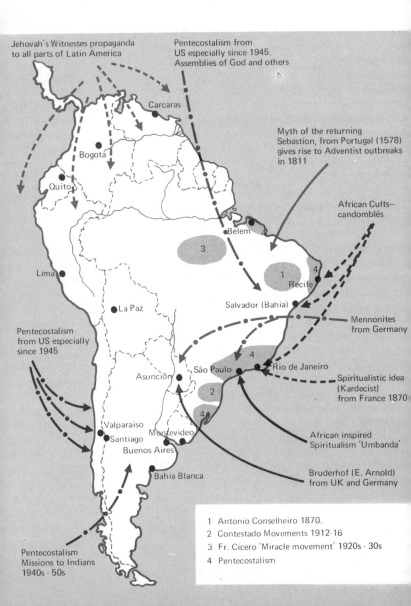

Jehovah's Witnesses propaganda to all parts of Latin America

Pentecostalism from US especially since 1945. Assemblies of God and others

Myth of the returning Sebastion, from Portugal (1578) gives rise to Adventist outbreaks in 1811

African Cults— candomblés

Mennonites from Germany

Spiritualistic idea (Kardecist) from France 1870

African inspired Spiritualism 'Umbanda'

Bruderhof (E. Arnold) from UK and Germany

Pentecostalism from US especially since 1945

Pentecostalism Missions to Indians 1940s - 50s

Carcaras
Bogotá
Quito
Lima
La Paz
Belem
Recife
Salvador (Bahia)
Asunciòn
São Paulo
Rio de Janeiro
Valparaiso
Santiago
Buenos Aires
Montevideo
Bahia Blanca

1 Antonio Conselheiro 1870.
2 Contestado Movements 1912-16
3 Fr. Cicero 'Miracle movement' 1920s - 30s
4 Pentecostalism

Oliver Lodge, a distinguished physicist, became devotees of the new practice. In France, Victor Hugo became morbidly obsessed with spiritualistic phenomena. Mary Baker Eddy was associated with Spiritualists in the years in which she first began mental healing before she pronounced Christian Science hostile to Spiritualism. Madame Blavatsky, a quick-tempered and erratic woman, for a time became a successful and magnetic medium. She finally abandoned Spiritualism, declaring it ethically and philosophically sterile, and established Theosophy, which emphasised the 'culture of the spirits of the living' rather than 'commerce with the souls of the dead'.

The appeal of Spiritualism lay in several factors: it explained telepathic phenomena, it proved the existence of life after death, it assuaged the grief of the bereaved, and satisfied man's demand for salvation as well as the morbid curiosity that induced many to attend seances. Scientific interest in Spiritualism has never entirely abated, but the difficulty of providing empirical proofs and the lack of a coherent and testable set of propositions about life after death and the state of the spirit world have made evident the essentially religious character of commitment to it. Because thaumaturgical beliefs and practices are so highly particularised, however, movements with a clear body of teaching and organisational stability have grown less easily than in the case of other sectarian responses. Some spiritualists have not abandoned other religious beliefs – seeing in Spiritualism confirmation of conventional Christian eschatology. Others have taken up Spiritualism simply at times when they have felt personal need for the comfort it affords. Even the highly committed may not see spiritualist practice as requiring allegiance to an organisation, since mediums are not ministers and command credibility by performance rather than by formal certification. More abstract thinkers, such as Mrs Eddy and Madame Blavatsky, who have been drawn to Spiritualism, have wanted more theoretical formulations than thaumaturgical practice has need of, and they have moved on to establish manipulationist sects with elaborate metaphysical ideologies. Thaumaturgical sects are particularistic in their operation, needing little more than the 'proofs' of performance. Manipulationists demand intellectual commitment: thaumaturgy needs only faith that a suitable agent can work a miracle for his client.

Spiritualist associations provide some organisational coherence for the groups that meet as religious gatherings, and ensure a supply of mediums and speakers, many of whom travel on circuits. Local cults do exist, but Spiritualism appears to thrive on a system of itinerancy. The associations are essentially federations of local autonomous groups: they give some coherence to the movement by establishing a body of orthodox teaching and by defining the movement's relation to Christianity, over which Spiritualists differ. The associations all have their own membership, but Spiritualism as a social phenomenon transcends them all, and there are many occasional participants. Spiritualist churches have adopted an order of service similar to that of the less liturgical Protestant denominations, but very little time is devoted to worship. Sermons are sometimes even given by mediums who are in trance. Because thaumaturgical movements are organisationally weak, they lack firm criteria for admission and expulsion. In the organisational sense the thaumaturgical response is only rarely constituted as a properly defined sect. Spiritualists are largely lower-middle and working-class people.

Spiritualism in developing nations

There is some evidence that interest in Spiritualism was very considerably revived by the widespread bereavements of the First World War. Despite the many exposures of mediums as frauds, the exaggerated claims for automatic writing, and the many discredited cases of mediums claiming to act as amanuenses in setting down literary works from the spirit of a famous dead person, Spiritualism continues to exercise its appeal. Nowhere has it had greater success than in Brazil, principally through the writings of Allan Kardec (pseudonym of Léon Hippolyte Denizard Rivail). His works *Le Livre des esprits contenant les principes de la doctrine spirite* and

Le livre des médiums, were written in the 1850s and 60s and still circulate (together with those of his two disciples, Flammarion and Denis), and have sold more copies in Brazil than anywhere else in the world. His theories, which include a doctrine of reincarnation, have been popularised by Chico Xavier, and are accepted by Brazil's hundreds of thousands of Spiritualists.

Kardecism is, however, to be distinguished from a second form of Brazilian thaumaturgical faith, the Umbanda cult, the origins of which lie in Africa, and which is practised with many variations in the coastal cities. In this cult, mediums become possessed by gods, and provide advice and comfort for their clients, but this is a more primitive form of thaumaturgy for less sophisticated audiences, whereas Kardecism does have a body of coherent teachings. The Kardecists believe in communication with the dead, in reincarnation, in the plurality of inhabited worlds, each of which represents a stage of spiritual progress and through which an individual passes by virtue of his own merit in previous reincarnations, and in the remoteness of God and the operation of spirit guides to help men. They practise levitation and materialisation. The directors and mediums of Kardecist centres are doctrinally well-informed and practise the system of ethics that Kardecism embraces. The bulk of adherents, less committed to the ethical principles, look to Spiritualism for solace and reassurance. Wide divergences occur in local practice, although the federation of Kardecists has existed since 1884. Numbers are difficult to assess, since many are transient or occasional adherents, who do not always abandon their other religious affiliations (in this case almost invariably Roman Catholics). Kardecism is strongest in the large cities, where it shows some commitment to social reform (which was an element in early Spiritualism in Europe and America, but one that has dwindled). In 1958, in Saõ Paulo alone, the Kardecists maintained thirty-one dispensaries or infirmaries, and 435 schools. Agencies of material assistance are an unusual element in sectarian religion, and especially in thaumaturgical religion, but particularly in a country lacking adequate medical facilities, and where those needing cures must

174

Some ecstatic holiness churches in Kentucky and Tennessee
have taken up snake-handling as evidence of faith.
Here a poisonous rattlesnake is handled at a meeting
of the Dolley Pond Church of God with Signs Following.
The lay preacher holding the snake subsequently died
from snake bite at a later meeting.

almost of necessity turn to spiritual healers of one sort or another, welfare agencies can readily be integrated with the search for spiritual help that is the main concern of adherents.

Thaumaturgical sects—healers and snake handlers

Although Spiritualists represent the principal form of thaumaturgical sects in the western world, there have always been other wonder-working groups. Most of these have remained small and local, and whilst none has attained the diffusion of Spiritualism and most have demonstrated the typical difficulties of thaumaturgical practice in acquiring stable organisation, some of these movements have attained a degree of permanence. An independent movement, the Antoinists, has spread in Belgium and France since the end of the last century. The sect is a mixture of thaumaturgical and manipulationist responses to the world. It developed after a Belgian miner, Antoine Louis (1846-1912), became convinced by revelations that his magnetic fluids could cure sickness, overcome evil and even conquer death. The teachings of the Antoinists, like those of other sects with strong thaumaturgical and spiritualistic orientations, are occultist and obscure. There is a marked sentimentality of religious expression which is also found in some Spiritualist groups, but which, in this case, betrays the lower-class interpretations of Roman Catholicism which existed in the social milieu from which the founder and his early devotees came. In addition to healings, the movement emphasises distinctive dietetic ideas, particularly vegetarianism. The sect has been estimated to have something approaching 50,000 followers in France and perhaps twice this number elsewhere – particularly in Belgium, Italy and Brazil, but these figures should be treated with caution. The principal centres in France are Paris (where there are three temples), Lille, Aix-les-Bains, Cherbourg, Nice, Orleans, Reims, Rouen, Saint-Etienne, Tours, Valenciennes and Vichy.

A distinctive and dramatic form of thaumaturgy that has spread somewhat in the United States, but not, as far as is known, else-

where, is snake-handling. Its practice draws on the text in St Mark (a gospel that strongly emphasises Christ's thaumaturgical performances) that promises the faithful that 'they shall take up serpents and not be harmed'. Snake-handling was begun in 1909 in Tennessee by George Went Hensley, and was subsequently introduced in a number of fundamentalist churches in Kentucky, particularly at the Dolley Pond Church of God with Signs Following. Once the service has reached a pitch of intense excitement, dangerous rattlesnakes are handed round as a test of faith. Handling the snake is the test of faith, regardless of the outcome. The snake represents the devil, but at an unconscious level it probably symbolises a capacity to dominate dangerous sexual desire among these ecstatic puritans. The idea of the snake as a primeval phallic symbol or as a pre-Judaic deity that had to be anathematised (in Genesis and Exodus) is probably quite unknown to snake-handlers. These often semi-literate people in culturally retarded areas are concerned only with the manifestation of miraculous power. The excitement, the reassurance and the sense of superiority it provides can transcend and re-interpret life-circumstances that are otherwise restrictive and harrowing. By a miraculous agency their poverty and ignorance are transformed into greater blessings than are offered by all the material, social and cultural advantages of cities.

Death from snake-bite (including that of Hensley in 1955) has periodically brought the movement into the headlines, and the state legislatures of Tennessee, Kentucky and Virginia prohibit snake-handling. Nonetheless the practice continues in these states, and has spread to a number of churches in North Carolina, Georgia, Alabama, Florida and West Virginia, and further afield to California.

Thaumaturgy and organisational adaptation

The incidence of the thaumaturgical response in primitive societies is ubiquitous but random. Since it has not easily established itself in stable and enduring separate (hence sectarian) organisations even in western societies, *prima facie* it might appear unlikely that it should acquire specifically sectarian accommodation in less developed countries, where the principles of voluntary organisation are so much less fully understood and practised. Paradoxically, it is precisely in such societies that thaumaturgical religion has its most coherent expression, nowhere more so than in the Church of the Lord, Aladura, which flourishes in Nigeria, Ghana, Liberia and Sierra Leone. What has occurred is that the organisational structure of the mission-founded churches has been adopted for a faith which is a syncretism of Christianity and African traditional religious concerns. These principally involve the search for supernatural blessings, in particular for healings, fertility, influence on others, the elimination of witches and the neutralising of evil magic.

Thus, although Aladura has a formal structure established by the Nigerian founder, J. A. Ositelu, with a hierarchy of bishops, prophets, captains and deacons, and although it retains a Protestant evangelical hymnology and a Roman-type liturgy, the central preoccupation is with revelations, guidance, prophesies and miracles. The principle of exclusivity of allegiance is not easily accepted in Africa, but it operates in the Aladura churches probably as well as it does in the more orthodox missions. Unlike European Spiritualists, Aladura ascribe the guidance they receive to God and not to particular spirits, which, as in the older tradition in Christian countries, are regarded as evil and potentially harmful. Protection is provided in the specifics prescribed by the officials who receive particular revelations from God for every individual at the service. As in other west African religions, there is special emphasis on the use of holy water (consecrated by the officiating priest at each ceremony). Almost all preventative measures prescribed in Aladura revelations enjoin the individual to recite (usually at night) psalms revealed as specifically appropriate to his case. The sect services encourage a degree of ecstacy, vigorous, emotional prayer for healing, drumming, rhythmic dancing and possession.

Reformist sectarianism

The reformist type of sect is a rarity and arises only in advanced societies. Even then, it arises only among groups which, by a long process of intensive socialisation, have acquired a very strong and perhaps partly collective conscience towards the wider world. Many diverse sectarian groups, despite their separation from the world, in fact feel some responsibility to do what they can for it. This is least true of revolutionist and introversionist groups, but even among these there is sometimes a warm humanitarianism. The withdrawn members of the eighteenth-century Moravian community at Bethlehem in Pennsylvania befriended the Indians; the local Shakers showed great kindness to the Indians who, in 1805, gathered around Tecumsah and his prophet-brother Tensk-watawa near Vincennes; the Ephrata perfectionists, although eschewing war, tended the wounded of both sides in the American Revolution with a dedication that impressed observers. The revolutionist Christadelphians strained their resources to aid Jews in nineteenth-century Palestine. Theosophists were often strongly committed to humanitarian good works, and even the early Spiritualists espoused the idea of a society reformed by a new goodwill among men. But all these manifestations of benevolence were at best secondary to the central concerns of these movements.

Perhaps our only example of a fully developed reformist sect is the Society of Friends (Quakers), particularly in its English branch, which has remained an essentially lay organisation. Social reform is itself essentially secular, and thus it is unlikely that any sect would arise primarily to promote social reform. The reformist approach to society is, then, a derived position of a sect that has undergone development. The early Quakers of the 1660s were millenarians. At times George Fox was disposed to be a prophet of doom, and James Nayler took his apocalyptic expectations even further, entering the town of Bristol as a messiah. Quakers learned to withdraw from society in preparation for a more glorious future. They were, however, always more disposed to seek inspiration from the Spirit than from the scriptures: the 'inward light' was the essence of their teaching, and eighteenth-century Quakers regarded it as more fundamental than the Bible. This doctrine came to justify reference to conscience as the criterion of action. Quakers became introversionist in this period, and cultivated a distinctive and separate way of life in which their ethical standards were continually referred back to the inward light. Although they insulated themselves by, for instance, their old-fashioned forms of speech and dress, it was their ethical standards that came to impress contemporaries as the real mark of the Quaker.

Conscience became the guide to a Quaker's everyday life, and particularly to his business life. A reputation for shrewdness *and* honesty undoubtedly facilitated the success of the merchants among them. They epitomised the Puritan ethic: they worked hard, and (with the exception of such aberrancies as those families who became known as 'Gay Quakers') they abstained from needless luxury. In the eighteenth century the movement was increasingly recruited from those who were inborn Quakers. Although Quakers accepted new converts, they were primarily concerned with their own piety manifested in their ethical practice. In the age of individual enterprise, when personal standards were so much more significant in business activity than they have become in role-articulated societies, asceticism and commitment to work produced a considerable number of wealthy men within the sect. Wealth, however, had to be justified, and justification had to be sought by reference to conscience. In the eighteenth century, the Quaker conscience and the long tradition of at least formal lay equality in Quaker societies had been responsible for the rejection of slave-trading and of slave-owning as sources of wealth. As industry developed, Quaker manufacturers became noted as employers of exceptional integrity and high standards (matched only by the Unitarians). Just as prosperous Catholic merchants had done before the Reformation, so rich Quakers now began to justify by philanthropy the wealth that otherwise might be seen as a threat to their standards, if not a departure from them. Quaker charity grew in the nineteenth century, particularly at a time when Quaker insularity was diminishing. Their conscience prompted an interest in political affairs, and prominent (and usually wealthy) Quakers entered the House of Commons. Perhaps more important was the impact on Quakerism of the current evangelical ideas, and the conscience of many Quakers urged support for missionary societies, welfare agencies, and other good causes.

During their evangelical period, in the mid-nineteenth century, Quakers reduced their 'peculiarities' and came to share much more of their life with the world outside. Their concern for the wider society was expressed in this acceptance of the need for men to be converted to Christ (although this was not the way that Quakers recruited). They began more systematically than before to engage in missionary activities (especially in east and central Africa). When the age of great individual merchant fortunes passed – and it was marked by some spectacular bankruptcies among Quakers, as well as by the shift from private ownership to joint-stock companies – Quaker philanthropy was an established way of manifesting Quaker

conscience. The movement remained a small sect (between 15,000 and 20,000 in the century 1850-1950 in Great Britain) and to this day many English Quakers are personally known to each other. The largely middle-class and professional people who constituted the Quakers in the early twentieth century had less money for philanthropy, and perhaps too, money seemed a less adequate means for the expression of Quaker conscience. Quakers as a group came to transform the old monetary philanthropy into the dedication of individuals and the use of their time and energy for social good works. These were mainly voluntary activities undertaken through agencies which, whilst largely Quaker-supported, were not officially Quaker. They became prominent in relief teams, in ambulance work in the war, in the defence of conscientious objectors (who included many sectarians besides Quakers, as well as non-religious objectors), in petitions for peace, and in voluntary service in under-developed countries. Individual Quakers have been active in campaigns for legislative reform, particularly in regard to prison conditions, capital punishment, protection of minorities, and the reform of laws on morality for the greater liberty of the individual.

Quakers have thus taken upon themselves the task of being

By the First World War the Quakers had ceased
to be an introversionist sect, and took part in
philanthropic activities on an increasing scale.
Their good work as non-combatants in the
war earned them the respect of many who did not
share their pacifist principles.

181

society's self-appointed conscience. The sect did not come into being with this goal in mind: it has grown up among a group pre-selected on other criteria, that has persisted as a self-conscious and segregated collectivity, among whom conscience, as the test of all things, has been intensely cultivated. Other sectarian movements have sometimes espoused humanitarian ideals – this is true of some branches of Theosophists, and of Anthroposophists – but their effort has been formed more as deliberate policy, and even as a programme. Among Seventh Day Adventists, and even among Salvationists, good works have been related to recruiting members. Much more spontaneously among the much less organised Quakers, social reform has arisen as a primary orientation. Quakers in the twentieth-century may be regarded as a reformist sect.

Utopian sects – the Oneida community

Utopian sects are always colony builders, and usually (though not exclusively) communitarian, but not all communitarians have been utopian in their orientation. Utopians are seeking a perfect society as the model for the world, and those that take a religious premise for such a community we may term utopian sectarians. Many colony builders have, however, been introversionists and simply concerned, as were the Rappites and the Society of the Truly Inspired (Amana Society), to get away from the world. They found that a separate community organisation was the expedient means. Utopianism, as such, has generally been less specifically religious than political, but the idea of remaking the world as a perfect community has inspired many sectarians for whom it was at best an auxiliary concern and not a basic response to the problem of salvation. It was such for William Booth; for the Philadelphians who were millenarians of late seventeenth-century England; it was important to Zinzendorf and to the Moravians, despite their eagerness for the second advent. We reserve the term utopian, however, for those for whom model colonies are the *sine qua non* of salvation.

Colonies are difficult to establish. Since even the minute details

The Oneida community was the most thorough-going and successful of all
Utopian sects and practised community of property, of sex and of children.
From about 1849 the women of the Oneida community adopted the distinctive
dress shown here. It was intended to conform to standards of hygiene,
utility and modesty, with especial emphasis on modesty to counteract the
public scandal caused by the sexual irregularities at Oneida.

of daily life have to be reorganised, there is considerable strain in
providing them with stability. Colonies are not brought into being
by merely legislative acts: the norms of social behaviour and the
texture of social relationships must acquire settled character. The
tasks of socialising the recruits to a radically new way of life and of
establishing that way of life in the first place have often caused the
break-up of such colonies before they have long been in being. But
religious utopian colonies have shown far more capacity to persist
than have those founded on purely secular premises. Some have
faded quickly, such as the colony of the New Dispensation formed
in the New Forest, England, by Mrs Mary Ann Girling in the 1870s.
Others, such as the Tolstoyan communities founded in England in
the 1890s through the Brotherhood Church, broke up because their
principal supporters had divergent conceptions of what exactly they
believed and what they wanted to achieve. As one Tolstoyan leader,
Aylmer Maude, afterwards acknowledged:

To hold a commune together requires either a great identity and immutability of life-habits, or a stereotyped religious tradition: so that the members,
from force of habit or from religious hypnotism, may not wish to do anything
that runs counter to the communal customs.[10]

Immutability of life habits are what the Hutterians and Amish
enjoy, and the strong leadership that Maude recognised as the only
way that communism could be *imposed,* was exactly what the
Rappites had. Strong initial leadership, good management, and
common religious commitment are the features of successful
utopian colonies. One which had these features was the Oneida
Community of Perfectionists of New York State.

The Oneida Community grew out of the attempt to institutionalise
perfect holiness as a way of life. It arose in the backwash of early
holiness ideas, particularly as held by Methodists and by the revivalist Charles Finney. John Humphrey Noyes, a Congregationalist
minister, espoused the idea that man could attain total security
against the commission of sin: he could be perfect. This position in
itself did not lead to the antinomian conduct – particularly 'bundl-

ing' and promiscuity – that was already advocated by some New York perfectionists. Noyes' position was more credible and more subtle. In the late 1840s, he and his followers established the community that settled at Oneida. They believed that they were totally secure from sin; that only those descended from the early saints were perfect; that the second coming had occurred in AD 70; that for the perfectly holy, marriage was abolished – a woman was the bride of Christ, the bride of all the saints. Communism was to prevail among those who were holy, and this was appropriate in sexual matters as in regard to property. Through their common life God would be glorified. The essential feature of Oneida was the clear conviction that personal sanctification was a prerequisite for social reconstruction: the community (numbering more than a hundred within a couple of years of settling at Oneida reservation) saw itself as the continuation of the primitive Christian church. They began with sufficient funds, and undertook manufactures as well as agriculture. After early hardships they flourished in a way unparalleled by most other communitarian ventures and quite unapproached by the purely political foundations.

To Noyes, the evils of the wider society were to be found in selfishness. This was evidenced in devotion to property, in monogamy, and in the possessiveness of mothers towards their children. The sinless were above selfishness, and were so, not simply because they had good social institutions, but because their social institutions reflected their spiritual state. His advocacy was not promiscuity, but sexual communism among the totally sanctified; thus, sexual relationships were not casual but were organised and disciplined. Oneida stood opposed to the type of spiritual wifery that had caused scandals when practised among the perfectionists in New York state. Noyes advocated a eugenic policy of selected mating for the scientific propagation of the race, and thus demanded considerable sexual continence.

Sinlessness implied a degree of bodily perfection and the Oneidans were believers in faith-healing. Sickness was as inappropriate as sin, and would be so in a regenerated world. Each could be exorcised, and for the exorcism of faults the community evolved an ingenious device, since used by other groups, including Buchmanites and political communists. This was the practice of self-criticism and mutual criticism. An individual laid bare his faults to the group, and others proceeded in turn to enumerate his failings. The technique, with a final summary and exhortation by Noyes himself, released tensions among members of the community as individuals purged themselves of shortcomings, re-dedicated themselves to the community, and found satisfaction in acceptance in spite of acknowledged deficiencies. This system depended very much on the remarkable authority and skill of Noyes himself. The community attained considerable stability under his leadership until, in his later years, there was some internal disruption. The Perfectionists did not, however, keep their practices and beliefs secret; indeed they circulated literature free of charge in full accordance with communistic principles. In 1880, the hostility of vociferous opponents exacerbated internal tensions and in 1881 the community abandoned sexual communism and the community of goods. The Oneida industries continued to flourish as joint-stock companies after the community was dissolved.

The Bruderhof: failure of an introversionist model

Two principal factors have helped utopian sectarianism in common with most forms of communitarian sectarianism to flourish in Anglo-Saxon countries, and, in lesser measure, in Latin American countries and Russia. These have been tolerance of deviant religious groups (sometimes in direct consequence of recognising their value as pioneers) and readiness to receive them as immigrants; and, particularly in the New World countries, cheapness of land and the ease of settlement. Utopian sects have, however, arisen elsewhere, as the many migrations of German sects illustrate. One of these was the Bruderhof, founded by Eberhardt Arnold (1883-1935), at one time secretary of the German Christian Student movement, as an informal colony at Sannerz in Hesse-Nassau in 1920. Arnold was subsequently influenced by the Hutterians in Canada, and in the early 1930s he established the Almbruderhof in Liechtenstein. His death in 1935, the financial difficulties of his German following, and the imposition of military conscription in Germany, caused the group to migrate to England, where they established a community in the Cotswolds. Although the group flourished, the war caused these, mainly German, communitarians to leave England and in 1940 about 350 of them fled to Paraguay.

Paraguay was a country which, despite its Jesuit tradition was ready to grant freedom to colonies of such diligent agriculturalists. There, with the help of Mennonites already settled in Paraguay they founded three settlements despite enormous difficulties. A small group remained in England, attracted newcomers, and with some returned members from Paraguay, established a new colony in Shropshire. The Paraguayan communities sought to identify themselves more fully with the Canadian and American communities of Hutterians, and for a time it appeared that the new movement would be merged with the descendants of sixteenth-century Anabaptism. The Paraguayans received considerable help from the North American Hutterians, but the two groups were essentially different in motivation. The Hutterians were an introversionist sect of peasant people who had maintained peasant interests (although accepting modern equipment). They were simply educated and did not need further education for the way of life they followed. The followers of Arnold were very much more intellectual and idealist. Their religious beliefs were much less consolidated into a fixed ethic, and they were largely concerned with stimulating others to accept their new way of life. The Hutterians had a genuine folk culture; the Arnoldians were merely folk-culture enthusiasts. In short, the Hutterians were introversionists and the Arnold followers were a utopian sect. Hutterians became disenchanted with the worldliness and the frivolity of the Paraguayan Bruderhof. Many of the Bruderhof members in Paraguay eventually settled in New York State, and established a Bruderhof there. There are now three colonies in the United States; until recently two colonies existed in Britain, and one in Germany at Bad Brückenau.

Utopian sects – the Brotherhood of the New Life

Utopian sects have frequently relied on the vision of one particular leader, whose mission to transform society has provided a clear programme for community organisation. Utopian groups are activists, for whom strong leadership seems essential. Community life is not merely an expedient, as it has been for some groups (the Amana Society, the Shakers, and, perhaps, the Rappites), nor a cloistered way of salvation for an élite: it is seen as a model for the world. It must succeed, because it is the very programme of salvation; and for this, positive leadership is essential. Such leadership was provided by Thomas Lake Harris, a frequently maligned sect leader. After periods as a Universalist minister and as a member of a spiritualistic community at Mountain Cove, Virginia, and a few further years as minister to a Swedenborgian church, Harris founded a new order, the Brotherhood of the New Life.

Harris drew on the principles of his early enthusiasms in establishing his new sect: social reforms, communitarianism and spiritualism were all part of his faith. He called into being first in the east of the United States and eventually at Fountain Grove, California, a community that was not strictly communistic but in which there was an emphasis on the equality of men and their value one to another. Labour was for the common good and the important thing was not strictly the amount that men did so much as the spirit in which it was done. Humility in work was vital and work was more than activity for economic ends. Crafts were fostered that had little economic worth, and the community undertook charitable works. Work indeed was a form of community devotion, and in this Harris emphasised his own particular form of socialism, which reiterated something of Edward Bellamy's movement of Nationalist Clubs; but to Harris, as to the Theosophists who surrounded Bellamy, socialism was not enough. He called his system Theo-Socialism. At Fountain Grove, private property was not abolished, nor communism enforced. There was, rather, an amiable using of each other's possessions. Devotees often made over their property to Harris, but when they left the community – as eventually did Laurence Oliphant, the English member of Parliament and *The Times* correspondent, who, with his mother, lived at the Harris settlement for a number of years – they were able to regain their contributions.

Despite the wild stories that circulated about Fountain Grove, Harris was a celibate, and believed only in spiritual counterparts. He expressed himself in vivid sexual imagery in verse and prose, but there is no reason to suppose that his behaviour at Fountain Giove was ever other than the celibacy that he believed to evidence a state of heightened spirituality. The inmates were segregated and were often directed to menial and difficult work, perhaps as an aid to sexual sublimation. Harris believed that every man and women should be married to God, who was both the only real Bride and the only real Bridegroom. Where individuals had not attained an adequate spiritual state, Harris permitted marriage in the community, but in seventeen years only five children were born among his following. At its various locations, the Brotherhood of the New Life flourished from 1861 to the 1890s, when hostility from the outside world forced Harris to leave: thereafter the community struggled on for only a few further years, becoming increasingly a commercial venture. Without his leadership it seemed that the prospect of realising the 'Harmonic Civilisation' in which there should be 'abolishment of all antagonisms' could not be achieved even in one small community: the antagonisms of the world were themselves too much for utopia.

Honest sociological analysis always recognises that empirical reality is more complicated than the theoretical framework employed in its comprehension. It has been convenient to establish logically a set of responses to the world, and to categorise sects in terms of these responses. But man is less rational than our categories which relate, in any case, only to broad orientations and which do not cover the important variability of the forms of organisation. Furthermore, men and sects experience change, and – as we have seen in the case of the Quakers – dominant responses at one time may undergo considerable mutation, even if such change is limited by received traditions and earlier response to the world. The matter of sect development we may leave for a final chapter, but mixed cases of sectarian response (mixed in terms of the categories of analysis here employed) must be acknowledged. And so must the impress of organisational forms on responses to which they are ill-accommodated, or which (as in the case of Aladura) are borrowed from other contexts.

Charisma and the transcendence of consistent responses

Sects that manifest responses to the world and to salvation that fluctuate over time, or combine divergent gestures at a given time, are usually those that have come into being at the behest of a strong charismatic leader capable of enunciating contradictory principles that go unchallenged because of his standing. Most leaders of sects are complex personalities; few are wholly single-minded, and the diverse elements in the scriptures, where these provide the basis for sectarianism, have frequently led them into ambivalent positions. With the distinctly charismatic leader, self-contradiction may only serve to deepen mystery and to enhance the dependence of devotees, particularly when the leader claims to be a prophet or messiah. Where charisma is institutionalised, or where it is distributed among a congregation, its expression is necessarily rationalised and systematised in any sect which is to persist. But where charisma is attributed to one leader, devotion to him may be enough to sustain a sect. It follows, therefore, that sects that arise round charismatic leaders may not readily conform to the categories of response that we have constructed. In a sense there is a more primary response in these cases: salvation is not so much by conversion, withdrawal, revolution or miracles, but in and through the leader himself.

Claimants to messiahship have not been uncommon in Christian countries in the past, nor have they been lacking in the twentieth century. What is known about them and their followers is often vague: understandably such figures do not expose themselves to investigation, and their followers are marked more by their implicit faith in the self-styled messiah than by their detailed knowledge of him. Just as adventist sects do not always disband after the disappointment of their predictions, so messianic movements do not always disappear with their messiah. Thus, when Oskar Ernst Bernhardt, who claimed to be the new Son of Man come to fulfil the mission unfinished by Christ by bringing God's final world to mankind, died in 1941, the *Gralsbewegung* that he had founded on Vomperberg in the Tyrol did not disappear. His movement, patronised by some wealthy people, persists in Munich, Zürich, Württemberg, and elsewhere. Salvation then shifts from belief in the person, to loyalty to his memory, writings and principles. If such a movement is to endure, however, some reinterpretation of events, and some reorganistion of its practices must occur.

The claims of a self-styled God would be of little sociological interest if such figures did not acquire a following. Self-identification with deity is a well-known psychopathological condition; but where a following comes into being, a genuine sociological phenomenon exists. Only rarely, however, has it been possible to investigate such movements, and the ways in which the messiah maintains credibility. From 1950 onwards Louwrens van Voorthuizen, a Dutch fisherman (born at Anna Paulowna, N.H., in 1898) claimed that God had become man incarnated in himself. Whereas Christ had defeated Satan in the spirit, he, Lou, would defeat him in the body. The Bible would not avail men as a means to come to God, nor would obedience to particular moral rules: they could do so only through him. He proclaimed that he could not sin or be ill or die, and his followers could become as Christ was on earth, the sons and daughters of God. The time of the end was at hand, in the decade 1970-80, when Satan would be vanquished, and when Lou's followers, *Lou-mensen,* would attain deathless salvation. Although Lou died early in 1968, his followers, who were mainly lower-class, continued to believe that they must reject their own wills, and be possessed only by Lou, God. Another such self-styled messiah of recent times, was Georges Roux, the French post inspector of Montfavet near Avignon, who, after some time as a faith healer, announced in 1954 that he was Christ. His following, of about 4,000 or 5,000, styled themselves *Témoins du Christ Revenu,* and their church, *L'Eglise Chrétienne Universelle.* As with the *Lou-mensen,* Roux's followers are taught that salvation exists in accepting his will. Their principal churches are at Cannes, Marseilles, Nîmes, Paris, Strasbourg and Toulon, with some adherents in Germany, Switzerland and Belgium.

The members of the Father Divine Peace Mission in the United States believed absolutely that their leader, the Negro, George Baker, was God. After undertaking missions elsewhere, Baker took the title Father Divine in 1930 at Sayville, Long Island, New York. Throughout the 1930s the Peace Mission grew; thousands of its members lived in the 'Heavens', a chain of small co-operatives that Father Divine set up, but non-resident adherents were even more numerous. For the full members there was a rigorous ethical code, including abstinence from sexual intercourse, even between spouses, from tobacco and alcohol; there was special emphasis on honesty; gambling, insurance and government welfare were all strictly eschewed. The success of the movement lay in the service that was provided for adherents: jobs were found for them, the needy were cared for, lavish banquets became the much-publicised symbol of the communion meal between God and his followers. Members, more than ninety per cent of whom were Negro, learned to depend on 'Father' and his efficient organisation. The full members believed that they acted essentially in response to the will of

their God, who was ubiquitous and omniscient. As with the *Loumensen* in Holland, and with other messianic sects, the Bible was superseded and little used in the Peace Mission. True believers, it was held, would not die, and death was regarded as shameful: like other messiahs Father Divine promised that death would be overcome. When God is on earth a movement needs no eschatology. The death of Father Divine himself, in 1965, was ignored: his wife maintained that nothing had changed, he was still beside her directing the movement.

Salvation in such movements depends essentially on faith in the messiah: response is highly personalised, and cannot be conveniently categorised except in these terms. Father Divine, Lou, Georges Roux, Oskar Ernst Bernhardt and other claimants to deity were certainly thaumaturges, but they were more than that. These messianic sects are best regarded as volatile in response – personal miracles, special wisdom, withdrawn communities (such as Lou's converted inn, Father Divine's 'heavens', or the divine encampments of South African messianic leaders) may all feature in their

ather Divine serves his followers at a banquet at one
f the 'Heavens' of his Peace Mission. His movement grew
apidly in the 1930s and '40s. His followers readily identified
heir leader with God and credited him with performing
miracles – one of the most famous being his ability to
our innumerable cups of coffee from one small coffee pot.

dispensations. The leader is more than a medium through whom
access to spiritual power may be had, and more than a magician –
men are saved by giving over their will to their chosen god.

Non-messianic charisma

Not all charismatic leaders claim to be God, of course. Some claim
only to be God's emissary, or, more typically in advanced industrial
societies, the leader claims to be the discoverer of special wisdom
that will enable man to overcome sickness, anxiety and, above all,
death. Such charismatic figures live in curious relationship with
their own teachings – knowledge of which is often claimed as in itself
sufficient for salvation. Because in modern society it is necessary to
emphasise the objectivity and scientific character of their ideas, such
leaders might be eclipsed by their own intellectual systems. Often
they maintain leadership by affirming the 'progressive' character of
revelation. This provides such a leader with flexibility in directing
his movement, but it also admits volatility and mutation of response,
ambiguities and even contradictions. Mutation and plurality of
response concerns us most, and these phenomena are even more
marked where one charismatic leader is succeeded by another. Such
shifting orientations, from millennialism to manipulationism (with
communitarian elements) occurred in the *Eglise du Royaume de
Dieu* or *Les Amis de l'homme* both under its original leader, and, in
the French branch of the movement, in the transmission of leadership from the founder to his successor.

The sect began as a separate organisation when F. L. Alexander
Freytag, head of the Geneva office of International Bible Students
(known as the Watchtower Movement and later as Jehovah's
Witnesses) broke with the movement in 1918. At this time
Rutherford was gaining control of the Watchtower movement, and
many splinter groups broke off. This change of control, together
with Freytag's differences with Belzereit (head of the German
Watchtower branch under whose jurisdiction he came), and disappointment that the millennium, prophesied by Watchtower

people for 1914, had not come about, no doubt stimulated Freytag
independent ideas about the establishment of God's kingdom. H
believed that God intended men to overcome death, and that th
might be achieved if men obeyed what he had discovered as God
'universal law' – altruism. Man suffered because he was sinful, an
because he was egoistic. By obeying God's universal law man woul
transcend all shortcomings and weaknesses, including death.

Freytag's theory was a type of organic perfectionism, some o
which reads like a religious echo of ideas drawn from Herbe
Spencer and Kropotkin, every part of creation functioning t
maintain all other parts. Men had a sixth sense, receptivity to God'
love which man must imbibe as a 'life fluid'. But egoism had cause
this sense to atrophy, and man's blood and nerves had been physi
ally affected by his self-centred preoccupations, which promote
such illnesses as cancer, gallstones and rheumatism. There was a la
of 'just deserts' in which men made their own sufferings by the
departure from God's law of love. God did not punish men – the
punished themselves. In all of this, there was much that resemble
New Thought and Christian Science, but such ideas were wedde
to the millennial dream that Freytag got from the Watchtowe
movement. He now stressed an imperative ethical condition for th
realisation of God's kingdom. The time of the advent *had* come
men should rejoice now, and obey God's universal law of altruism
Man's character would be transformed and the new world woul
come into being. Man's life span would immediately lengthen, an
eventually he would triumph over death.

To make evident the actuality of the kingdom, Freytag set u
experimental stations, in France, Germany, Belgium, Switzerlan
and elsewhere. These were colonies in which life was to be live
according to the universal law, and where his other ideas, in particula
those on agricultureal methods free from chemical fertilisers, woul
be put into practice. Apart from the relatively small numbers livin
in the colonies, Freytag recruited two groups of believers, essenti
ally similar to the two classes of votaries found among Jehovah'
Witnesses (see page 113 above). Followers were known as the *peti

troupeau who composed the 144,000 of the completely dedicated, and who were regarded as 'little Christs', participating in his redeeming work by taking on the sins of others. They would occupy a special place in the coming kingdom. Other members were known as *l'Armée de l'Eternel* who would live according to God's universal law on earth and populate God's kingdom. The resurrection would occur when the law of altruism was sufficiently obeyed. As the Ambassador of the Age (*Messager de l'Eternel*), Freytag wrote a detailed constitution for the Kingdom of God. Apart from his system of government, his programme included re-afforestation to alter the world's climate, rejection of medicines, in favour of vegetarian diet, abstinence from, among other things, alcohol and tobacco, breathing pure air, and the character-transformation demanded by the universal law.

Freytag's periodicals were circulating in tens of thousands in the 1930s, but the exact number of adherents remains obscure. Banned in the Second World War the movement re-emerged in 1945 and entered a phase of activity and growth. Fourteen thousand visitors were reported at its Paris congress in 1946. In 1947, Freytag – always preoccupied with overcoming death – died. Almost at once the movement split into two, when Bernard Sayerce, a Basque school-teacher (born at Ahetze near Biarritz in 1912) who had kept the French adherents faithful throughout the war, assumed control of the French branches of the movement, claiming to be the designated successor to Freytag – a claim not recognised by the leaders at headquarters in Cartigny, Switzerland. The schism was not over doctrine, but essentially over leadership. Sayerce became known as 'Fidèle Berger', who claimed that 'le flambeau passait de Suisse en France'. He was joined by Lydie Sartre, a former Huguenot, who came to be known as 'la chère Maman', and together they became the elders, 'le cher Noyau', of the movement. Through them God now spoke, and through them the new kingdom would be established.

Freytag's teachings were retained, but from his headquarters in Paris (and later in Bordeaux) Sayerce interpreted his accession as a new step, leading beyond altruistic belief to altruistic action. Sayerce was a dynamic figure, while Lydie Sartre was represented as the kindly mother to whom all should bring their troubles, and from whom all would gain strength, love, and light for the times. The action in which Les Amis de l'homme now engaged was social relief. Well equipped workshops were set up, and at the Grange Neuve estate in Ville-neuve-sur-Lot, foodstuffs were produced. At the Bordeaux headquarters material was collected for distribution wherever it was needed. The new message was that the earth's possessions were not to be stored up, but to be distributed to the needy: men could help themselves only by helping their neighbours. This was altruism in action, and by these means the kingdom of God would be established, as men transformed themselves, and acquired new characters. The transformation of the world would begin in France, and from France spread to other nations. Les Amis de l'homme were the new conquerors, who did not dispossess men, but distributed well-being towards their reclamation for God's kingdom. Although Sayerce died in 1963, Lydie Sartre has maintained the drive of the movement.

Active propaganda through periodicals and by house-to-house calls was introduced. (The Sayerce branch has been less vehemently opposed than the Cartigny branch to orthodox churches, which Sayerce regarded as dead rather than evil.) The French movement (which appears to have dropped the old title *Eglise du Royaume de Dieu*) has become well known also through its social works, and is estimated to have a following of about 12,000 to 15,000 in France, with perhaps a fifth or more of these in Bordeaux and Toulouse. It is also active in Vienna, Linz, Salzburg, Nuremburg, Stuttgart, and in Belgium. The Cartigny branch appears to have made less progress in recent years, although it probably has a following of several thousands, principally in Switzerland and Germany.

The many-sided sect – Mormonism

Movements with such a muted charisma as Les Amis de l'homme are of greater significance than the directly messianic modern sects. Of particular sociological interest are sects that, either because of complexity of circumstances, or diversity of leadership claims, have institutionalised their offer of salvation in divergent forms. None is more complex than the Church of Jesus Christ of Latter-Day Saints, the Mormons. Mormonism began in New York State in the late 1820s. Its founder, Joseph Smith, was a farmer's son who had dabbled with a 'luminous stone' that helped him to find things that had been lost, and who – like many others in the curious, naive and superstitious atmosphere of the heart of the 'burned-over district' – had been an adolescent digger for secret buried treasure. Whilst still a young man, he claimed to have been visited by the angel Moroni, who had given him the golden plates from which the book or Mormon was translated. Undoubtedly, Mormonism was affected by the current enthusiasms of millennialism, perfectionism, revivalism, the campaigns against freemasonry, and the temperance crusades. It embraces something of them all. Although Mormonism asserted a fund of ideas common in adventism, such as the literal gathering of Israel, the restoration of the ten tribes (the Indians) and also the Jews, and Christ's personal reign over a renewed earth, in practice the emergence of a new prophet with a new revelation may be said to have fulfilled adventist expectations. America was now given its due place in the divine scheme, and the cultural retardation of up-state New York farmers was assimilated to the

198

general cultural retardation experienced by Americans in their early days as a new nation. The new gospel affirmed that America had been the scene of Christ's past activity on earth, just as much as had the Middle East, and would be so again: it was *there* that the true church would arise to indict the apostate church of Europe. America was designated by God as the Zion to come. The new religion thus provided more than mere compensation for those who had chosen, or would choose to settle so far from what had hitherto been regarded as the centre of the world – it gave them especially prestigeous identity as Americans, and sanctified their chosen land.

Mormonism embraced conventional adventism, but without the attribution of importance given to these teachings in contemporary Millerism. In its own stage-by-stage movement westwards, it replaced in practice the passive watching for the Lord and the interpretations of the old prophecy, with physical endeavour towards the realisation of the new. The movement's millennial doctrine remained, but to it was added the teaching that all men would evolve into gods, just as God himself had evolved. Thus was millennialism assimilated to contemporary American belief in progress and the inherent goodness of man. Even the fall of Adam was reinterpreted as a blessing, since it allowed Adam to fulfil God's command to replenish the earth, and this too became a strong Mormon preoccupation. The family became central to the faith, since children provided bodies for waiting spirits to occupy: a teaching well adapted to a struggling sect in a vast continent urgently needing people.

Mormon withdrawal from the 'Gentiles' – to Kirtland, Ohio, to Missouri, to Nauvoo, Illinois, and finally (for the majority) to Utah, was a mixture of millennial and introversionist responses, neither of which was a consistent or unalloyed theme in Mormonism. Mormons were neither pacifist nor quietist, and their withdrawal was principally an avoidance of persecution, rather than a strong desire to escape untainted from an evil world. Desire for insulation was strong, however – in 1855, a special alphabet and type-font were designed (but never used), and had a new language actually been created it might have served Mormons in some measure as German had served the Hutterians in Russia, or the Rappites and Amana Society in America. Mormons were too numerous for the typically intimate social relationships of the introversionist sect. Social control was never *gemeinschaftlich,* and in the early days rapid expansion brought many raw characters into the movement, who were not quickly socialised. (Even in San Bernardino, the early Mormon outpost in California, which was smaller and almost communitarian, drunkenness, gambling and other vices were difficult to control.) In government, their theocratic ideas resembled those of other sects, but Mormons adopted the patterns of organisation known in the outside world. Despite their conflict with secular authorities, Mormons did not reject the idea of such authority: Joseph Smith announced his candidacy for the presidency of the United States, and, in Utah, Mormons contended vigorously for political office. In one sense, Mormonism was almost a type of surrogate nationalism. Mormons took advantage of cheap land to achieve both segregation and autonomy, building up a homeland, just as many Zulu sects became surrogate tribes by acquiring a territory. Yet, although Zion was to be in Utah, America was also the promised land, and as with the British-Israelites in England, this exaggerated identification with the nation and its destiny, was a curb on retreatism and sectarian separatism.

The Mormons were also evangelistic, but theirs was not a simple revivalistic faith with a conversionist justification. Nor were their converts simple frontiersmen: they came rather from the rapidly growing townships, full of immigrants, for whom Mormonism became a charter of America's destiny. Many came from Scandinavia and Britain – where Mormons missioned vigorously, and where in the late 1840s, they had more members than in America. A simple conversionist sect would not – given the existing competition – have succeeded so well. America was the promised land, where men should gather to the new Zion, scene both of a physical utopia and of the temporal millennium. Its scriptures were rich and many-sided. The Book of Mormon reflected, as critic Alexander

Campbell, leader of the *Disciples,* commented, 'every error and almost every truth discussed in New York for the last ten years'. As a religion it possessed prophetic leadership, institutionalised in the presidents of the Church, a lay priesthood, instituted through 'laying on of hands', a lay and unprofessional hierarchy of apostles, prophets, pastors, teachers and evangelists, and rituals that had much of the richness of contemporary masonic practice. With all this the movement provided novelty, and yet had traditional appeal. The organisation acquired a certain objectivity and apartness as an external entity, more characteristic of a long-instituted church than of a new sect.

A churchly, worldly sect

Yet Mormonism arose as a sect, whatever churchly styles it subsequently adopted – and its churchly character was very much assisted by its dominance in what became the state of Utah. In the early days, Mormons made plain that they had voluntarily sacrificed the honours and flatteries of the world, as Sidney Rigdon, an early leader, put it. And much later, the sympathetic commentator Thomas Leiper Kane noted 'the mutual sympathy of Indians and Mormons growing out of their common identity as dispossessed peoples'. The assertion that full salvation was to be had only through the Mormon Church is another feature of the exclusiveness of the sect, although Mormon soteriology is complex and allows for many different conditions of men.

Mormonism differs from most sects in its acceptance of a wide range of activities that many sectarians would regard as distinctly worldly, in particular recreation, including the theatre, dancing and sport, and the adoption of modern facilities in their various enterprises. Whilst a typical, Puritan work ethic was always strongly expressed in Mormonism, this was dissociated from the tensions of Puritan asceticism. Some Mormons enjoy affluence and comfort, but this is not taken as evidence of laxity in religion: since Mormons tithe (give ten per cent of their income to the church), the movement

Although in early days the Mormons encouraged their converts to go to Utah where they had established their temple, in recent decades they have built temples in various parts of the world which are not open to the general public after dedication and where secret rites are performed. The one pictured here is in Switzerland.

202

has benefited from its prospering members. By the use of their elaborate territorial divisions – the *stake* and ward system – in their extensive welfare work and semi-communal enterprises, the Mormons have combined a churchly structure with a very largely lay organisation. Part of the socialisation of young men for their life in the church is achieved through the obligatory two-year period of missionary activity required in the movement.

Mormonism in its many-sidedness has provided activity for the young in recreation, corporate charitable endeavour for the middle-aged, and a unique occupation for (often) the elderly and leisured. The accent on ritual in Mormonism includes a strong emphasis on baptism, and part of the duty of a good Mormon is to ensure that those who died in ignorance of the truth, before the church was restored by Joseph Smith, should posthumously receive proxy baptism, with living substitutes undertaking the ceremony. The search for one's ancestors, in order to give them prospect of salvation, is strengthened by the idea that the salvation of the living depends on the salvation of the dead. The Mormons have accumulated vast microfilm archives in Utah, so that the faithful may engage in research to discover ancestors for whom they can institute ceremonies. What is a pleasurable game for many Americans – seeking to discover their pre-American descent – is more than that for Mormons, who combine recreation, research and ritual in their devoted use of leisure. Scientific activity is thus joined to mysticism in manifestation of faith and the performance of good works. Charity, solidarity with the church, reinforcement of kinship identity, and businesslike and *useful* scholarship are all encompassed in this activity which again reflects the early preoccupation with the need for identity and the assertion of continuity with the past.

In its early days, Mormonism drew its European converts to Utah by subsidising the journey of most of them; but this policy eventually changed, and today Mormons who do not intend to migrate to the United States are found in most European countries. Even so, about eighty-five per cent of the two million Mormons were, in the mid-1960s, resident in North America. The movement claimed some 15,000 members in Germany, about 10,000 in Britain at this period, and smaller numbers in other European countries. About 5,000 Maoris in New Zealand are Mormons. Although Mormons have been active in Polynesia, they have avoided missionary work in Africa and have very few American Negroes among their adherents. The reasons for this are curious. Joseph Smith once gave an inspired 'translation' of a piece of papyrus that came his way from a travelling showman, and declared it to be the Book of Abraham. Although the papyrus has since been acquired by the Metropolitan Museum in New York, and has been shown to be no more than fragments of a copy of the Book of the Dead used for funerals in Egypt for many centuries, Smith's translation declaring that Negroes were cursed with regard to the priesthood has never been disavowed by the Mormon Church. Since priesthood is a vital element of full church membership for men, this commentary has been sufficient to keep Negroes from becoming adherents of the movement. Unlike the doctrine of polygamy, which was espoused by the church soon after its establishment in Utah (although the doctrine had been circulating secretly in the Mormons' earlier location at Nauvoo, Illinois, and at least one apostle, Adams, had openly taken a second wife in 1843), neither Joseph Smith's inspired but erroneous 'translation', nor its racist implications, have ever been disavowed by the church authorities.

The response to circumstances

In some degree the initial response to the world of any sect is modified as its circumstances change. In long continuing sects, a pattern of change from one of the dominant responses to another, and then to a third, as with the English Quakers, may be produced. In other cases, no such obvious sequence is evident: responses are more mixed. One example is the Shakers, as the members of *The United Society of Believers in Christ's Second Appearing* were known, who came into being in Manchester, England, in the mid-

204

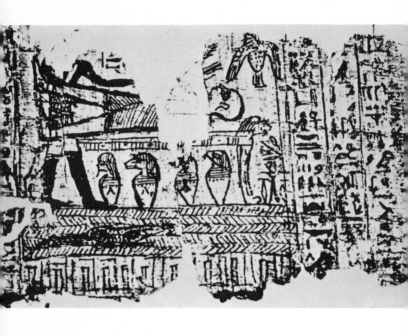

eighteenth century, under the influence of refugee *Camisards* from the Cevennes. From the beginning the Shakers had experienced ecstatic trances, in which they received revelations and uttered prophecies. They taught that Christ would soon return to earth, and urged the world to repent. The little groups of enthusiasts were brought, in the 1760s, under the leadership of Ann Lee, an illiterate woman, who, after having four stillborn children, came to the conviction that sex was the principal evil in the world. The still ecstatic worship of the sect, in which tongues and shakings occurred, led to prosecutions, and in 1774 nine Shakers sailed for America.

From the beginning, the Shakers were evangelistic, eager to convince men of sin and to recruit them to their own celibate group,

Left A fragment of the papyri which Joseph Smith, founder-prophet of the Church of Jesus Christ of Latter Day Saints (Mormons) acquired in 1835 from a travelling showman in Ohio and which he took to be the writings of Abraham and Joseph. Opinion today considers that the papyri are part of the conventional funerary texts of the Egyptian Book of the Dead.

Right A replica of the periodical in which Smith announced the discovery of the fragments, and offered his inspired translation of them.

A FACSIMILE FROM THE BOOK OF ABRAHAM

No. 1.

EXPLANATION OF THE ABOVE CUT.

Fig. 1. The Angel of the Lord. 2. Abraham fastened upon an altar. 3. The idolatrous priest of Elkenah attempting to offer up Abraham as a sacrifice. 4. The altar for sacrifice by the idolatrous priests, standing before the gods of Elkenah, Libnah, Mahmackrah, Korash, and Pharaoh. 5. The idolatrous god of Elkenah. 6. The idolatrous god of Libnah. 7. The idolatrous god of Mahmackrah. 8. The idolatrous god of Korash. 9. The idolatrous god of Pharaoh. 10. Abraham in Egypt. 11. Designed to represent the pillars of heaven, as understood by the Egyptians. 12. Raukeeyang, signifying expanse, or the firmament over our heads; but in this case, in relation to this subject, the Egyptians meant it to signify Shaumau, to be high, or the heavens, answering to the Hebrew word, Shaumahyeem.

3

and the endemic revivalism of the United States brought them new recruits. They were millennialists in a sense, but they taught that they were already the children of the new generation, who had confessed, repented, abandoned sin (particularly sexual intercourse) and thus were saved and resurrected. Mother Ann Lee was credited with thaumaturgical powers, and was represented messianically as 'the woman of the Apocalypse'. Yet salvation was to be had only by leading the righteous life of celibacy, since concupiscence was the root of all hatred, envy and destruction among men. Enquirers thus were brought to a realisation of their own sinfulness in a way that might be found in a conversionist sect, but the consequence was a life of separation that was thoroughly introversionist.

The communitarian solution that the Shakers eventually adopted was to set up elaborate colonies, in which work and worship formed a complex and well-institutionalised order. This development, occurring after Ann Lee's death, rationalised Shaker practice, adapted the sect to external circumstances, provided the basis for mutual 'family' help (necessitated by the abandonment of the real family) and confirmed the introversionist tendency. Shakers did, however, permit a 'secular order' of believers who had not yet abandoned property and involvement with the world. Nor was their retreat from the world simply contemplative. They took in orphans in considerable numbers; they befriended Indians; and they produced a range of ingenious inventions, many of which have passed into wider use in the world. They maintained their strong inspirationalist convictions, and even evolved a form of spiritualism (albeit of a rather different kind from that which the followers of the Fox sisters were contemporaneously developing). Eventually the evangelistic orientation of the Shakers gave way to a more enclosed pattern of life: patterns of routinised dancing displaced the early 'shaking in the spirit', and eventually they too ended. Internal differences arose in the latter half of the nineteenth century between the prominent elder, Frederick Evans, who saw Shakerism as a type of socialism and whose conception of the sect was essentially a utopian response to the world, and the more conservative, quietist Shakers,

The Shakers engaged in one of their
more elaborate dances. Dancing became
an important feature of the worship of
this sect during the nineteenth century.

207

such as elder Harvey Eads, who maintained an introversionist
position. Shakers established nineteen separate communities, all
but three in the period between 1787 and 1810, which had about
17,000 members over the period from their beginnings to the late
1950s, when the last dozen Shakers still maintained two communities.

The search for comprehensiveness

Although many sects have arisen with one strong preoccupation that
constitutes a primary response to the world, emphasising certain
ideas in scripture, exhorting votaries to particular practices, and
regarding salvation as dependent specifically on these, some sects
have sought a universality and a comprehensiveness that more
typically characterises the church. These sects have, not surprisingly,
regarded themselves as reformed churches (or, more typically, as
restored churches), but their separation, their competition and their
implicit rejection of existing religious agencies, warrant their
discussion as sects. Most conspicuous of these has been the *Catholic
Apostolic Church,* and its German offshoot the *Neue Apostolische
Kirche,* but there have been others such as the Liberal Catholics
and the Free Catholics (the choice of titles is itself an indication of
the orientation of these sects). These movements most typically
question the warrant of the existing churches, and in particular
challenge either the validity of their orders, or the faithfulness of
those within them to the Christian mission. The concern about
church authority was particularly prevalent in England in the early
nineteenth century. Apart from its consequences for the major
parties in the Church of England, it led to a variety of new movements. One of these was the *Plymouth Brethren,* whose early founders, even though several of them were Anglican priests or
ordinands, came to reject the ecclesiastical structure of the church,
and, in particular, the sacerdotal principle it embraced.

The *Catholic Apostolic Church,* whose leader was Edward Irving,
the successful Presbyterian minister of a fashionable London
church, arose partly from a similar concern, and partly from con-

The Shakers showed extraordinary
ingenuity in mechanical inventions.
Depicted here are two stages in
their development of a washing machine.

cern about the state of the church in what were regarded as the last days before the second advent of Christ. When Irving was expelled from his church for heresies (particularly in Christology) many of his congregation left with him to found a new church where his adventism was given full expression. The basis of the church order of the new movement was derived from the incident of spontaneous outbreaks of speaking in tongues in Scotland. Irving and his associates, so keenly expecting the literal millennium, accepted the outbreak of glossalalia both as a further sign of the end of the age – the 'latter rain' of the scriptures – and as one of the 'gifts' which St Paul attributed to the Spirit's provision for the work of the church, but which the church had long neglected. Only if the apostolic gifts and competences, as defined by St Paul, were restored, would the church accomplish its work in the last days. The gift of tongues continued in Irving's separated congregation, which now designated itself the *Catholic and Apostolic Church*. Church officers were appointed as the Spirit directed, in accordance with the distribution of the Spirit gifts, and Irving himself accepted, for the few remaining years of his life, a subordinate position to the twelve Apostles who now became the leaders of the church.

Although the movement had been expelled from the Presbyterian church as unorthodox, its votaries believed that they had received the power of the Holy Spirit, not to establish a new sect, but, rather to bear witness to the churches concerning the approaching advent and the need for apostolic church government. The Apostles visited various countries, not to evangelise the masses, but in an attempt to influence orthodox church leaders. Their failure to convert the churches, and their steady recruitment of a following, especially in Britain, Germany and the United States, in effect established a new sect. After controversies about the simulation of the Spirit gifts, the movement settled down to an ordered pattern of worship with special concern for the sacraments and elaboration of liturgy which, in some ways, anticipated the development of Anglo-Catholicism. It adopted the complete structure of the church, as indicated by Paul, with prophets, angels, pastors, and evangelists, serving under

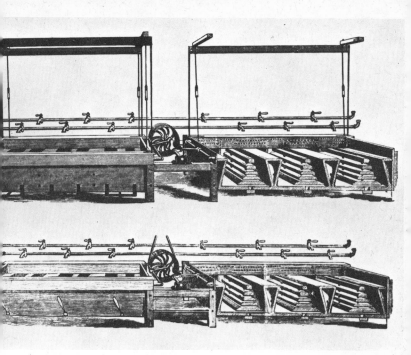

the Apostles. The advent was expected to occur by, or at the time of, the death of the last Apostle. That death occurred in 1901, and thereafter the church abandoned further extension, although it declined only rather slowly, and, even in the 1930s, counted its following in thousands in Britain, the United States, and in Europe. It had in the early days, largely through the spontaneous outbreak of tongues at Karlshud, Donaumoos, acquired considerable impetus in southern Germany and Switzerland: the Roman Catholic priest at Karlshud eventually became a Catholic Apostolic, and acted as Angel at Bern.

What the Catholic Apostolic Church lacked was a distinctive ideology to justify its separate existence: such an ideology would, of course, have run counter to the assumptions of its founders. Although the movement emphasised pentecostal phenomena, particularly in its early days, and also adventism, neither of these emphases was taken to be more than indications of the way in which the Roman, Anglican and Presbyterian churches had gone astray.

Most of all they had failed to realise the proper nature of church government. Because they established church government on charismatic lines, the Catholic Apostolics were driven into a partial separation for which they were ill-prepared, and which went against their own hopes and intentions. After the failure of their millennial hopes, the raison d'être of the movement was exhausted, and in Britain many of its members drifted into the Church of England.

Not all members of the church accepted the interpretation of the early leaders however, and some felt that the office of apostle was not one that should die with its first incumbent. The dissentients were particularly prominent in Germany, and through the exercise of the spirit of prophecy, new appointments were made. Two movements evolved, the more powerful being *Die Neue Apostolische Kirche*, in which those designated as Apostles became a continuing line of leaders far more authoritative than the original conception. Redemption was to be laid only through the work of the Apostles who became God's representatives on earth, and the new movement became an independent sect rejecting all association with existing churches. As a movement it has suffered serious and repeated schisms as well as the shock of disappointed adventual hopes fostered by its leader in the decade 1950-60.

Eclectic and non-separatist sects

The sects discussed in earlier chapters answer the question of what men must do to be saved uncompromisingly in terms of one dominant response that differs sharply from orthodoxy. Those discussed in this chapter promise salvation either through a living messiah, or by obedience to the teachings of a charismatic leader, or give an equivocal answer to the question. This equivocation is evident to the analyst but not to the adherent. It arises either from the volatility or inventiveness of their founders, or because no single orientation appears adequate to attain so complex an end as salvation. Such sects are eclectic and syncretistic, adopting diverse procedures some of which may be instituted in the churches. The most vivid example is Mormonism, which was never simply a sect in a world of churches, but which imitated orthodoxy in attempting to recreate and institutionalise a pattern of life for a people rather than for a minority group.

The equivocation of other groups arises because they strongly identify with a race, a nation, an existing church or some other collectivity whose salvation in toto is their preoccupation. These groups seek to convince a specific but wider constituency of their destiny, and resist being forced into separation from them. The Black Muslims seek to convert the black race; the Catholic Apostolics sought to restore lost teachings to the churches; the British-Israelites sought to convince the British (and by extension other Anglo-Saxon peoples) of their identity with the ten lost tribes of Israel for whom God would still honour the promises recorded in the Bible. Although they do not separate themselves, such groups are commonly regarded as sects.

11 Sects in two developing societies

It is a commonplace of the sociology of religion to assert that sects arise in conditions of social change, when social organisation and social relationships have been disrupted. It has sometimes been said, more specifically, that sects are a product of industrialisation and urbanisation, and those who have concentrated on European sectarianism have sometimes been impressed by the frequency with which weavers – one of the earliest industrial types of worker – have been active sectarians. In western history, social change has been most conspicuously a process of industrialisation and urbanisation, and in the nature of social structure, steadily changing over the course of a thousand years of history, it would be difficult to regard sects as anything but associated in greater or lesser degree with this process. Nonetheless, sects have arisen in the contexts of very different types of social change, particularly in conditions of cultural contact. Sects in the two societies in the world that appear to be the most prolific spawning grounds of sectarianism, South Africa and Japan, appear to have been more influenced by cultural contact than by industrialisation, and this is also true of Indonesia and the West Indies, where sects are numerous.

Sects in other societies – South Africa

The burgeoning of sects in South Africa since the beginning of the twentieth century makes evident the search of the indigenous population both for freedom of expression and the continuance of familiar patterns of religious activity. By the early 1950s over 2,000 native sects were known in the Union of South Africa, many of them small and entirely local meetings, but others with impressive organisations and a following of thousands. The Swedish ecclesiastic, Bengt Sundkler, differentiated between two (and later three) distinct types among these sects, and although his nomenclature is inadequate and unfortunate, it has been widely adopted.

The *Ethiopian* sects were those that had separated from western mission churches, largely because aspiring African ministers and catechists wanted to run their churches themselves, free of European supervision. The name *Ethiopian* was adopted by the Africans themselves, who sought, by use of the reference in Psalms to Ethiopia stretching her hands towards God, to justify their schismatic movements. These particular sects frequently remained similar in style to the missions from which they had broken away, although some of them became more aggressively anti-white. In recent years, the Ethiopian sects have been more conspicuous for the extent to which they have imitated white patterns of church practice and ethical principles, and some of their leaders have not dissented from *apartheid* policies.

The other principal group of sects which Sundkler distinguished he designated *Zionist,* because some of the early ones found their origin in imitation of the Christian Catholic Apostolic Church in Zion, founded by John Alexander Dowie, who in 1900 built Zion City on Lake Michigan, and whose missionaries were active in Africa. The Dowie adherents were fundamentalists, faith-healers, pentecostalists and pre-millennialists, who worshipped (at least initially) with wild enthusiastic spontaneity. The African sects which arose in imitation quickly produced divergent faith and ritual by incorporating African thaumaturgical practices which were not difficult to assimilate to what had been learned from Dowie. Faith-healing, ecstasy, revelations and, as in Dowie's own case, the establishment of communities, all became typical for these sects. Subsequently, Sundkler designated some South African sects *messianic,* but this category was not well distinguished from the Zionist category.

African sects fulfilled many subsidiary functions, not least of which was to provide a context in which adherents might see in their sect leaders an African in possession of great power and status. But these sects also manifested the search for salvation in ways essentially similar to those recognisable in western sectarianism. Some of their responses, particularly the thaumaturgical, were indigenous. Others, certainly the conversionist, and perhaps the revolutionist were learned by imitation of European or American Negro sectarian movements that evangelised in South Africa. An

A baptism of total immersion taking place in the River Jukskei. Baptism is a ritual of central importance in the many hundreds of Zionist sects in South Africa because it combines Christian symbolism with the initiation ceremonies of indigenous religions, and also because of the importance attached to water in South Africa.

American Negro revolutionist sect influenced Enoch Mgijima, whose followers called themselves *Israelites* and believed that Negroes were a chosen people. Mgijima's tendency to visions and prophecy eventually led to the separation of his followers from the American parent group. They refused to pay taxes, assembled and encamped illegally, and expected the divine annihilation of Europeans. Despite the efforts of a patient government to disperse them, the Israelites refused to go to their homes, predicting that God would help them to eliminate the Europeans, to which end they had already armed themselves. The conflict that eventually came in 1921 at Bulhoek, led to the deaths of 183 Israelites and the imprisonment of Mgijima for three years.

Few South African sects have taken adventist preaching quite so far, although there is, even in the thaumaturgically-oriented groups, often a strong anti-white disposition. This was strongly pronounced in the *Zion Christian Church* of Edward Lekganyane at 'Zion City' in the North Transvaal, where several thousand followers acknowledged this son of their founder as 'king' in 1950. Edward Lekganyane presented himself as a thaumaturge who could destroy witches and whose potency was such that those in search of healing might get it by burning paper that he had blessed. The rules of the movement were exacting, and part of its appeal was its obvious strength and size, the elaborate hierarchy by which it was governed, and the manifest power of Edward, who dressed like a monarch and maintained a sumptuous style of life. Worship was ecstatic in the way typical of such groups, with dancing and processions.

The settlement at Zion City and the transcendence of sect allegiance over tribal allegiance make clear that this sect was very much the surrogate-tribe in a society undergoing detribalisation, where individuals were suffering loss of the sense of identity. Some sects were drawn very largely from particular tribes, and in these chiefs were frequently accorded the special standing increasingly denied to them in the missions of the white men. But such sects have also been vehicles for the assertion of power by other men, and in these contexts the muted struggle for power between warriors and pro-

phets is re-enacted: the African situation clearly favours prophets,
since religious independence persists while political and military
autonomy has gone. Such a prophet is John Galilee Shembe of the
Nazareth Baptist Church (known as *Shembe's Church*) whose
following is mainly Zulu. He maintains ceremonial similar to that
of the ancient Zulu chiefs and is honoured more than any living chief
among the Zulus. Shembe, who became leader in succession to his
father, is virtually a messiah-thaumaturge, equated with Christ.
His movement too is the great salvation from witchcraft (to which
all illness is attributed) and it maintains its 'territory' in the tradition
of a tribe. Church government, hierarchy and etiquette are modelled
on Zulu tribal practice, but the movement also enjoins a variety of
taboos and injunctions derived from the Old Testament. The life of
the sect stands in some continuity with traditional Zulu life, and the
power of the movement evokes the power of the Zulu past.

In the cultural confusion of African life, the functions of sects
become more apparent than is always the case in western society –
partly because their constituency is so much more self-evident. The
conversionist sect of Nicholas Bhengu in East London and Durban,
which is more conspicuously influenced by white conversionist
sectarianism (particularly Pentecostalism) than most African sects,
demonstrates the significance of this type of religious response in
the assimilation of immigrants to town life. Healing and public
confession (traditional among the Xhosa, who are his main votaries)
are associated with tolerance of traditional ancestor cults. A
considerable proportion of his following are people from the
countryside, and this sect acts as a protection against the temptations of the city, and as an agency communicating high ethical
standards that help a new immigrant from the farm to get on in
employment in the town. The Bhengu-ists acquire both a strong sense
of apartness, and of community, the cost of which is separation from
outsiders and commitment to a way of life, emphasising honesty,
thrift, cleanliness, prudence and industriousness. In this sect, which
is very much influenced by European evangelical movements, we
come closest to the conversionist sect of Europe and America, which,

whilst preserving the rural values of its constituents in some measure, communicates to them – often in idealised form – the ethical standards of urban society. Its effectiveness is attributable in large part to its provision of a new and meaningful community life for its members. In this case it is the migrants to the city who adopt sectarianism : but we may not overlook the persisting and more numerous thaumaturgical sects, by which others escape urban influences and reassert the traditional rural values of the past.

Sects in Japan

The complex process of social change that Japan has experienced since the country was thrown open to foreign trade in 1854 has been far more than merely a process of industrial development, although that has been a significant part of it. It has included the complete transformation of social structure; tense, and often violent political activity; enforced, state-sponsored development of new industrial activity; conscious and systematic cultural borrowing; and the attempt, and failure, to establish imperial dominion. In the process, class structure has been transformed; the religious basis of society has been undermined; the myths of greatness have been destroyed; and the Japanese people have experienced, after dramatic victory, defeat, conquest, and enforced political and social re-organisation. Circumstances of social crisis were endemic in Japan over a long period, and the nation, in some ways so well-integrated, and enjoying the coherence of its insular geography and centuries of social and political isolation, has undergone an acute crisis of identity. It is largely in these circumstances that new religious movements have come into being.

In many ways, the contemporary Japanese have been presented as a highly secular and materialistic people, whose religious concerns have been shallow and casual. Yet new sects have proliferated. Despite the divergence of received traditions, much the same comment was often made about the United States in the nineteenth-century – at a time when new sects were burgeoning there. Sects grow readily in secular societies, where national (or societal) ideologies have fallen into disrepute, or where, in the welter of diverse traditions, they have not been firmly established.

New sects may be a reassertion of old values or an accommodation to new conditions: sometimes they manage to be something of both. Japanese sects have been, in large part, accommodative, even to the point where their own teachings have been consciously adjusted to meet changes in political climate, and the changing social needs of their votaries.

From 1868, the Japanese recognised thirteen distinct religious sects of the traditional Shinto faith, as well as Buddhism and Christianity, but even before this time some new religious movements had arisen. In the 1890s, in the early twentieth century, and in the 1930s, others emerged, preceding the profusion of new sects that came into being after the surrender of the country at the end of the war in 1945. There are today more than two hundred new Buddhist sects, over two hundred and fifty Shinto sects (schisms of old sects, and new movements combined), and more than one hundred and fifty new sects that are neither Buddhist nor Shintoist in character. Some have been of short duration: others have become movements claiming between them the allegiance of tens of millions of Japanese. Several now command vast resources, with impressive headquarters and temples, and exercise considerable political power.

Although the Japanese sects draw on various divergent traditions – Buddhism, Shinto, and occasionally Christianity for their teachings, western organisational ideas for their structure, and sometimes on modern international ideologies for their programme – there are a variety of very general attributes that are common to many of them. Most immediately impressive of these is the particular Japanese tradition of thaumaturgy, in terms of which their founders have usually legitimated themselves. The founders are often regarded as *ikigami*, somewhat more than human shamans who become possessed by a deity. Although presenting their founders and their successors as thaumaturges, the sects themselves are not specifically thaumaturgical. More typically they approximate to the

manipulationist type, which reflects Japanese development from the primitive conditions appropriate to thaumaturgy, to the more sophisticated social circumstances in which a manipulationist response to the problems of security and salvation becomes acceptable. (The same shift from crude spiritualism, with emphasis on miracles and manifestations, to a more elaborate metaphysical doctrine is also evident among sects in Brazil.) The earlier new religions are, appropriately, most committed to the legitimation of their founders in thaumaturgical terms. Thus, *Tenri-kyō*, 'Divine Wisdom', makes this claim most vigorously for its foundress, Nakayama Miki (1798-1887). She claimed that ten deities had 'forced themselves upon her', she experienced trance and performed healings. Kawate Bunjiro, founder of *Konkō-kyō*, became, after a lifetime of crisis, possessed in 1859 by an entirely new deity, who was presented as higher than the traditional local spirits, and whose favour, through the founder, was now available to others. The *toritsugi,* way of meditation (or intercession) of this sect, consists in consultation of votaries with their spiritual head, who by

'Holy labour' is, like artistic appreciation, a common feature of a number of Japanese sects. Here the wife of the Patriarch of Tenrikyō, a sect founded in the nineteenth century, joins others in public service activities. Its founder, Miki Nakayama, claimed to be herself the shrine of the gods. The sect emphasises miraculous healing.

wisdom of the deity offers solutions to their problems. In a much less dramatic way, the system is reminiscent of what occurs in the *candomblés* of Brazil, where possessed mediums advise clients, or in the spirit-medium cults of Singapore. At a more sophisticated level, the toritsugi suggests some resemblance to the 'quiet time' of Buchmanism (Moral Re-Armament). It is clearly a practice bridging the transition from what was initially a type of developed thaumaturgical practice, to styles nearer to those of a modern manipulationist sect.

Even in those sects that trace their inspiration to specific Buddhist tradition, these elements of mixed thaumaturgy and manipulationist ideas are evident. *Reiyūkai* is one of these sects, and takes the Lotus Sūtra of the Mahayana Buddhist tradition, presented to Japan by Nichiren, a Buddhist monk of the thirteenth-century as its special source of inspiration. Reiyūkai itself began incipiently in the years after the First World War, and emphasised the veneration for the spirits of the dead. It acquired its modern form in 1925, and in that difficult period, presented itself as an optimistic, nationalistic faith. Power was believed to be concentrated in the *mandalas,* scrolls of graphic illustration of teachings, created by its own founder and by Nichiren, which alone could bring men into direct contact with the Buddhas and Boddhisattvas. Like the Mormons, the adherents of Reiyūkai believe that they could confer merit on their ancestors, in this case by reading the Sūtra. The particular institution of Reiyūkai, however, was the *hōza*, a system of group consultation, in which votaries revealed – in a way quite at variance with Japanese tradition – their problems and personal difficulties. The hōza system was taken over by one of the very successful schisms from Reiyūkai, known as *Risshō Kōseikai*, a sect that, in the early 1960s, claimed more than 1,600,000 adherents. Group counselling, undertaken everywhere where the sect has adherents, and at the movement's impressive central headquarters in Tokyo, is organised under a leader for groups of between ten to twenty people. The solution of the problems of individuals is a vital part of the faith. Risshō Kōseikai also inherited preoccupation with ancestral

The *Risshō Kōsekai* movement, a procession of whose members is seen here, is one of the group of neo-Buddhist sects in Japan which emphasises the importance of the Lotus Sutra (Hokekyō) a cult originated by Nichiren, a thirteenth-century Japanese Buddhist monk.

spirits from its parent sect, Reiyūkai, and ancestors are registered at sect headquarters, although since the death in 1957 of Naganuma Myōkō, (known as Myōkō Sensei) the woman who was the principal shamanistic leader of the sect, this spiritualism has been somewhat reduced. The veneration of Myōkō, who in her lifetime was sometimes regarded as a living Buddha, has also been curbed. Again, the change from more thaumaturgical and charismatic elements to more institutionalised procedures, and the shift of emphasis to mental discipline and the counselling system more typical of manipulationist sects suggest that the movement is experiencing secularising and modernising influences.

Typically for sects of this kind, the new sects in Japan emphasise their utility, in every-day life. This is a characteristic manipulationist orientation, but in Japan it has the special importance of providing a modern faith for a society whose traditional faith is not easily accommodated to modern conditions. In an extension of this orientation, and as if to illustrate its importance corporately and publicly as well as privately and individually, many of the sects sponsor public works of one kind or another. This is a feature of sects of this kind in Brazil (Kardecism and, in increasing measure even the cruder African-inherited spiritualism of Umbanda). In countries like Brazil and Japan, traditions of voluntary service and disinterested goodwill have been very much less developed than in Protestant Europe, partly because national religion has had a different focus, and has exercised much less organised control. In Japan, the public works of a movement like Risshō Kōseikai, and the syncretistic sect, *Ittoen,* which regards only toil as ennobling, are an interesting indication of a vacuum in social organisation that sects can readily fill.

Public activity, however, does not eclipse the unabashed emphasis on personal benefit in many of the Japanese sects. Even in the early days, Konkō-kyō was characterised as having a deity who was 'the god of money-making'. The most powerful of the new sects, *Sōka Gakkai,* the 'Value Creation Society', which, whilst denying that it is a religion, is paradoxically most intolerant of other religious

allegiances, has vigorously proselytised by promising great personal benefits to those who believe. 'Value', indeed, is tantamount to profit – everything that is associated with long and happy life. Testimonies to its beneficial effects by votaries of Sōka Gakkai are a principal feature of the movement's literature, just as they are of Christian Science.

Nowhere more than in the emphasis on the cure of sickness have the new sects shown the strong similarity of their orientations. The original goals of Tenri-kyō were healing and the realisation of the bright and cheerful life through the exercise of the mental discipline of perseverance. Although its original teaching has undergone some changes the movement still claims, by sweeping away dust from the soul, to perform healings. But today it also builds hospitals, and maintains that illness may be overcome by methods other than mere healing of the body. This is also a typical adaptation for a sect that begins in social circumstances where very little medical attention is available, and which continues into times when the competition of medicine induces it to find other functions. In the west, the process has occurred largely through slight and almost imperceptible shifts of emphasis (for example in Christian Science) and by the emergence of new movements. In Japan, where doctrinal consistency has been less demanded, a sect with a long life, like Tenri-kyō, undergoes considerable overt change of orientation. A few sects have rejected all physical causes of healing, however, and they have continued to present themselves as alternatives to medical practice. Several sects, including *P L Kyōdan* (Perfect Liberty Church) emphasise the condition of the mind as the cause of sickness: it is the claim of this sect to be able to point out to any individual the specific mental cause of any illness, through the agency of an official with the gift of spiritual discernment. Here, as in other sects, practice amounting almost to divination is associated with a modern psychological religious emphasis: in some sects, particularly Reiyūkai and its schisms, and in the *Ōmoto* group, sickness is attributed more readily to the influence of ancestral spirits, and sometimes to animal spirits.

Japanese sects have shown a marked capacity to adopt organisational techniques learned from the west. Many are mass-movements with highly efficient central agencies and extremely disciplined following – this is most conspicuously true of Sōka Gakkai. In many of the sects there is the strange association within a very short time of saintly and charismatic leadership and luxurious and impressive headquarter buildings. What took a long time in western Christianity has occurred in a matter of decades for some modern Japanese movements. As in Africa, there is the paradox of emphasis on the originally humble circumstances of leaders and on the simplicity and hardship of their lives, with the evident satisfaction that the followers have in the prestige, influence and wealth of contemporary leaders of their movement. Many of the sects have vigorous publishing houses, radio stations, hospitals, recreational centres and welfare institutions. A notable exception to this tendency is the Christian sect, *Mukyokai-Shugi*. This is a churchless religion whose founder was committed to completing the Protestant Reformation, which Luther had not taken far enough, by eliminating all organisation, except Bible study groups gathered about a teacher. The founder knew of the Quakers, but rejected their inspirationalism for a Bible-centred faith.

A peculiarity of the new Japanese religions is the emphasis on artistic living. This is most pronounced in P L Kyōdan. Its slogan is 'Life is art': every man should be an artist. Really to live is to express one's quality in life, and this is to become an artist, which is the truly happy condition, for then man is expressing God. The strong liturgical orientation of this sect is an extension of this idea. The somewhat older Ōmoto sect, with its strong concerns with spirits, also considers life to be the quest for art and beauty. Perhaps the most distinctive expression of this ideal is in *Tenshō Kōtai Jingu-hyō*, a religion founded in 1945 by a charismatic middle-aged woman, Kitamura Sayo, who claimed to be possessed by a Shinto deity who speaks through her. This religion, in which the leader is the only preacher, emphasises the need not to exorcise but to redeem evil spirits and thereby to improve life. The individual reaches a heightened state in dance, and by dance moves along the road to God. Like other new religions, God's abundance is emphasised, but man's access to it is held to be exclusively through Tenshō Kōtai Jingu-kyō. In asserting this degree of exclusiveness, this sect differs from most others in contemporary Japan, although Sōka Gakkai is also an exception to the general principle of toleration.

12 Origins, functions and development

Cultural contact is a conspicuous element in the background of sectarianism in Africa, Asia and Melanesia: it consists in multiform processes of social change, including the effects of highly industrialised societies on societies at very different stages of development. Sects do, however, arise among rural tribal people and peoples whose societies have not themselves been affected by industrialisation. Such a new religious movement is the Peyote cult among North American Indians, which, although an innovation, is introduced as a continuance of traditional Indian culture. The spread of this introversionist faith occurred after the failure of the advent promised in 1890 by the Ghost Dance religion which had spread among Indians. The cactus-button called peyote became regarded as a saviour for all Indians and was taken up by a minority in one tribe after another. Peyotism is a sect arising among an undeveloped people in response to conditions of acute cultural despair. Although it claims to be traditional and conservative, in effect it is pan-Indian rather than tribal.

The sects of Württemberg arising in the late eighteenth century, some of which we have examined, were the sects of rural people. So were the Doukhobors who came into being in the Ukraine in the eighteenth century, the Hutterians, the Amish Mennonites, and a number of small sects that emerged in Britain in the eighteenth and nineteenth centuries. So too are many of the holiness sects that still thrive in Kentucky, Tennessee and neighbouring states. Many of these sects have been small and local: their growth, where they have grown, has often been by the association of local Gemeinschaften into a league of sectarian congregations, who recognise each other as forming the community of the faithful. Although most sects are comprised of intense local primary groups, it is less true of the large, international organisations, and least true of all of thaumaturgical practice and of the urban, sophisticated manipulationist movements, who do not celebrate community as in itself a vital element in religion.

Sects are often a consequence of the disrupting social processes that occur with new productive techniques and new products, but sects respond at the level of values. Sometimes, as in medieval movements, it is the workers who are themselves employing the new techniques, and facing the new life circumstances, who are disposed to accept new ideologies, and who reinterpret their life values in sectarian terms. In societies where thought was couched in essentially religious terms, all reactions to change were themselves likely to be religious. As societies have been secularised, it becomes less likely that those engaged in new technical and industrial processes will seek religious legitimations of their aspirations. Rural populations, however, who may regard themselves as more threatened by new industrial developments, may seek ways in which to enshrine their own values, to preserve their way of life, and to protect it. In particular, they may have some sense of cultural retardation as they compare themselves with urban and industrial centres, about which, in an age of more effective communication, they learn a great deal more than in the past. In such areas, of which the prairies of Canada are one, recourse to sectarianism is frequent. The orthodox churches train their ministers in the cultural centres, and these men, therefore, represent the values that rural populations find alien. Church, state and the city become the symbols of things evil, since they represent values alien to the rural context and which cannot be readily assimilated in rural conditions. A readier response is to sectarianism of a restorative and preservative kind – a sectarianism that promises the continuance of the values and life-styles of the past in face of the apostasy of the city. So vigorous did this response become in Alberta that in the 1930s a prominent fundamentalist preacher who had his own 'prophetic' Bible Institute became the Prime Minister of the state.

Although it cannot be offered as a firm generalisation, the sectarianism of the new urban working classes in medieval times was often of a revolutionist type. Adventist sects have generally prospered in towns, even in the nineteenth and twentieth centuries. It must be acknowledged, however, that millennial enthusiasm has, in many periods – in England in the mid-seventeenth century, and America in the early nineteenth, for instance – been no respector of

classes or of conditions of men! On the other hand, rural sectarianism has been restorative, often of a conversionist (although
occasionally of an introversionist) kind. The conversionist type has
been more common in more recent history, and in rural movements set against a background of industrialism, whilst introversionist responses were more common in the eighteenth century.
Sects arising among rural immigrants to the town are usually
conversionist, and function to reassure their votaries of their personal adequacy (through experience of being 'born again'). They
legitimate for them, in highly idealised form, the values and morality
of the society, to which, in the case of immigrants from another
culture, they are introduced, and which they take on as the appropriate standards for their new life in the new society. In this instance,
the change is in the life circumstances of the immigrants themselves, rather than in the life and productive activities of society.

The proposition that sects arise in conditions of social change is a
truism. But social change has a differential impact on different
groups; equally, responses to change occur within groups and not
from groups as a whole, since sects are always a minority phenomenon. The type of response varies with historical periods and social
and cultural contexts. Thus, today, new sects are no longer arising
amongst industrial workers, nor, in the western world, among the
rural population, nor among the marginal 'independent men' who
were drawn into some Puritan movements (including the Plymouth
Brethren in the nineteenth century). They arise less in response to
specific economic circumstances than to the conditions of social and
cultural uncertainty in affluent, pluralistic advanced societies.
They recruit not so much in industrial centres, as in the metropolitan
cities, among populations which are not merely rootless but which
also increasingly come to contain a large proportion of isolated individuals. Their salvation is not by the re-creation of a Gemeinschaft,
since often they have never experienced stable community life, but
rather in the legitimation and celebration of anonymity and impersonality. Ultimate values are easily eclipsed by instrumental values
for such people, and consequently their sects are less concerned

with eschatology than with present happiness and freedom from neurosis. Where whole populations have been affected by conditions of widespread social and cultural change, traumatic loss of all the traditional terms of national identity, and dramatic confrontation of ancient thaumaturgy with modern psychology, philosophy and diverse ideologies, the extraordinary mixed sectarianism of Japan, for instance, is a result.

National cultures and sectarian expression

Countries undergoing profound social re-adjustment in the modern world – such as Japan or Brazil – provide circumstances conducive to the proliferation of sects. Most of our analysis, however, has had to do with established sects, the most prominent among which are of Anglo-Saxon, and particularly of American origin. Why should this be? And why have countries such as France and Italy so few indigenous sects? Several reasons may be advanced. In the first place, America underwent, especially in the nineteenth century, a process of social expansion and change, and an absorption of alien cultures of similar proportions – if in a very different historical context and of very different cultural content – to that experienced in the twentieth-century new nations that produce new sects. Secondly, the countries in which industrialisation had its earlier dramatic effects, Britain, America and Germany, were all largely Protestant countries, and the tolerance of Protestantism was itself propitious for sectarianism. Sacerdotal authority, of the kind entrenched in the Catholic church, is not easily reconciled with the authority structure and rational procedures of industrialism. Thirdly, the expansionism of American society in particular (but also of nineteenth-century Britain) and the missionary vigour of evangelistic movements, added to a type of Protestant patriotism against what was seen as the obscurantism, authoritarianism and perhaps even the wickedness of the Roman church in continental Europe, induced many sectarians – John Nelson Darby is an example – to proselytise on the continent. In the American case this missionary zeal was enhanced by the adoption of the rational bureaucratic style of efficient organisation typical of a technically advanced society, and familiar in the twentieth century in the work of the Mormons, the Seventh Day Adventists, and Jehovah's Witnesses. Sectarian ideologies – themselves almost a proof of the liberty, tolerance and pluralism of American society – have been a major American export, particularly successful since the end of the Second World War. The great sects of continental Europe have American origins, even if they have acquired – as have many Pentecostal groups – local autonomy.

Protestantism encouraged strong lay involvement in religion and a tradition of independent religious thinking that Catholic countries have not shared. The effective suppression of heresy in Catholic countries accounts for the absence of those little groups of independent seekers that were common in America. Britain and parts of Germany in the eighteenth and nineteenth centuries, some of which have persisted to the present day. Although French and Italian society underwent, at different times, dramatic political changes, these were not comparable in their intensity and pervasiveness to the radical social changes of nineteenth-century America, much less of twentieth-century Japan. Where the hold of the Roman church was shaken, it was shaken not by sectarian impulses (the Waldensians in their remote mountain valleys excepted) but by more outright secularism.

In the more secular twentieth century, sectarianism has found expression in countries such as France, Belgium and Italy. The bigger American sects have recruited quite widely, and, in Italy in particular, returning immigrants have converted relatives to the joys of the gemeinschaftlich sectarian experience with its expressive spontaneity. Where indigenous sects have arisen in Catholic modern Europe, they have centred much more dramatically on charismatic leaders – on figures such as Davide Lazzaretti, Père Antoine, Bernard Sayerce, Oskar Bernhardt or Georges Roux. The Protestant tradition of independent searching of the scriptures has been absent, and the complete authority claimed by the Catholic church has necessarily been challenged by a counter-authority, an alternative charisma, centering on a dominant personality, and frequently on his claim to messiahship. Charisma is difficult to institutionalise, but in the twentieth century persisting sects have arisen around such figures. They are more radical, more bizarre, less biblical than most of the sects of Protestant countries, but their more colourful, and often more romantic, appeal still competes against the international organisations of the great American sects.

Sectarians and relative deprivation

Contemporary explanations of social deviance frequently invoke the theory of relative deprivation: deviants are said to be people who have been (or who feel that they have been) deprived of satisfactions. Their deviance is a form of compensatory behaviour. This thesis is sometimes applied to religious deviance – to sectarianism. Before it is too readily accepted, it must be recalled that sectarianism has its own dynamism: sects sometimes arise in schism from existing sects, without the operation of external causes. There is a distinction to be made, too, between the availability of a teaching and its adoption. A sect may come into being in one historical or cultural context, but grow only in another: thus the Shakers were begun in England, but grew only in America. Mormonism developed in small towns in New York State, among a population that was often agricultural, and that certainly lived in a predominantly agrarian society, but in Britain its success was largely in the industrial towns. Christian Science was first tried in small manufacturing towns, but really flourished only when it found the soil of metropolitan Boston. A corollary of this point is that sects, being exportable, acquire differing cultural connotations in different societies. In America, used to religious pluralism from early days, a sect such as the Disciples was early recognisable as a denomination, but its tiny offshoots in Britain were sectarian in the eyes of the church and the population. The Seventh Day Adventists are a respectable middle-class denomination in some Californian communities: they remain distinctly a sect in France, Italy and Britain. If sects arise in social change, they often persist in conditions quite different from those that gave rise to them. They also undergo internal change, and to this we shall turn shortly.

It is evident, in discussing social change in broad terms, that the effects of change must be mediated to particular groups and, within those groups, to particular individuals, as a type of personal dissatisfaction, a sense of insecurity, and anxiety in individuals, before it gives rise to sectarianism, and even then, there are intervening processes by which those who experience hardship, anxiety, and insecurity are made aware of, drawn to and recruited into sects. There are, obviously, other ways of dealing with such experiences. Not least among them is migration, and sometimes – as in the case of rural people moving to the city and becoming Methodists, in early nineteenth-century England, or industrial workers leaving their country to go as Mormons to the new Zion in mid-nineteenth-century America – the two are associated. The relationship between religious conversion and migration is, however, almost uncharted territory.[11] We may suppose that in the conditions of hardship and insecurity there is an awareness of change, and also, perhaps, an inability to perceive exactly what social processes are at work, and to understand the implications. The sense of cultural retardation among rural people, the sense of lost community among newly arrived urban immigrants, the feeling of inadequacy among native populations impressed by the evidence of more advanced technology, and the awareness of life-styles and opportunities available only to others – are all conditions that may be conducive to new 'world-changing' responses. All these conditions may give rise to a sense of relative deprivation. Men feel deprived because the traditional legitimations of social differences have broken down, because the accepted meanings of social relationships have, by some process of change, been destroyed. (The process of change may be an objective economic process, a new basis of social status, an increase of information and knowledge that has acted as a solvent of old ideologies, a growing clash of representatives of diverse cultures –

among perhaps many other things.) The sect is not an inevitable consequence of such circumstances. It is merely one way in which new circumstances, or newly perceived circumstances, may be explained. Sects arise to establish new religious explanations of the differences by assuring votaries

1 of compensation for discrepanices (conversionist, revolutionist, introversionist responses)

2 of means by which to overcome them (manipulationist, thaumaturgical responses)

3 of ways in which they can be eliminated (reformist and utopian responses)

The sect may itself stimulate, or induce, feelings of relative deprivation. It may assuage them, as in conversionist movements: or it may legitimate and perpetuate them as do revolutionist ideologies. Always, it provides a radical transformation of the situation for its votaries: it gives them a response to the world and a community of the like-minded with whom to share it.

Sect development

It used to be frequently asserted, particularly by American observers, that new sects steadily became old denominations. In particular H. Richard Niebuhr believed that with the birth of a second generation, a sect necessarily underwent transformation. He believed that the second generation was much less committed to the principle of voluntary adherence, simply inheriting their sectarian persuasion. Following John Wesley, he noted, too, that many nonconformist religious groups prospered, particularly by becoming thrifty, ascetic, and dedicated to work. Each of these propositions needs modification. Some sects have persisted as sects, continuing to assert a strong contra-cultural position, demanding exacting tests even of their own young people before admitting them, and holding themselves aloof from the wider society. Again, whilst thrift and industry have been factors in sectarian change, what has sometimes been more basic to the process has been the intensive way in which sectarians often socialise their children to particular sets of values. Where these have been the idealised values of the wider society, presented in specially elevated form, they have produced men of high integrity, strong moral dispositions, and heightened sense of responsibility to whatever group they regard as theirs (if in the beginning, only the sect, sometimes, later, and in particular departments of life, the whole society, or even mankind). In Anglo-Saxon countries, in particular, these sectarian values have some-times had – as Quaker, Baptist and early Methodist influences indicate – significance for the whole society.

Niebuhr's hypotheses were derived from the evidence of American society, where sects were somewhat lightly transformed into denominations, for a number of reasons. America lacked an established church, so that sects, although out-groups, were not so clear about what it was that they protested against, at least in reference to institutional religion. America was an expanding and an egalitarian society, and in consequence sects grew in size and in social respectability. The formal and legal equality of men implied the formal equality of their religions, and this degree of tolerance permitted sects to become denominations fairly easily. New immigrants, who, especially because of language difficulties, tended to occupy the most menial roles in their new society at the bottom, caused older settlers to count themselves as more fully American, and no longer of the lowest class: where older settlers were sectarians their sect was pushed up in the social scale with its clientele. As social advance occurred for such sectarian groups – and the Methodists in America, the Disciples and the Church of the Nazarene all trod this familiar path – so their religious peculiarity diminished. They came to accept the wider culture and to claim a part in it.

The process of denominationalism has affected the most recent crop of conversionist sects, as much as did those of earlier proven-ance. The Pentecostalist sects, particularly in Europe and America, have steadily acquired respectability. Initially the emotionalism of these movements was difficult to bridle, and led, at times, to excesses and to scandals. Gradually, a pattern of order was evolved, and the Pentecostalist sects became institutionalised. The gifts were no longer encouraged to operate so freely and texts were found that circumscribed their operation. Even the strong lay tradition of the sects was, in many cases, modified, and whilst lay expressiveness continued to be the ideology of the movement, most Pentecostal sects evolved a ministry, and the function of that ministry has been, paradoxically, to sustain a lay ideology, whilst simultaneously limiting the freedom of lay expression. Because Pentecostal sects were largely recruited by revivalism, the after-care of those converted became a primary preoccupation, and steadily this concern became more important in the various sects that developed than the recruitment of the outsider. The organisation that emerged, which, in some part, contradicts the very ideology of Pentecostalism (and which for that reason perhaps is more of a latent than a manifest structure in these sects), was also necessary for the continuance of particular movements. If Pentecostalism was not to burn itself out in a congeries of small meetings, with ecstatic styles of worship, regulation and routinisation had to occur. As it did so, with increasing effect, so Pentecostal sects came to be increasingly nearer to the denominations from which originally they had distinguished themselves.

The sects that were denominationalised, that moved from a position of protest and separation to one of general cultural conformity and whose members lost that distinctive religious identity which characterises a sect, were not, however, a cross sample of all types of sect. They were conspicuously the conversionist sects. These were sects relying on revivalism for recruitment, emphasising a change of heart as the condition of salvation, generally reasserting traditional moral values and religious imagery, and doing so, initially, with intense emotionalism and expressiveness. Lay involvement in them was not so much a matter of lay government as freedom of expression and the absence of ministerial decorum and order. As these groups were stabilised, and as they adjusted to the new condition of salvation that they proclaimed, so the emotionalism diminished. As their members gained in wealth and social respectability, so their disapproval of the wider culture declined. Having expected salvation in another world by conversion, they often first discovered the 'kingdom of heaven' in the sect meeting itself, in the reassurance and security it provided, and then, through socialisation to high moral standards, they attained salvation in the wider world, where they were no longer so insecure. The paradox of the conversionist sect has often been that, having promised its votaries social mobility after death, it has provided it for them in real life – but by means it had not envisaged. Faith in God has been, at least in the past two centuries, a frequently indirect means to earthly salvation. Social adjustment has been a latent function of the conversionist sect.

Self-evidently, however, not all sects become denominationalised. The revolutionist sects have not shown so consistent a tendency. It is clear that the Seventh Day Adventists have undergone some change in this direction. Their preoccupation with the seventh day as the Sabbath gave them a strong reason to embark on evangelism, and although this has not made them conversionist (in the sense of making a change of heart the one crucial criterion of salvation) it has led them into evangelistic activities not dissimilar from those of conversionist groups. Most important has been their inheritance from early times of a separate, full-time ministry, which has led to increased concern with professional training, differentiation of ministry and laity, and which has given the movement some impetus towards intellectual orientations, which are in their nature not easily reconciled with sectarian separatism. Obviously, within a movement that has a diversified set of concerns – the advent, the seventh day Sabbath, dietetic principles, affirmation of the special revelations it has received, and extensive missionary activity – there is room for diverse opinions, and diverse adjustments, and there is evidence that different sections within the movement have somewhat different orientations to the world and to the movement's role in relation to it.[12] The Seventh Day Adventists, in adopting a variety of beliefs that were necessary to sustain faith in the advent after initial disappointments had been experienced, sometimes manifest diverse responses to the world. Adventist sects, in their purest state, are sects that place great emphasis on the one tenet that really matters – the coming of the Saviour and the overturn of the world. In the case of Seventh Day Adventism, and it is a case strongly affected by the fact that the sect arose *after* the disappointment of firmly promised dates, the sect has moved from strong affirmation of one thing to the additional affirmation of many different things. It was only in virtue of this that the sect could arise as an integrated organisation, and by virtue of this also, it has been possible to shift emphasis from the advent to other concerns. In this respect, without as yet being wholly denominationalised, this sect has shown some tendency to move in that direction. As long, however, as the idea of the advent persists, and the tendency to interpret prophecy in the traditional way that identifies state and church (particularly the Roman Church) as the evil beasts depicted in prophetic scripture, the movement marks itself off as opposed to the general culture, and so can be considered a sect.

Other adventist movements have in different ways remained sectarian. Jehovah's Witnesses are as vigorously and single-mindedly adventist in their doctrine as they ever were. They have undergone some process of change but not towards denomination-alism. The movement transformed itself from being an élite body into becoming a mass-movement under the direction of its second leader, Judge Rutherford. House-to-house and street canvassing were introduced. Its leadership gradually became more anonymous, and its publications were produced as if they came from God, without other indications of authorship. What was accomplished in this case was the development of the dual system of organisation – a loose, unstructured movement of Bible Students, and the tight, highly organised activities of a publishing concern. The control in the movement is effectively concealed: apparently Jehovah leads his people, and his government is theocratic. There are no mediators, and there have been no revelations, no mysteries, no sacraments but the vestigial communion ceremony, no aesthetic gratifications, no liturgical activity – but only the catechising of the students, who need qualifications in the truth in order to go out and proclaim the good news, to which end the movement as such is wholly dedicated. The local meeting is less a fellowship than a working-party. The Witnesses have come to terms with the disappearance of Gemeinschaft in the wider society, and they perpetuate it only marginally. Their followers are not typically rural people, nor recent immigrants to cities (who, having much to hope for in this world, are less immediately disposed to adventism) but are drawn from the lower classes and lower-middle classes of the cities.

Jehovah's Witnesses are kept heavily involved in evangelism. They are not, however, a conversionist sect: they do not want to induce a heart-experience, but only to persuade men of the truth of the scriptures and of prophecy as they interpret it. They are a recruiting campaign in the last days before Armageddon. They are still an adventist sect, but one that has found a solution to the problem of waiting for the day. Their activity becomes self-sustaining, and the march forward of the movement is itself regarded as a sure indication of the approach of the end of the dispensation. A sect as such is not an interest association, of course: it has ultimate values, and the Witnesses have recognised that Bible Students themselves cannot be – according to scripture – organised in rational-legal form like a modern corporation. Hence they have a scriptural form of association of believers, and, in the background, a firm modern organisation to provide its members with instrumental activities, similar to those that dominate, for example in salesmanship, the modern world. The movement has become a surrogate nation, and a substitute voluntary organisation at the same time, allowing rational criteria to apply in a wide field of its activities, with intense concern about deployment of effort, increase of size, and trends of growth. The ideological justification for this is Jehovah himself, who is concerned primarily to proclaim and justify his name. In some respect this movement represents an extraordinary case of goal deflection – from knowing the truth and quietly awaiting God to work out his will, to business in the world in the promotion of publishing – but it is a deflection almost consciously undertaken. It is the only way in which organisation can be sustained, and organisational survival has become an important subsidiary goal, in a movement that is committed to belief in the forthcoming end of the world as it is now known. The revolutionist response persists: it becomes, however, the justification for activity in society, to occupy the time and energy, and sustain the enthusiasm, of members.

In the case of adventist sects which reject formal organisation, we must expect to see a very different pattern of change. Here, too, the problem of maintaining the pristine revolutionist response has been met. Among the Christadelphians, who have neither a central headquarters for subsidiary concerns like that of the Witnesses, nor a ministerial order like that of the Seventh Day Adventists, original belief persists much as it was first enunciated. Early writings have not been superseded by new ones (whereas the Witnesses, to sustain their organisation, are of course obliged to pour forth new material and to allow the old to go out of print – a procedure that is both economically necessary, and useful both in sustaining interest, and in permitting changes of emphasis in teaching). Christadelphians have not added subsequent revelations, or new injunctions for believers, as did the Seventh Day Adventists. Yet, although they remain adventists, some of the intensity has also gone from Christadelphian advocacy. As they have come, in large part, to recruit internally, and to sustain their segregation from the wider society, so they have also come to adopt a more introversionist position. There has been some shift from preoccupation with the kingdom to more emphasis on the cross: the movement has become somewhat more devotional, and there has been a loss of the angular and contentious characters who, in the early days, were so joyously convinced of the early overturn of this dispensation. In recent years there has also been some indication that Christadelphianism might follow the path formerly taken by the Quakers, moving from introversionism to a more reformist position. Some Christadelphians have become increasingly concerned about social problems, refugees and famine relief.

Nor have introversionist sects shown a disposition to become denominationalised. They have been generally small, and they have often preserved their values by the fullest possible insulation from the surrounding society. This insulation has been vital to their continuance in a world in which they suffer increasing interference in various matters – particularly education, health, military conscription, sometimes compulsory political involvement, increasingly extensive social legislation (in respect, for instance, of trades unions, planning, zoning) and the conformity demanded by a wide range of technical processes. Where such sects have attempted to hold a balance between their own ethic and limited commerce with the outside world, they have gradually succumbed, as did the Amana Society (Inspirationalists), to the allurements of the world. The response to external pressure by the Exclusive Brethren, for instance, has been to intensify the sectarian ethic and the devices of insulation.

Manipulationist sects appear to undergo no one process of change. As between such sects arising at different periods, there is a changing focus of concern, from physical to mental health. There is also some evidence of increasing secularity of aim and style, particularly in the more developed movements. And yet, there is also a tendency for psychotherapeutic systems, such as Scientology and The Process to adopt the style of religious movements. There is, frequently, a merging of styles imitated from educational agencies, psychotherapeutic practice and religious movements. Many such movements have votaries who are not lifelong adherents, however: they enter, undergo an experience, and drift away again. Typically there are many isolated individuals in such movements, and even in a movement like Christian Science that has assimilated itself strongly to a church style of organisation (maintaining a secondary and separate system of healing practice), there is far less likelihood of lifelong family commitment and transmission from one generation to the next than in most other types of sect.

We have seen the variety of forms adopted by thaumaturgical sects principally by comparing such movements in different cultures, and particularly in those where the needs they fulfil are more commonplace than the concerns of thaumaturgical movements in the west. Despite the difficulty of establishing stable movements from among those who seek thaumaturgical relief, a variety of styles of organisation has been adopted. In societies undergoing rapid transition, that are influenced both by indigenous cultural traditions and ideas imported from the more advanced nations, the mixture of thaumaturgical and manipulationist orientations is evident, and there are strong indications that the old thaumaturgy gradually gives place to the new metaphysical and therapeutic systems introduced from abroad. Styles of explanation change, and more universalistic orientations are adopted. And these are more congruous with secular styles of large-scale organisation that are being simultaneously introduced in government and business. Undoubtedly this process reflects wider changes in education, general cultural awareness and sophistication. It also reflects changing material and medical provision. While personal insecurity persists, men may seek personal dispensations from it by oracle and miracle. As conditions of insecurity become more widely known, men may look for more general principles and laws that promise a better experience of the world when once they have learned how to manipulate it. As medical agencies increase in number and efficiency, the shift of preoccupation from physical to mental health may also occur, as it has in western society. Clearly, exotic methods of attaining peace of mind may have special appeal – as have Indian meditation cults in America and Britain, and, increasingly, western styles of manipulationist cult, as found in some of the sects of Japan. In many respects, manipulationist sects do represent a more secularised, less traditionally religious, orientation to the world, and, as is evident in Japan, they fulfil diverse functions as voluntary associations in a society with little tradition of voluntary organisation.

Sects represent a wide range of functions to their votaries, and sometimes are creative agencies in society. The public has often been made aware of them because of some bizarre episode, or some extraordinary demonstration of faith, and even today is frequently aroused to intolerance by politicians and journalists, who, for their own purposes, have represented sects as enemies of the people, sinister influences, destroyers of families and decent ways of life. All too rarely is it recognised that sects have sometimes helped men to adjust to their social circumstances and have provided them with hope, fellowship and security when no other agencies could have done so. At their best they have been agencies of self-help and social integration. If, at their worst, they have encouraged fanaticism, intemperance and even self-destructiveness, and if, to the general public, they work on mistaken assumptions, and propound dangerous theories and ideals, it cannot but be acknowledged that all these things have been the property of all religion at some stage in its development. In advanced and free societies, sects have no sanctions over their following other than those provided in their own belief-systems. Belief, it is true, may be very compelling, and sanctions – when they may mean, through excommunication, loss of all those whom one has respected and loved – may be severe. But this is true of other human relationships, particularly of the intimate relationships of those who are in love. Sects represent, in many ways, a community of love – whatever they may manifest to the world outside, and whatever hostility they may feel to be warranted in their relations with the wider society. They participate fully in the tensions and paradoxes of that condition. The tensions are only assuaged when the love – and perhaps the hate – itself cools into the temperateness, or tepidity, of the denominations and the churches.

Notes

1 For an excellent account see Norman Cohn, *Pursuit of the Millennium,* London, Secker and Warburg, 1957.

2 See, in particular, Ernst Troeltsch, *The Social Teachings of the Christian Churches,* New York, Macmillan, 1931.

3 Different designations have been employed in the attempt to distinguish types of sect. The term *transformative* is used by David F. Aberle, *The Peyote Religion Among the Navaho,* Chicago, Aldine, 1966. The terms followed here were developed in Bryan R. Wilson, 'Typologie des sectes dans une perspective dynamique et comparative', *Archives de Sociologie des Religions,* 16 (1963) pp. 49-63. See also Bryan R. Wilson (ed), *Patterns of Sectarianism,* London, Heinemann, 1967, pp. 22-45, and Peter L. Berger, 'The Sociological Study of Sectarianism', *Social Research,* 21, (winter, 1954), pp. 467-85.

4 See E. D. C. Brewer, 'Sect and Church in Methodism', *Social Forces,* 30, (May, 1952) pp. 400-8.

5 Cited by O. R. Whitley, *Trumpet Call of Reformation,* St Louis, Bethany Press, 1959, pp. 82-3.

6 Emile Durkheim, *Elementary Forms of the Religious Life,* Glencoe, Ill., The Free Press, 1954.

7 For an account see Elizabeth Isichei, 'From Sect to Denomination among English Quakers', in B. R. Wilson (ed.), *Patterns of Sectarianism, op. cit.* pp. 161-81.

8 For an unintentionally revealing account of Mrs Eddy written by one whom she made into a Director of the Mother Church of Christian Science, see Adam Dickey, *Memoirs of Mary Baker Eddy,* Robert G. Carter: London and Boston, 1927.

9 This influence in American orthodoxy is well recorded in Louis Schneider and Sanford Dornbusch, *Popular Religion: Inspirational Books in America,* Chicago, University of Chicago Press, 1958.

10 Aylmer Maude, *A Peculiar People: The Doukhobors,* London, Grant Richards; and New York, Funk and Wagnalls Co., 1904, p. 261.

11 See, on this subject, Renate Poblete and Thomas O'Dea, 'Anomie and the "Quest for Community": The Formation of Sects among the Puerto Ricans of New York', *American Catholic Sociological Review,* XXI, 1, (Spring, 1960), pp. 18-36; Anne Parsons, 'The Pentecostal Immigrants', *Journal for the Scientific Study of Religion,* 4, 2, (1965), pp. 183-97; Margaret L. Sumner, 'Mexican-American Minority Churches, U.S.A.', *Practical Anthropology,* 10, 3, (May-June, 1963) pp. 115-21; Philip

Hammond, 'The Migrating Sect: An Illustration from Early Norwegian Immigration', *Social Forces,* 41, 3, (March, 1963) pp. 275-83. See also, although they are less concerned with sectarianism, Nicholas Tavuchis, *Pastors and Immigrants: The Role of a Religious Elite in the Absorption of Norwegian Immigrants,* The Hague, Nijhoff, 1963; A. Grumelli, 'Il compartmento religioso degli immigrati', *Studi Emigrazione,* 1, 2, (1965). pp. 1-17; J. S. Roucek, 'On religion and immigration', *Sociologia Religiosa,* 7, 9-10, pp. 52-64; J. J. Mol, *Changes in Religious Behaviour of Dutch Immigrants,* The Hague, Research Group for European Migration Problems, 1965.

12 This has been investigated by J. T. Borhek, 'Role Orientations and Organizational Stability', *Human Organization,* 24, 4, (winter, 1965) pp. 332-8.

Acknowledgments

For his time in so carefully and discerningly reading the typescript of this book before publication, I am most grateful to Professor Allan W. Eister of Wellesley College, Massachusetts. Although I have not adopted all his valuable suggestions, I have profited a great deal from considering them in relation both to this book and more widely in the context of our mutual discipline. Mr John Whitworth of Simon Fraser University very kindly put his expert knowledge of the Oneida Community, the Bruderhof and the Shakers at my disposal. Dr S. von Kortzfleisch of the Evangelische Zentralstelle für Weltanschauungsfragen in Stuttgart was helpful in regard to some of the photographs reproduced. At the proof-reading stage I had the help of Mr T. P. Bull, whom I should like to thank for all his care.

Acknowledgment is also due to the following for the illustrations (the number refers to the page on which the illustration appears): 17, 129 Transworld Feature Syndicate Inc; 33 National Film Board of Canada, 1963; 46, 180 The Friends Service Council (Quakers); 56 Mansell Collection; 60 Salvation Army; 79 Sender Freies Berlin; 86-7 World Revival Crusade; 121 Vancouver Sun; 145 Radio Times Hulton Picture Library; 158, 160, 161 The Theosophical Society; 162 Paul Popper; 165 Hubbard Scientology Organisation; 167 The Christadelphian; 175 J. B. Collins, Chattanooga News-Free Press; 197, 207 Church of Jesus Christ of Latter Day Saints, Information Service; 204, 205 *Dialogue: A Journal of Mormon Thought*; 206 Deming Andrews, E. 1953. *The People Called Shakers*, Oxford University Press, London and New York; 208 The Shaker Museum Foundation, New York; 214 J. L. Moss; 217 (top) K. Schlosser; 217 (bottom) Dept of Information, Pretoria.

The maps were drawn by Design Practitioners Ltd.

Bibliography

The literature on sectarian movements is immense, but the strictly socio-logical literature is, although growing, much less extensive. This bibliography attempts to do no more than to indicate important sociological works and some of the more important historical studies about movements discussed in the text. In general, theological works and polemical works have been omitted, except in a few instances where there is a paucity of other material. The bibliography includes a few classic works in the sociology of religion that are of special importance for the study of sectarianism, a list of works of general importance on sects, covering sects in various countries, and works of particular relevance to the subjects in this book.

Classic works in the sociology of religion

Niebuhr, H. Richard, *The Social Sources of Denominationalism,* New York, Holt, 1929.

Pope, Liston, *Millhands and Preachers,* New Haven, Yale University Press, 1942.

Troeltsch, Ernst, *Social Teachings of the Christian Churches,* New York, Macmillan, 1931. (Translation by O. Wyon of *Die Soziallehren der christ-lichen Kirchen und Gruppen,* Tübingen, Mohr, 1912.)

Wach, Joachim, *Sociology of Religion,* London, Kegan Paul, 1947.

Weber, Max, *Gesammelte Aufsätze zur Religions-soziologie,* Tübingen, Mohr, 1920.

Weber, Max, *Wirtschaft und Gesellschaft,* Tübingen, Mohr, 1925. The parts of these works of principal interest in the sociological study of religion and of sectarianism have been translated into English as: *The Protestant Ethic and Spirit of Capitalism,* London, Allen & Unwin, 1930. *The Sociology of Religion,* London, Methuen, 1966. *Essays* (edited by H. H. Gerth and C. W. Mills), part III, London, Routledge, 1948.

Works of general importance

Algernissen, K., *Die Sektenwesen der Gegenwart,* Aschaffenburg, Pattloch, 1962.

Blanke, Fritz, *Kirchen und Sekten,* Zürich, Zwingli Verlag, 1963.

Boerwinkel, F., *Kerk en Sekte,* Den Haag, 1953.

Braden, C. S., *These Also Believe,* New York, Macmillan, 1949.

Cassin, H., 'Quelques facteurs historiques et sociaux de la diffusion du protestantisme en Italie meridionale', *Archives de Sociologie des Religions,* 2, (1956), pp. 55-72.

Chéry, H-Ch., *L'Offensive des Sectes,* Paris, Editions du Cerf, 1959.

Clark, Elmer T., *The Small Sects in America*, New York, Abingdon Press, 1949.

Clark, S.D., *Church and Sect in Canada*, Toronto, University of Toronto Press, 1948.

Dagon, G., *Petites églises et grandes sectes*, Paris, SCE, 1962.

Damboriena, P. and Dussell, E., *El protestantismo en America latina*, Friburgo-Bogotá, Feres, 1963.

Desroche, Henri, 'Approches du nonconformisme français', *Archives de Sociologie des Religions*, 2, (1956), pp. 45-54.

Glock, Charles Y. and Stark, R., *Religion and Society in Tension*, Chicago, Rand McNally, 1965.

Gründler, J., *Lexikon der christlichen Kirchen und Sekten*, Vienna, Herder, 1962.

Gustafsson, B., *Svensk kyrkogeografi, med samfundsbeskrivning*, Lund, Gleerup, 1958.

Highet, John, *The Churches in Scotland To-day*, Glasgow, Jackson, 1950.

Hoekema, Anthony, *The Four Major Cults*, Grand Rapids, Mich., Eerdmans, 1963.

Hutten, Kurt, *Seher, Grübler, Enthusiasten*, Stuttgart, Quelle-Verlag Rev.Ed. 1966.

Hutten, Kurt, *Die Glaubenswelt des Sektierers*, Hamburg, Furchte, 1957.

Kraemer, P.E., 'Enkele Haagse buitenkerkelijke religieuze groeperingen', *Sociologisch Bulletin* 1, (4), 1952, pp. 117-43.

Kraemer, P.E., Enig materiaal over sectarisme in een achtergebleven gebied, *Sociologisch Bulletin*, 13 (3), 1959, pp. 98-108.

Léonard, E.G., *Le protestant français*, Paris, Presses universitaires, 1953.

Littell, F.H., *The Origins of Sectarian Protestantism*, New York, Macmillan, 1964.

Poulat, Emile, 'Les Cultes dans les statistiques officielles en France au XIXème Siècle', *Archives de Sociologie des Religions*, 2, (1956), pp. 22-6.

Robbins, John E., 'Sources of Information on the Smaller Christian Denominations in Canada', *Canadian Church History Society*, Bulletin 12, 1959.

Séguy, J., *Les sectes protestantes dans la France contemporaine*, Paris, Beauchesne, 1956.

Séguy, J., 'Les problems de la typologie dans l'étude des sectes', *Social Compass*, 12 (3), (1965), pp. 165-70.

Sunström, E., *Trossamfund i det svenska sämhallet*, Stockholm, 1962.

Whalen, W.J., *Faiths for the Few: a Study of Minority Religions*, Milwaukee, Bruce, 1963.

Wilson, B.R., *Sects and Society*, London, Heinemann, and Berkeley, University of California Press, 1961.

Wilson, B.R., 'Typologie des sectes dans une perspective dynamique et comparative', *Archives de Sociologie des Religions*, 8, 16, (1963), pp. 49-63.

Wilson, B.R., *Religion in Secular Society*, London, Watts, 1966.

Wilson, B.R., (ed.) *Patterns of Sectarianism*, London, Heinemann, 1967.

246

Additional bibliography

CHAPTERS 4 and 5

Alonso, Isadoro, *La Iglesia en América latina: Estructuras ecclesiasticas*, Friburgo-Bogotá, Feres, 1964.

Bloch-Hoell, N., *The Pentecostal Movement*, London, Allen & Unwin, 1964. (Translation of *Pingsebevegelsen*, Oslo, 1956.)

Brien, Efraim, *Dem moderna Pingströrelsen*, Stockholm, 1924.

Calley, M.J.C., *God's People: West Indian Pentecostal Sects in England*, London, Oxford University Press, 1965.

Cleveland, C.C.., *The Great Revival in the West*, Chicago, University Press, 1916.

Collier, Richard, *The General Next to God*, London, Collins, 1965.

Cross, Whitney R., *The Burned-Over District*, Ithaca, Cornell University Press, 1950.

Davenport, F.M., *Primitive Traits in Religious Revivals*, New York, Macmillan, 1905.

Elsbree, Oliver W., *Rise of the Missionary Spirit in America, 1790-1815*, Williamsport, Williamsport Printing Co., 1928.

Fleisch, P., *Die Pfingstbewegung in Deutschland*, Hanover, 1957.

Gee, Donald, *Pentecostal Movement*, London, Elim Publishing Co., 2nd Edn., 1949.

Hollenweger, W.J., (ed.) *Die Pfingstkirchen*, Stuttgart, 1968.

Hollenweger, W.J., *Enthusiastisches Christentum: Die Pfingstbewegung in Geschichte und Gegenwart*, Zürich, Zwingli Verlag, 1969.

Hollenweger, W.J., *Handbuch der Pfingstbewegung* (microfilm, from Yale University), 10 vols., 1965-7.

Inglis, K.S., *Churches and the Working Classes in Victorian England*, London, Routledge, 1961.

Johnson, Benton, 'Do Holiness Sects Socialize in Dominant Values?', *Social Forces*, 39, 4, (1961), pp. 309-16.

Kelsey, M.T., *Tongue Speaking*, New York, 1964.

Loewen, Jacob A., Buckwalter, A. and Kratz, J., 'Shamanism, Illness and Power in Toba Church Life', *Practical Anthropology*, 12, 6, (1965), pp. 250-80.

McLoughlin, Wm., *Modern Revivalism*, New York, Ronald Press, 1959.

Mecklin, John M., *The Story of American Dissent*, New York, Harcourt Brace, 1934.

Miegge, Mario, 'La Diffusion du Protestantisme dans les Zones sous-développées de l'Italie méridionale', *Archives de Sociologie des Religions*, 8, (1959), pp. 81-96.

Mosiman, E., *Die Zungenreden geschichtlich und psychologisch untersucht*, Tübingen, 1911.

Nida, Eugene A., 'The Indigenous Churches in Latin America', *Practical Anthropology*, (1961), 8, 3, pp. 97-110.

Poblete, R. and O'Dea, Thomas, 'Anomie and the "Quest for Community":

the Formation of Sects among Puerto Ricans of New York', *American Catholic Sociological Review* (1960), XXI, 1, pp. 18-36.

Robertson, R., 'The Salvation Army: the Persistence of Sectarianism', in B. R. Wilson (ed.), *Patterns of Sectarianism, op. cit.*

Read, W. R., *New Patterns of Church Growth in Brazil,* Grand Rapids, Mich., Eerdmans 1965.

Schmidt, Wolfgang, *Die Pfingstbewegung in Finnland,* Helsingfors, Suomen Kirkkohistoriallisen Seuran Toimituksia 27, 1935.

Smith, T. L., *Called Unto Holiness,* Kansas City, Nazarene Publishing, 1963.

Thörnberg, E. H., *Fralsningsarmen: en engelsk skapelse i svenskt samhällsliv,* Stockholm, 1939.

Voipio, Aarni, 'Sleeping Preachers: a Study in Ecstatic Religiosity', Suomalaisen Tieteakatemian Toimituksia (Annales Academiae Scientiarum Fennicae), Sarja Ser. Bnide Tom. 75, 1, Helsinki, 1951.

Warburton, T. R., 'Holiness Religion' *Journal for the Scientific Study of Religion,* VIII, 1, (Spring, 1969) pp. 130-9.

Whitley, O. R., *Trumpet Call of Reformation,* St Louis, Bethany Press, 1959.

Wilson, Bryan R., *Sects and Society, op. cit.*

Wilson, Bryan R., 'The Pentecostal Minister' in Wilson (ed.), *Patterns of Sectarianism, op. cit.*

CHAPTER 6

Barzellotti, G., *Monte Amiata il Suo profeta,* Milan, 1910.

Bush, George, *A Treatise on the Millennium,* New York, Harper, 1832.

Case, Shirely J., *The Millennial Hope,* Chicago, University Press, 1918.

Cohn, Norman, *The Pursuit of the Millennium,* London, Secker & Warburg, 1957.

Cole, Marley, *Jehovah's Witnesses,* New York, Vantage Press, 1955.

Froom, LeRoy E., *The Prophetic Faith of Our Fathers,* vol. IV, Washington DC, Review & Herald, 1954.

Gaebelein, Arno C., *The Hope of the Ages,* New York, Our Hope Pub., 1938.

Hébert, G., *Les Témoins de Jéhovah,* Montreal, Editions Bellarmin, 1960.

Hobsbawm, E., *Primitive Rebels,* Manchester, University Press, 1959.

Lazareschi, E., *Davide Lazzaretti,* Bergamo, 1945.

Manwaring, D. R., *Render Unto Caesar: the Flag Saluting Controversy,* Chicago, University Press, 1962.

Meijer, J. A., 'Jehova's getuigen in Amsterdam', *G.S. I. Nieuws,* 6, 1, (1960), pp. 1-14.

Nicol, Francis D., *The Midnight Cry,* Washington DC, Review and Herald, 1944.

Pike, Royston, *Jehovah's Witnesses,* London, Watts, 1954.

Rogers, P. G., *The Fifth Monarchy Men,* London, Oxford University Press, 1966.

Rogerson, Alan, *Millions Now Living Will Never Die,* London, Constable, 1969.

Salt, Leo F., 'The Fifth Monarchy Men: Politics and the Millennium', *Church History*, XXX, 3, (1961), pp. 314-24.

Stevenson, W. C., *Year of Doom, 1975*, London, Hutchinson, 1967.

Stroup, H. H., *Jehovah's Witnesses*, New York, Columbia University Press, 1945.

Williams, George H., *The Radical Reformation*, London, Weidenfeld & Nicolson, 1962.

CHAPTER 7

Arndt, Karl J. R., *George Rapp's Harmony Society, 1785-1847*, Philadelphia, University of Pennsylvania Press, 1965.

Bennett, John W., *Hutterian Brethren*, Stanford, University Press, 1967.

Correll, Ernst, *Das Schweizerische Täufermennonitentum*, Tübingen, Mohr, 1925.

Eaton, J. W. and Weil, R. J., *Culture and Mental Disorders: a Comparative Study of the Hutterites and Other Populations*, Glencoe, Ill., Free Press, 1955.

Erbe, Hellmuth, *Bethlehem, Pennsylvania. Eine Kommunistische Herrnhuter Kolonie des 18 Jahrhunderts*, Stuttgart, Schriften des Deutschen Ausland-Instituts, Stuttgart, 1929.

Fischer, Hans, *Jakob Huter: Leben, Frommigkeit, Briefen*, Newton, Kansas, Mennonite Pub., 1956.

Friedmann, Robert, *Hutterite Studies*, Goschen, Ind., Mennonite Hist. Soc., 1961.

Gardiner, A. J., *Recovery and Maintenance of the Truth*, Kingston-on-Thames, Stowe Hill Bible Depot, 1963.

Holloway, Mark, *Heavens on Earth*, London, Turnstile Press, 1951.

Hostetler, J. A., *Amish Society*, Baltimore, John Hopkins Press, 1963.

Hubrý, Frantisek, *Die Wiedertäufer in Mähren*, Leipzig, 1935.

Kaplan, B., and Plaut, T. F. A., *Personality in a Communal Society*, Kansas, University of Kansas Pub., 1956.

Noel, Napoleon, *The History of the Brethren*, Denver, Col., Knapp, 1936.

Nordhoff, Chas., *The Communistic Societies of the United States*, New York, Hillary House, reprinted 1961.

Peachey, Paul, *Die Soziale Herkunft der Schweizerische Täufer*, Karlsruhe, 1954.

Peters, Victor, *All Things Common: the Hutterian Way of Life*, Minneapolis, University of Minnesota Press, 1965.

Schambaugh, B. M. H., *Amana That Was and Amana That Is*, Iowa State Historical Soc., 1932.

Steimle, Theodor, *Die Wirtschaftliche und Soziale Entwicklung der Württ. Brudergemeinden Korntal und Wilhelmsdorf*, Korntal, 1929.

Wilson, Bryan R., 'The Exclusive Brethren' in Wilson (ed.), *Patterns of Sectarianism, op. cit.*, pp. 287-342.

Wolkan, Rudolf, *Die Hutterer*, Nieuwkoop, de Graaf, 1965 (repr.).

CHAPTER 8

Bach, Marcus, 'The Life and Death of Psychiana', *Christian Century*, LXXIV, 1, (Jan. 1957), pp. 11-14.

Braden, Chas. S., *Christian Science To-day*, Dallas, Southern Methodist University Press, 1958.

Braden, Chas. S., *Spirits in Rebellion: the Rise and Development of New Thought*, Dallas, Southern Methodist University Press, 1963.

Dakin, E. F., *Mrs Eddy – Biography of a Virginal Mind*, New York, Scribners, 1929.

Dresser, H. W., *The Quimby Manuscripts*, New York, Crowell, 1921.

Gardener, Martin, *Fads and Fallacies in the Name of Science*, New York, Dover, 19.

Griswold, A. W., 'New Thought: a Cult of Success', *American Journal of Sociology*, XL, 3, (1934), pp. 309-18.

Hine, Robert V., *California's Utopian Colonies*, New Haven, Yale University Press, 1953.

Isherwood, C., *Ramakrishna and His Disciples*, London, Methuen, 1965.

Kennedy, H. A. S., *Mrs Eddy*, San Francisco, Farallon, 1947.

Kuhn, Alvin B., *Theosophy*, New York, 1930.

Lutyens, Lady E., *Candles in the Sun*, London, Hart-Davis, 1957.

Nethercot, A. H., *The First Five Lives of Annie Besant*, Chicago, University Press, 1959.

Nethercot, A. H., *The Last Four Lives of Annie Besant*, London, Hart-Davis, 1963.

Rosten, Leo (ed.), *Guide to the Religions of America*, New York, Simon & Schuster, 1955.

Steiner, Rudolf, *The Story of My Life*, London, Anthroposophical Publishing Co., 1928.

Swihart, A. K., *Since Mrs Eddy*, New York, 1931.

CHAPTER 9

Castelli Y., *Le Spiritisme*, Paris, Presses universitaries, 1954.

Cross, W. R., *Burned-Over District*, Ithaca, Cornell University Press, 1950.

Doyle, Sir A. C., *A History of Spiritualism*, London, Cassell, 1927.

Elliott, A. J. A., *Chinese Spirit-Medium Cults in Singapore*, London, London School of Economics, 1955.

Ferreira de Camargo, C. P., *Kardecismo e Umbanda: Uma Interpretação Sociólogica*, São Paulo, Livraria Pioneira Editora, 1961.

Ferreira de Camargo, C. P. and Labbens, J., 'Aspects socio-culturels du spiritisme au Brazil', *Social Compass*, VII, (1960), pp. 407-30.

Hine, R. V., *California's Utopian Communities*, op. cit.

Kloppenburg, B., 'Der Brasilianische Spiritismus als religiöse Gefahr', *Social Compass*, V, (1959), pp. 237-55.

La Barre, Weston, *They Shall Take Up Serpents*, Minneapolis, University of Minnesota Press, 1962.

Léonard, E. G., *L'illuminisme dans un protestantisme de constitution récente*,
Paris, Colin, 1953.

Nelson, G. K., *Spiritualism and Society*, London, Routledge, 1968.

Noyes, J., *History of American Socialisms*, Philadelphia, Lippincott, 1870.

Parker, R. A., *Yankee Saint: John Humphrey Noyes and the Oneida Community*, New York, Putnams, 1935.

Peel, J. D. Y., *Aladura*, London, O.U.P., 1968.

Turner, H. W., *An Independent African Church*, London, O.U.P., 1967.

CHAPTER 10

Andrews, Edward D., *The People Called Shakers*, New York, Dover, 1963.

Brodie, Fawn M., *No Man Knows My History*, New York, Knopf, 1945.

Drummond, Andrew L., *Edward Irving and His Circle*, London, Clarke, n.d.

Fauset, A., *Black Gods of the Metropolis*, Philadelphia, University of Pennsylvania Press, 1944.

Eggenberger, O., *Die Neuapostolische Gemeinde*, München, Chr. Kaiser
Verlag, 1953.

Mulder, William, *Homeward to Zion: the Mormon Migration from Scandinavia*, Minneapolis, University of Minnesota Press, 1957.

Mulder, William and Mortensen, A. R., *Among the Mormons*, New York,
Knopf, 1948.

O'Dea, Thomas, *The Mormons*, Chicago, University Press, 1957.

Shaw, P. E., *The Catholic Apostolic Church*, London, Crown Press, 1946.

Taylor, P. A. M., *Expectations Westward*, London, Oliver & Boyd, 1965.

CHAPTER 11

Benz, Ernst (ed.), *Messianische Kirchen, Sekten und Bewegungen im heutigen
Afrika*, Leiden Brill, 1965.

Blacker, C., 'Le Soka-Gakkai japonais. L'activisme politique d'une secte
bouddhiste', *Archives de Sociologie des Religions*, 9, 17, (1964), pp. 63-7.

González de Zarate, R. M., 'Soka Gakkai: una religión del valor', *Razón y Fe*,
171, (804), (1965), pp. 53-66.

Kohler, W., *Die Lotus Lehre und die modernen Religionen in Japan*, Zürich,
Atlantia, 1963.

Lanternari, V., *Les Mouvements religieux des peuples opprimés*, Paris,
Maspéro, 1962.

McFarland, H. N., *The Rush Hour of the Gods*, New York, Macmillan, 1967.

Mayer, Philip, *Townsmen or Tribesmen*, Cape Town, O.U.P., 1961.

Mühlmann, W. E., *Chiliasmus und Nativismus*, Berlin, Reimer, 1961.

Offner, C. B. & van Straelen, H., *Modern Japanese Religions*, Leiden, Brill.
1963.

Schlosser, K., *Eingeborenenkirchen in Süd- und Südwest-Afrika*, Keil, Walter
G. Mühlau, 1958.

Sundkler, B., *Bantu Prophets in South Africa*, London, Butterworth Press, 1948.

Thomsen, H., *The New Religions of Japan*, Rutland, Vermont, Tuttle, 1963.

Index

Principal references are denoted by italics